"My students speak of learning to observe more closely; of getting back to the forests as simple and free people; of living in harmony with nature; and most of all, of building a confidence and security for their families that is not dependent on outside events. Yet there is no simple and comprehensive series of books which can teach them how to do these things. It is because of this need that I have decided to write a four-volume series of *Survival School Handbooks*."

Tom Brown, Jr.

Berkley books by Tom Brown, Jr.

THE SEARCH (with William Owen)
THE TRACKER (as told to William Jon Watkins)
TOM BROWN'S FIELD GUIDE TO WILDERNESS SURVIVAL
  (with Brandt Morgan)

TOM BROWN'S FIELD GUIDE TO WILDERNESS SURVIVAL

Tom Brown, Jr., with Brandt Morgan

Illustrated by Heather Bolyn

BERKLEY BOOKS, NEW YORK

This Field Guide contains material, knowledge of which could be invaluable in dealing with a sudden wilderness emergency—an unexpected "survival situation" when knowledge of fundamental survival techniques could be life-saving.

Neither the publisher nor the author claim that all techniques in this Guide will insure survival in all situations. Some of the techniques and instructions described in the Guide may be inappropriate for persons suffering from certain physical conditions or handicaps. Misuse of any of the techniques described in the Guide could cause serious personal injury or property damage, for which the publisher and author disclaim any liability.

TOM BROWN'S FIELD GUIDE TO WILDERNESS SURVIVAL

A Berkley Book / published by arrangement with
the author

PRINTING HISTORY
Berkley trade paperback edition / June 1983
Second printing / January 1984
Third printing / July 1984
Fourth printing / April 1985

ISBN: 0-425-07702-0

A BERKLEY BOOK ® TM 757,375

The name "BERKLEY" and the stylized "B" with design are trademarks belonging to Berkley Publishing Corporation.

PRINTED IN THE UNITED STATES OF AMERICA

TOM BROWN'S DEDICATION:
To my dad, Tom Brown, my first and most loving teacher.

BRANDT MORGAN'S DEDICATION:
To Charlie Johnson for his generosity and enduring friendship.

A SPECIAL THANKS TO:
Melinda Denton, Loren Foss, Marc Schmitt, Ivan Doig, Jean Bryant, Arthur and Ruth Morgan, Rose Ann Cattolico, Dave Boyd, Michelle Kaestner, Lee Hillman, Rob Traver, Paul Brown, Al Moser, Frank and Karen Sherwood, Rob Sherwood, Lou Green, Craig Hook, Neil McKee, Paula and Randy Miller, Laurie Serianni, Wayne and Linda Blais, Jim Spina, Joe McDonald, Eric Heline, Steve Lee, John McCoy, Bob Dickson, Dick and Vicki Mills, (Haioka) Ralph Panaro, Bill Leavens, Gary Eiff, John Roman, Mac C. Oreiro, Jr., Pacific Northwest Tracker Association, Debbie Skougstad, Ann Hessel, Shannon Whalen and Trip Becker and all my former students for their expertise, dedication, field testing, and making the term brotherhood a reality.

CONTENTS

INTRODUCTION

Every year the number of people using North America's wilderness areas is increasing. Outdoor recreation, with its bewildering array of activities (from hunting and backpacking to rafting and RV travel), has mushroomed into a huge and complex industry. It is a hopeful sign that so many people are answering the call of the great outdoors, since it is also the call of our ancient heritage beckoning. But, unfortunately, the enthusiasm with which many people take to the woods is not always tempered with the skills and understanding our ancestors once had.

Tragically, the growth in outdoor recreation has led to a steady increase in the number of accidents and deaths resulting from carelessness and lack of knowledge. All too often I have come upon the results of such mishaps. A hunter becomes hopelessly lost and wastes all his energy in a flight of panic. A hiker sprains an ankle and dies of hypothermia during a night without shelter. A downed pilot nearly starves to death in the midst of a bounty of edible plants and animals. A desert traveler is hospitalized for dehydration. The list goes on and on.

Most of these mishaps are needless. They could be prevented with the most basic understanding of wilderness survival. Yet many people die and millions more travel the backwoods in peril because they have never been properly taught the skills that can give them and their families peace of mind. This book is written partly for such people.

More generally, this book is written for people with an interest in self-reliance. Dwindling resources, rising prices, and natural or human-caused disasters are all a part of modern living. Every day the newspapers remind us that society under stress cannot always provide for us. In fact, we need only imagine what would happen if all the supermarkets closed down to see through the veil that separates us from survival living. It is uncomfortably thin. In the face of such possibilities, a basic survival knowledge offers a kind of security that no insurance policy can provide.

But there are other reasons for writing this book, too. For one, learning the art of wilderness survival can help you enjoy the outdoors more fully. Perhaps you already feel relatively comfortable in the woods but want to get even closer to nature. Perhaps you would like to travel without heavy gear, sleep comfortably under the stars without a tent, learn to see more wildlife, or spice your prepackaged foods with fresh edible plants. Learning these skills will help you on your way. And as you go, you may begin to see the wilderness with new eyes.

Much of what I have learned about wilderness survival was passed on to me by an old Apache scout and medicine man named Stalking Wolf. I met Stalking Wolf through his grandson, Rick, when I was seven years old. For the next ten years, he passed on to both of us the priceless gift of

9

his Apache heritage. He taught us how to track and stalk like Indians, how to enjoy rain and snowstorms, and how to feel more at home in the wilderness than we did almost anywhere else.

For many years since, I have explored wilderness areas all over the country—gathering, testing, and experimenting with old and new skills to see how a trained person might fare in varied conditions and environments. Usually, except when tracking lost people, I have done this for no other reason than the sheer love of it. But that love has been fraught with a great deal of pain over the widespread destruction and disregard for the landscape I have seen in my travels. It does not take long, living intimately with nature, to realize that such destruction is caused by our alienation from the forests and fields. Very quickly, while gathering wild edibles or picking an animal from a trap, you will realize that you are as intimately connected to the web of life as the snake and the spider.

Learning wilderness survival, then, is not only an insurance policy, but a way of getting back in touch with your roots. It can be an adventure in which you discover not only how to survive, but how to live well— whether your home is an Alaskan bush cabin or a New York apartment house. At its best, a survival situation will heighten your senses and enhance your abilities. Through necessity you will discover you can do things you never dreamed you could do. And at particularly high moments, you will feel not only your connection to the earth, but the flow of the spirit-that-moves-in-all-things. If you can open your heart to the wisdom of the universe, you will come to know that man, animals, trees, rocks, rivers, and skies all speak a common tongue. Sensing this, you cannot help but care more for the earth and all its creatures.

How to Use This Book

One of the first things you may notice about this book is that it deals very little with commercial survival aids. This does not mean that you shouldn't use them—far from it. Tents, stoves, lighters, ultra-light foods, and modern navigational equipment have made wilderness travel safer and easier for millions of people, while at the same time decreasing its impact on the environment. But the problem is that you never know when you may be faced with a survival situation or what gear you may need to have with you when it arises. When you board an airplane, you cannot always take along a high-powered rifle, a tent, a fiberfill sleeping bag, Gore-Tex raingear, several cases of waterproof matches, and enough insect repellent to ward off an army of mosquitoes. And even if you do have these things, you can never be sure how long they will last. Theoretically, then, with the exception of a few items you may choose to carry in a small belt pack on any outing, this book is geared for the survivalist who has nothing—no clothes, no backpack, no halazone tablets—not even a knife.

Most of the chapters in this book are arranged in order of importance to the survivalist. As much as possible, separate skills are explained in the same logical sequence you might expect to follow in a real survival situation. Where appropriate, cross references are included by page number to give you additional information. In general, then, you can use the chapter headings and subheadings as a checklist for survival priorities and procedures. But keep in mind that this sequence is not sacred. There may be times, for example, when fire is more important than shelter, or when it may be better to spend your energies catching animals instead of gathering plants. In the end, you should rely heavily on your own ingenuity and common sense as you adapt to each new situation.

Most of the chapters conclude with a short series of practical exercises. I include these for two reasons. One is to pass on ideas that have proven helpful in my survival classes. The other is to underline the fact that reading about survival skills is never enough. The mastery of any art comes only through practice. Don't wait for a crisis to begin developing your survival skills. Start right in your own living room or basement, using materials found in local parks or your own back yard. Each skill mastered will add to your reservoir of confidence, making your emotional and mental adjustments much easier in a real survival situation.

Practice these skills under controlled conditions at first, in places where you don't have to worry about freezing your fingers or baking under a hot sun. Then practice them under varied conditions until you feel comfortable in almost any situation. After you feel confident that you can build an effective shelter, go camping and leave the tent at home. When you've mastered the bow drill in your basement, leave all matches at home—and so on.

Practice whenever you can. By all means enjoy the aesthetic beauties of nature—the birdsongs, rushing streams, and glowing sunsets. But also observe things with the eye of a survivalist. Ask yourself the "What If" questions: "What if I got lost here? What if I sprained an ankle? What if I ran out of matches or my tent were blown away? Where would I build a shelter? Where would I find kindling and firewood? What about edible plants?" Keep that internal dialogue going.

Try also to look at nature from a utilitarian viewpoint. A tree is not just a tree, but a potential source of fire, shelter, and food. In time, you'll be able to look at a plant and know much more than its name. You'll know its food and medicinal uses, whether it will provide cordage or building materials, and what its presence says about the ecology of the area. Far from decreasing your aesthetic enjoyment, such mental games will actually add to your overall appreciation of the outdoors. You'll find, in fact, that there is much more in your surroundings than you ever dreamed was there.

In summary, I suggest that you use this book as a working manual. Take it with you on your wilderness outings or slip it in a small survival pack that can be taken anywhere. Better yet, read it clear through, then concentrate on learning each skill until all have become second nature to you. That way, you'll always have the tools to survive when you need them.

1. ATTITUDE

It is truly said that the most important survival tool is the mind. But to keep the mind functioning smoothly, you must establish and maintain a positive attitude. Within hours or even minutes after the onset of survival stress, the attitude you take—and the decisions that result from it—may mean the difference between life and death. Over time, how you feel about yourself will determine how well you adapt to your new environment and its changing conditions. And no matter how long the survival situation may last, your outlook will affect the quality of your experience, just as it does in everyday life. The only difference is that the wilderness offers no escape from problems and much less margin for error.

To a great degree, your attitude will depend on prior experience. Some years ago, I was flying over the slickrock and desert country of Utah, admiring the magnificent land formations below, when the man next to me looked down and said, "I'd sure hate to be lost down there!"

Without thinking, I quickly replied, "Are you kidding? I'd *love* to be living down there!"

Because of his experience, my fellow passenger saw the landscape as a place to be lost rather than a place to belong. He even thought of it as a place where it might be impossible for a human to survive.

It is only natural for a person who has been fed, clothed, and transported by modern conveniences to recoil at the thought of having to provide for his or her most basic needs. But frequently such experience fosters the idea that humans are too weak and frail to successfully confront the harsh conditions of wilderness living. Granted, we do not have the legs of the deer, the fur of the rabbit, or the claws of the cat. But we have the will and intelligence to adapt to almost any natural environment on earth. Most of us are much stronger and more capable than we realize. One of the first steps in a survival situation, then, is to realize and acknowledge that strength.

I am not talking as much about physical strength as a quality of spirit and character that is often hidden in modern society. Sometimes the physically strongest person is the first to give up, while the weakest may show a determination that can give new heart to an entire group. What is it that makes a person decide to live rather than to give up and die? There is no simple answer. Sometimes it is a burning desire to see loved ones again or to push on toward an unrealized goal. But just as often it is the ability to accept the present situation and to deal with each moment as it comes.

Fear and Panic

The onset of a survival situation can cause an overwhelming sense of fear. Suddenly you may feel cut off from friends, family, and everything famil-

13

iar. The security of home may be replaced by darkness and discomfort. Strange sounds may conjure up visions of predatory beasts and primeval dangers. Some of your life's foundations may be shaken.

To a certain extent, fear is a normal reaction to such change, and it can even be helpful if kept under control. It gets the adrenalin pumping and prepares the mind and body to cope with the unfamiliar. But fear can become very dangerous if you let it run away with you. The uncontrolled urge to run blindly in search of a highway or to flee from an imagined danger can destroy judgment, cause debilitating accidents, drain vital body energies, and—in extreme cases—bring on shock and death.

The most important rule, then, for anyone who is suddenly faced with a survival situation, is to *keep from panicking*. When calamity strikes, sit down and think things through before taking action. Talk to yourself out loud, if necessary, as you might to a frightened friend. Try to relax and take stock of the situation. It may not be nearly as serious as you think. Instead of giving in to panic, look upon the event as a challenge—or even as an opportunity to enjoy an unplanned vacation. If that isn't possible, at least follow the example of a nine-year-old boy I heard of, who confidently weathered a two-day blizzard under a fir tree because he knew rabbits use firs for shelter and figured their technique would also work for him.

Whatever your situation, don't make matters worse because you are afraid of looking foolish for getting yourself into a predicament. Instead, accept your problems as calmly as possible, form a definite plan of action to provide for your immediate needs, and then take action knowing that all the necessities for survival are within easy reach.

Comfort: Wants Versus Needs

You'll go a long way toward increasing your mental comfort by realizing that you cannot immediately have everything you want, but that you *can* have everything you need. Certainly you would want a comfortable place to sleep with perhaps a blanket or a sleeping bag for added warmth. You might even wish you had oil heating and a television set. But for survival purposes all you need is a simple shelter with enough insulation to keep you from getting hypothermia. On another level, you might want a steak and lobster combination when all you need for the moment is a cup of pine tea and a few edible roots. The point is, you can debilitate yourself beyond belief by dwelling on what you cannot have.

Adapting to a lower degree of comfort is not as difficult as it might seem. For example, during the 1970s, millions of Americans who had been living with thermostats at seventy-two degrees Fahrenheit were asked to turn them down to sixty-eight or lower to conserve energy. It was a little inconvenient at first to wear sweaters instead of simply turning the thermostat up. But with time, most people adjusted and even discovered unseen benefits. They felt more awake and alert, saved money on fuel bills, and even found a new sense of control in their lives. To some of these people, seventy-two now seems unbearably hot!

Researchers have discovered that children often adapt more easily to survival situations than adults. One reason is that children haven't been conditioned to so much comfort. Instinctively they crawl into protective tangles of brush or hole up under fallen logs because they are not afraid of getting wet or dirty. They are used to spending days in the woods building forts, sloshing in the mud, and lying on hard rocks—and they realize how much fun it can be!

So take a lesson from the children. If you approach a survival situation with a negative attitude, thinking, "I can't stand sleeping in a smelly, bug-infested shelter in the middle of these damp, scary woods," you will certainly have nothing but problems. But if you think, "Here I am all by myself in this magnificent forest, surrounded by the richest scents of nature, lying in the embrace of the earth, and sleeping in a shelter I made myself"—then your experience can actually be grand and harmonious.

Don't Complain—Do Something!

One snowy night I was sitting by a small campfire in the Pine Barrens, bemoaning the cold. Stalking Wolf was sitting back against a tree, totally relaxed, as though lying on a big feather bed. He looked at me and said, "What is your problem, Grandson?"

"It's cold," I said. "My hands are frozen."

Stalking Wolf agreed that cold hands could be a problem. Then he asked me if I had ever seen a chickadee or a fox complaining about the cold, and what might happen if they did.

Grudgingly at first, I got up and stomped around to warm my body. This act alone took my mind off my miseries and helped me to begin thinking positively. Next I began building a shelter. I quickly set up the sticks for the framework, then mounded up a huge pile of brush and other forest debris. By the time the hut was finished, I was already warm. Finally, I crawled into the shelter and nestled down into the pine boughs. For a long time afterward, I looked out to enjoy the falling snow and the beautiful silence of the night.

I had occasion to remember this lesson some time later when I fell through the ice on a lake a long way from home. The air was about fifteen degrees Fahrenheit, and a chill wind was blowing. It took me a while to get out of the lake. By the time I finally pulled myself up on the bank, I was shivering violently. I realized that unless I did something fast, I would probably die of hypothermia.

This realization alone got the adrenalin pumping, and I fed it by getting deliberately angry. I hurried toward home, cursing and kicking at things, beating at my numbed arms and legs. Much to my surprise, by the time I was halfway home, I had broken into a sweat. I slowed down to avoid overheating, munched on some energy-rich food to replenish my strength, and the rest was easy.

Normally I do not recommend anger as a survival tool. There are very few situations in the wilderness when anger is anything but destructive. When you are cold and depressed, though, you may also feel a strong tendency to give up. That's when you need to muster some energy to do something for yourself. And it is truly amazing what you can do when you suddenly realize you have no choice.

My survival students invariably learn this lesson one way or another. One chilly winter evening, six of my advanced students were having trouble getting a bow-drill fire going. Instead of really trying, though, they just sat there complaining. If they had been putting some real effort into it, I might have had some compassion. But I knew they were waiting for me to start a fire for them, so I simply said, "If you keep on complaining, you're all going to die."

I said it with conviction, and they knew that I was not going to help them. This started a flurry of activity. Within fifteen minutes, four out of the six had fires going, and before long everyone was warm and comfortable. As soon as you start doing something, the whole world looks a lot better.

One obvious value of activity is that it automatically bars the mind from negative thoughts. When you are productively involved, there is no time to reflect on how miserable you are. Another value of activity is that it wards off loneliness and boredom. These two emotions can become powerful forces in a survival situation—especially after several days in the woods. Time slows down. You can't watch TV or go to the movies. You can't even call a friend on the phone. Feeling cut off and hemmed in, some people panic and try to flee even after their physical survival is assured. Productive activity helps to prevent this.

There is always something worthwhile to do. You can make a more permanent dwelling and furnish it with a backrest or a sleeping bag made of grass fibers. You can make more animal traps to augment your food supplies. You can fashion useful implements with bone, stone, and natural cordage. The sheer act of doing has a powerful effect on the psyche. Every positive thing you do will help to ingrain in your mind that you are a survivor, and this realization can leave you with a sense of mastery and pride even in the most trying of circumstances.

Be Here Now

One of the most effective keys to survival is living each moment as it comes. This point is beautifully illustrated by the experience of an Alaskan friend of mine who once found himself caught in an ocean storm in a small canoe. All around him the wind was howling, and each wave threatened to swamp his little boat. He took the waves singly at first, carefully aligning the boat and paddling into each one. But then, at the crest of a particularly large breaker, he looked out at the endless walls of surf and spray, and suddenly he realized he didn't have a chance.

If my friend had maintained this attitude, he would certainly have perished. But fortunately he got ahold of himself. He realized that if he thought about what he had left to endure in the hours ahead, he would not be able to deal effectively with the wave that was here right now. So he snapped back to the present moment and paddled to meet the oncoming giant. It buoyed him up twelve feet in the air. He bobbed over the top like a cork as the surf crashed behind him. Then came a quick moment of relief and a deep breath as he sank into another trough to prepare for the next wave.

Needless to say, my friend rode out that storm. But he didn't do it all at once. He did it one wave at a time. In the wilderness it is the same thing: one survival problem at a time. Don't compound your problems into an ocean of troubles and you will come through just fine.

If you are in a particularly bad situation and can do nothing about it, your only alternative is to endure it. John Muir, the naturalist, and a friend were once forced by a blizzard to spend a perilous night on the summit of Mount Shasta. They were so cold they had to call to each other every few moments to make sure they didn't drift off and die. Yet in spite of his agony, Muir was still able to appreciate the beauty of individual snow crystals and the "marvelous brightness" of the stars.

In all, Muir and his friend lay thirteen hours in the open, covered with ice and snow. Every hour seemed like a year. But they survived those hours a minute at a time. So can you. Sometimes you may be so uncomfortable that you will have to back off every few minutes and ask, "Am I all right?" If you are all right in the moment, that is all you need. The next moment will take care of itself.

Sometimes an amazing thing happens when you live in such a way. You can become so attuned to "now" living that each moment seems like a gift. And the sense of gratitude over each gift can lead to such a joy that your spirits are uplifted and you find a reserve of strength you didn't know you had. Muir called it "a kind of second life," available only in emergencies.

Living in the moment is something you can practice every day—and the best teachers of this art are often the very young and the very old. Before his death, Chief Dan George wrote, "The young and the old are closest to life. They love every minute dearly." This is very true. Until they are bound by routine and expectation, children live in a haven of wide-eyed wonder and involvement. Old people know their day is coming to a close, and every sunset they witness is new and alive for them. That is the kind of involvement that is necessary for effective survival living—or, as you may gather, fruitful living of any kind.

Curiosity

Another thing that will keep you in the now moment is an eagerness to learn. Explore your surroundings with the open, questing mind of a child—especially if you do not feel comfortable there. If you're feeling lonely, take heart in the sparks of life around you. The plants, animals, winds, and waters all have their survival lessons to offer. Everything is a teacher, and learning can be your ever-present joy.

I was fortunate to have Stalking Wolf as my teacher during many of my learning years. He often sat for hours without saying anything. Rick and I would be sitting right beside him with our chins in our hands, waiting. Finally he might fix a flower with his glance and say, "Plant have much to teach."

Immediately Rick and I would drop down on all fours beside the plant, peering into its flowers, feeling its leaves, smelling its fragrance. We would spend hours—even days—trying to discover all it had to teach, but we could never exhaust its lessons. How much more there is to learn with an entire wilderness to explore!

As you explore your surroundings, you will make many valuable discoveries. Gradually, you will learn what trees are best for bow-drill wood, what plants yield the most nutritious foods or the best fibers, what animals live in your area and what their habits are. During this process, you may also discover that you are not really alone at all—that in fact you are one of a multitude of interlocking lives sharing the same environment. At that point, survival may begin to take on a deeper meaning.

Harmony

Many people today see wilderness survival as a desperate struggle—a situation in which a person is pitted against "that angry killer nature," fighting tooth and nail against insurmountable odds. It is only in our recent history that we have adopted this attitude. It is the attitude of separateness, and it is based on misunderstanding.

The truth is that there need be no fight for survival. In fact, the moment you begin to resist nature is the moment you will begin to lose.

Nature is much too powerful an entity to overcome. No amount of modern technology can prevent a volcanic eruption. No person alive can turn back a thunderstorm. But, like the tall grasses, you can bend with the wind; and like the wild animals, you can find shelter from the storm until it passes. If you flow with nature instead of resisting, you'll find that she will take care of you and provide everything you need.

I do not mean to say survival will always be comfortable, but you can minimize the discomfort by enjoying your oneness with nature. There is no point in going through life as a spectator, looking at nature from afar and not getting into it. The closer I can get to the earth, the more alive I feel. It is a thrill to live with the deer and the fox, a joy to share with the fish and the frogs. This is part of what survival is all about. This is what *life* is about—a sense of involvement and connection.

There is an old Indian saying that the farther man's feet are removed from the earth, the less respect he has for living, growing things. It follows that the less man realizes his dependence on nature, the more he is apt to foolishly destroy it. Unfortunately, that is what is happening today. It is difficult for us, when we go to the supermarket, to realize that the meat we buy is part of an animal that had to give up its life, or that the processed cereals we buy were once part of vast fields of grain waving in the wind. It is even more difficult to crumple a piece of paper and see trees falling in the forest. The final products are often so far removed from the natural materials that there seems to be no connection. Yet there is always a connection—and in spite of our need to use these natural materials, they are not easily replaceable.

For too long mankind has been fighting, resisting, and trying to control or destroy the pure and natural. This is a grave mistake, for in doing so we also resist and destroy ourselves. I am very much Indian in my beliefs. In the Indian world, even a rock is alive and has a spirit. The plants and animals are friends and brothers, communicating their wisdom and advice in times of need. How could the native Americans feel alone when they knew themselves to be part of the "spirit-that-moves-in-all-things"? With such an attitude, wilderness survival takes on a completely different meaning.

The native Americans considered all of life's necessities as gifts from the Great Spirit, and they never failed to show their appreciation for them. If they built a fire, they thanked the wood for giving them warmth. If they killed an animal, they made peace with the animal's spirit through prayer. Whatever they made with the gifts of nature, they made with perfection as a way of expressing their gratitude.

Regardless of your personal beliefs, this attitude makes excellent survival sense. For in many cases, survival depends on careful craftsmanship and thoughtful conservation. If you build a fire carelessly, it may be snuffed out by the first gust of wind or rain. If you squander your firewood today, you may have none left for tomorrow. But if you are mindful of your interconnection with all things, you will help to maintain the balance of nature and thus bring harmony into your own life.

In summary, the survival experience can be very difficult if you intentionally push yourself to your limits, move your camp frequently, or allow yourself to be bothered by cold feet, dirty hair, or other rigors of primitive living. But if you can separate your wants from your needs and see the beauties that surround you, if you can keep yourself in good physical shape and meet the challenge of survival with well-honed skills, you will live easily in a survival situation and come to know the sense of oneness that flows from the heart of the wilderness.

Exercises

The survival attitude can be practiced constantly. Following are some games you can play—anytime, anywhere—that will help strengthen your mind.

1. Problem Solving. Next time you have a pressing problem, stand aside mentally and observe your reaction to it. Do you tend to complain, feel listless or depressed, or do you try constructively to solve the problem? Whatever your reaction, don't make any judgments. Just learn from it. If your reaction is negative and passive, sit down and make a list of the positive things you can do about the problem. Then, no matter how you may feel at the moment, *do* them—and watch your attitude change for the better.

2. Facing Illness. Colds and other physical ailments are sometimes debilitating, but they are also opportunities for attitude growth. Next time you're sick or injured, see how gracefully you can get through it. Gear your mind and body toward healing and maintaining a high energy level. Above all, keep from complaining. See if you can stay active and get through it without anybody knowing you're not feeling well.

3. Comfort Control. Practice gearing yourself to a lower comfort level. Try turning the thermostat down and using a sweater. For a month, go without something you think you need—coffee or cigarettes, for example—to better understand the difference between wants and needs. Sample "uncomfortable" environments under controlled conditions. Take a swim in a cold mountain stream. Step into a swamp and feel the mud around your legs. You may find that the "discomfort" of such experiences is blotted out by exhilaration.

4. "Now" Living. Next time you're worried about something, practice "being here now." First, notice how your mind jumps to the past and the future like a drunken monkey, wasting precious time and energy. Then begin to harness your concentration. Imagine yourself incapable of seeing yesterday or tomorrow. Mentally put yourself into a day-tight compartment. Try relaxation exercises, meditation, physical exercise—whatever works to calm your mind and return you to the "now" moment.

2. SHELTER

Most people in a survival situation become overly concerned about what they're going to eat. This is understandable, since most of us are used to three meals a day. Yet of the four necessities for survival, food is usually the least important. Chances are you can survive for a month or more without eating. And though it may take a while to adjust to more meager rations, you can probably maintain a healthy body on a fraction of your present diet. By the same token, fire usually ranks low on the list of necessities unless there is an immediate danger of freezing or chilling. Under wet conditions without matches, your firemaking efforts may be frustrating at best. Even if you do get a fire going, it will probably not keep you warm and dry without added protection. Water, of course, is an important essential, because you can survive only a few days without it. But, as I'll explain, you can easily collect water in almost any environment. That leaves shelter as the most critical necessity in a survival situation. And with good reason. A person stranded in a harsh environment without adequate protection may not live more than a few hours (see "Hypothermia," page 265).

I can hardly overstress the importance of shelter. Like your own home, a good one will protect you, maintain your body heat, and provide a place you can identify with. If you are lost, it will also reduce your tendency to panic and keep you from wandering. This in turn will make it easier for searchers to find you. Moreover, you can build a good, warm shelter without the aid of a knife, blanket, or anything but your bare hands almost anywhere on this continent. While such a shelter may not provide all the comfort you want, it will at least bring you enough peace of mind to assess the situation and decide what to do about it. So remind yourself that home is where you make it, no matter how temporary. Then set about making it without delay.

Location

One day Rick and I were camped down by Cedar Creek in the Pine Barrens of New Jersey. We had found a spot in an open area beside a swamp. It was a gorgeous place. The smells in the air were delightful. We rejoiced at the sight of moss-covered banks and the sounds of birds and running water.

We built our shelter facing the creek with its back to the swamp. It was a large, luxurious debris hut with three-foot-thick walls. As we were admiring our handiwork, though, Stalking Wolf came by on a search for herbs and laughed as he passed us. This struck us as peculiar, but he said nothing, so we forgot about it.

23

That night it rained, and we quickly discovered the reason for Stalking Wolf's mirth. Our campsite was a flood area. By two in the morning, the shelter was inundated with water, and we were forced to move to higher ground. Even at that, our troubles were not over, because then the mosquitoes and other biting insects came out and ate us alive.

The next day, when Stalking Wolf strolled into our camp, he could tell from the pained, tired expressions on our faces that we had learned our lesson. He emphasized it gently by saying, "A camp that is pleasing to the eye is not always pleasing to the body."

Another way of saying this is that a good shelter in a bad location is a bad shelter. Before you start building, then, consider the following points:

1. Protection from weather. Pick a place that is away from wind, rain, snow, and glaring sun. Locate your shelter on the lee side of incoming weather systems—usually on the east side of existing ridges, tree groves, or protective outcroppings. Most North American weather systems move from west to east. But this can vary a great deal. Many mountains, for example, create their own weather systems where microclimates change dramatically from one location to another. Wind direction can also vary with time, warm air tending to rise during the day and cool air descending at night.

2. Protection from natural hazards. Keep an eye open for avalanche slopes, overhanging dead limbs, trees that might blow down in a wind, or rock formations that could collapse. If you find such hazards, either break them down or move to another area.

3. Dry, well-drained area. Locate your shelter away from valleys, washes, troughs, and depressions. You need not build on a hilltop—just high and dry enough so you don't wake up with a stream of water running under your bed. Ideally, build your shelter at least fifty yards from your water source. This will prevent you from inadvertently polluting the water, and it will also keep you free from the heavy dew that usually descends on lakes and streambeds during the night.

4. Open, southern exposure. Given a choice, do not build your shelter in thick woods. Such areas take a long time to dry out and usually have an abundance of needles or leafy boughs that block out the sun. Preferably, find the edge of a clearing with a southern exposure where the sun provides the longest-lasting heat and light.

5. Entryway facing east. Open your shelter toward the east so the entryway will catch the first warming rays of the sun. To take greater advantage of the daytime sun, you can face the entryway southeast. But don't face it directly south, where it could be subject to a quick rainstorm.

6. Fire safety. Locate your shelter well away from fire hazards. Since you will usually have a small fire for cooking and heating near the entryway, stay away from areas with peat bogs, dry grasses, flammable fir boughs, and the like. If you can't avoid such areas, then place the shelter so that sparks and coals will be least hazardous.

7. Plant and animal hazards. Avoid areas with dangerous plants and animals. That includes everything from poison oak to ant nests and grizzly dens. Several of my survival students quickly learned this painful lesson when they inadvertently built a shelter over a nest of ground-dwelling yellowjackets.

8. Abundance of materials. Pick an area with plenty of resources. If you're building a thatched hut, make sure you won't have to walk five miles to find thatching materials. If you're building a debris hut, find a place with lots of insulating material. If you want a fire, choose an area that offers a good supply of kindling and firewood. Also consider the proximity of edible plants and animals.

9. Comfort. Finally, look for a place that is relatively comfortable and cozy. Scan the ground for sharp rocks and root tangles that might make a less than satisfactory mattress. On the other hand, remember that comfort is not your primary objective. That nice fat easy chair in the spacious living room can wait for another day.

Shelter Size

Small is beautiful. Most people make their shelters much larger than necessary. This is not only wasteful of time and materials, but often self-defeating as well. The main purpose of the shelter is to keep your body's internal fire burning with as little heat loss as possible. The smaller the shelter, the less energy (from body, fire, or sun) it takes to keep it warm. Initially, all you'll need is enough room in which to sleep and sit up—and in a dire emergency, you can get by with little more than a well-insulated, body-sized cocoon. Start out small, then, and enlarge the shelter as you increase your level of comfort and security (see "Hut Logistics," page 43).

Conservation

Do not disregard Mother Earth while building your shelter. Spiritually, I cannot justify breaking down pine boughs, pulling up grasses, or using live shelter materials of any kind in a practice situation. If everyone went out tomorrow and practiced building lean-tos or thatched huts with live vegetation, the trees would soon be stripped bare. There is not enough wilderness left in this country for that kind of extravagance. So even in a survival situation, choose an area where your presence will have the least impact. In practice, build shelters with dead materials in areas you will be able to restore to their original condition. The beauty of most of the following shelters is that they can be made without tools and without killing any plants. If constructed properly, they can be used and dismantled later so that hardly anyone would notice they were there.

Natural Shelters

If you need a place to hole up quickly, you can find temporary protection in some kind of natural shelter. Almost anything that keeps out wind and weather will do. This might be a tree well, a fallen log, a matted clump of vegetation, a cave or rock outcropping—whatever you can squeeze into. If you are not sure what to look for, think about what animals use. Rabbits nestle into the thickest tangles of briars or bushes they can find. Foxes often den up in hollow logs or small rock caves. Birds usually roost beneath overhanging boughs. Almost all animals instinctively seek these natural shelters. You can do the same, keeping in mind some general guidelines.

First, make sure the shelter is safe. If you squeeze into a cave or under a fallen log, check to see that it won't collapse during the night. Try to make your natural shelter more habitable. Add sticks and boughs to "brush in" cave entries. Stuff hollow logs with a good supply of insulating leaves (see "Insulation," page 28). Add protective brush and bark coverings to tangles of branches. Always line your shelter on the bottom so there is something between your body and the cold, wet ground. Also stay mindful of the fact that natural shelters are only temporary. If you have to spend a miserable night in the damp gloom under a fallen log, remember that tomorrow you can add on to it or construct a more permanent shelter from scratch.

The Wickiup

The wickiup is one of the simplest and quickest shelters to build. It was used extensively by the Indians of the plains and the Southwest—especially in desert areas where building materials were scarce and warmth was not a critical factor. The name, appropriately, means "place of shelter."

To build a classic wickiup, find three strong ridgepoles and set them up tipi-fashion. If you have cordage, you can lash three ends together and open the poles like a tripod. If not, select ridgepoles with branches that will hook together at one end to form a sturdy base. Complete the skeleton by filling in the sides with branches.

Leave enough open space on the east side for an entryway. On top of the skeletal structure, pile any kind of brush you can find: sage, grasses, cactus pieces, bark slabs, creosote bush, rabbit bush, etc. Heap these materials into a dome. The more brush, the better the insulation. If grasses

or similar materials are available, you can also create a loose thatchwork by bundling handfuls of it to plug into obvious holes.

For two people, a wickiup six feet in diameter and five to six feet tall should be adequate. It can be made any size—even large enough to accommodate fifteen or twenty people. But remember that small is beautiful. For a cozy structure that still allows plenty of sleeping space, simply cut one of the ridgepoles shorter than the other two, forming a low, sloping, body-sized shelter.

Because of its low insulating properties, I recommend the wickiup primarily for desert and summer use. It provides good protection from sun and wind, but only marginal protection from rain and cold.

The Lean-to

This shelter is a classic, used by survivalists everywhere. Like the wickiup, it is quick and easy to build, and it can be made with similar materials. To begin, either pound in two forked sticks and join them with a strong ridgepole, or set a pole between the forks of two trees. Then, leaving the east side open toward your fire pit and the morning sun, fill in the west side with sticks and brush to create a forty-five-degree sloping roof. In bad weather you can brush in both sides and both ends of the shelter to form a low, protective tent.

The lean-to should be long enough so you can stretch out lengthwise in front of a fire, and high enough so that you can perform critical chores (such as firemaking and fashioning tools) without being exposed to the elements. Like the wickiup, it affords only minimal protection. In severe conditions, of course, you should add on to these structures to provide more insulation from the cold.

Insulation: Go Watch the Squirrels

The first time Rick and I slept out in the Pine Barrens was in November. It was the first night of a four-day Thanksgiving vacation. As it started to get dark, we asked Stalking Wolf whether it was time to go home, and he said no, that we were staying over.

At first Rick and I wondered where we were going to sleep. Then we remembered the lean-to described in our Boy Scout handbook and thought we had it made. We suspended a pole between two pine trees, leaned other poles up against it, threw debris on top of it (a piece of bark here, a pine needle there—nothing very thick). Then we built a small fire ten feet from the opening.

We slept about fifteen minutes before we woke up shivering. The rest of the night we alternated between going to the fire to get warmed up, back to the shelter to sleep, then back to the fire to get warmed up again. Finally we moved the fire closer and we got a few hours' sleep, but it was far from adequate. And we were covered with dew in the morning. Coincidentally, we had faced the shelter toward the east, and the morning sun was delicious when it finally hit us.

Stalking Wolf couldn't believe how stupid we were. "Have you ever watched the squirrels?" he asked. We said yes, and he asked, "How do they sleep?"

Rick and I watched squirrels all morning. Mostly we watched them scamper up and down pine trees, adding on to their big, leafy nests. We decided we needed more insulation. As the day wore on, we gathered leaves, needles, ferns, and dead pine branches. All this we heaped into a huge pile of brush that was big enough so we could both burrow into it. When we looked for Stalking Wolf's approval, he just turned the other way, ignoring us as he used to love to do.

At nightfall, Rick and I crawled into our brush pile and gathered armfuls of dry leaves about us. For the first half of the night we sweated. We were so hot we had to take off our coats and loosen our shirts. But there was one shortcoming. All night long, sticks and pine needles slipped down inside our clothing and poked at our skin. We reasoned that it was a lot better to be uncomfortable than to freeze to death. But by four in the morning, with all our tossing and turning, we had lost most of our insulation. And just before dawn we were freezing again.

Once more, Stalking Wolf seemed dumbfounded. "You haven't really watched the squirrels," he said. "Did you ever look inside their house?"

That day we climbed trees and peered into squirrels' nests. We discovered that their leaf piles were contained in a latticework of branches so they wouldn't shake free. Rick and I looked around and finally settled on a dead oak bush that left a skeleton of branches spreading low to the ground. We bent the branches all the way down and laid pieces of sandstone on the ends to keep them from springing back up. Then we placed a network of sticks on top and stuffed the inside with leaves.

That night it rained. The water trickled down into every nook and cranny. It soaked through the leaves and seeped right through our clothes onto our skin. It was then that Rick and I made a monumental discovery. We were wet, but we were still warm! In spite of the rain, we slept well all night long, and the next morning we ran excitedly to tell Stalking Wolf about our discovery.

As the steam rose off our clothes, we explained to Stalking Wolf how great it had been. He just looked at us and said, "You're wet. Do you wet your bed?"

Our pride turned to shame as Stalking Wolf berated us. "You do not believe the wisdom of the squirrels," he said. "You still think you can improve on their methods."

Soon afterwards, we realized that we had been looking at the squirrel's nest only from the inside. We had forgotten about the round, bulky exterior that protects it from the rain. We went back to our shelter, took all the wet leaves from the inside, and threw them on the top. We even added some more brush, piling it up into a steep dome so the water would run off. Then we refilled the inside with leaves that had been freshly dried by the afternoon sun.

The last night it got down to about twenty degrees Fahrenheit, but Rick and I slept comfortably all night long. The morning we left, we poked our heads out to find that the leaves on top of the shelter were frozen solid, and Stalking Wolf finally nodded his approval.

It was very clear to Rick and me, after our four-day campout, that insulation was the key to warmth. It did not even matter whether the insulation was damp, as long as there was enough of it. And neither did it make much difference what the material was made of, as long as it was light and airy. Gradually we realized that there were hundreds of things we could use for insulation: leaves, ferns, mosses, grasses, pine boughs, cattail down—anything that would provide thickness and create dead air spaces around our bodies.

Insulated Clothing

We also realized we could use insulation in many different ways. Not only could we stuff it into rock caves and hollow stumps to make instant sleeping bags, but we could use it for clothing, too.

Once I was out several miles from home in an oak forest, wearing a light jacket and a pair of jeans. It rained for a while and I got soaked. Then the temperature started to drop. By the time I was halfway home, I was dangerously cold. Then I remembered the lesson of the squirrels. I unbuttoned my pants and stuffed them with leaves all the way down to the ankles. Next I pushed my pant cuffs inside my socks to keep the leaves from falling out. Finally I tucked in my jacket and stuffed it with leaves— front, back, and down the arms to the cuffs. By the time I was done, I looked like a scarecrow, but I was already warm. After walking a bit, I had soon worked myself into a sweat. The more I walked, the more leaves I had to remove. And by the time I reached home, I realized just how smart squirrels really are.

Not long after this episode, Rick and I took the insulation theory a step farther. Instead of throwing out our old shirts, we sewed two of them together, leaving an opening in the back so we could stuff them with insulation when we needed it. Whenever the weather got too cold in the Pine Barrens, we filled our double-layered shirts with dried ferns, grasses, cattail down, mosses, or even shredded newspaper. Then when we got home, we just shook out the leaves and washed the shirts. In the winter, instead of buying down vests (which we couldn't afford), we simply filled our shirts with cattail down. We wore these for an entire season and dumped them out in the summer.

The Debris Hut

Over the years, Rick and I experimented with variations on the "squirrel" shelter we built in the Pine Barrens, and eventually it evolved into what I call the debris hut, or leaf hut. For warmth and ease of construction, this shelter is one of the best of all. You can build it either free-standing (making a tripod with two short stakes and a long ridgepole) or by placing one end of a long ridgepole on top of a sturdy base—for example, a stump or crook in a tree. Choose a sturdy ridgepole that is at least as thick as your arm and long enough to cover your sleeping and work area. Lift one end of the ridgepole onto the base and position it so your entryway will be facing east.

Once the ridgepole is well secured, prop large sticks all the way along both sides to create a wedge-shaped ribbing effect. The ribbing should be wide enough to accommodate your body, but steep enough to shed moisture. Fill in the entire structure, leaving a hole for the entryway just be-

side the base. Then place finer sticks and brush crosswise to make a latticework that will keep junk from falling through the ribbing onto your sleeping area.

Over the ribbing, heap on a pile of light, airy, soft debris. Leaves, grasses, sticks, brush, moss, bark slabs, tree boughs—almost anything but damp loam will do. The accumulating debris should eventually form a large, dome-shaped mound over the skeletal structure. Don't strive for architectural perfection. Just heap on more debris until the dome is at least two-and-a-half feet thick.

Check the thickness of the debris by working your hand down into it as far as you can. You should be in up to your armpit before you feel the ribbing. In cold weather, add another foot or two of debris. If all this junkpiling seems like overkill, remember that the thicker the pile, the better the insulation. Also, the steeper the dome, the better the rain protection. If your hut is well built, you should be able to pour a five-gallon bucket of water over the top and not get wet inside.

On top of the debris layer, add some protective shingling—say, flat bark slabs or large mats of absorbent moss to help keep the rain out. Finally, pile on a heavy layer of outer brush to prevent the lighter insulation from blowing away in a storm.

Bedding. When the exterior is complete, literally stuff the inside of the hut with the driest, fluffiest materials you can find. Dry leaves, ferns, cattails, and grasses are best, but any insulating material will work, even if it's damp. If you've provided for a work area, stuff only the bottom two-thirds of the shelter and pound in four or five vertical stakes to keep the leaves in place.

Next, squeeze your body inside and mat it all down. This will break down the insulating material and help to create the dead air spaces that are so crucial to maintaining body warmth. Repeat this stuffing and matting process twice more, building up a good, thick cocoon all around you. Then, just before you turn in for the night, collect a final heap of insulation and place it just outside the entryway within arm's reach. This is your sleeping plug. When you've snuggled inside the hut, simply pull the plug in after you. Use part of it as a pillow and part to stuff into cold spots around your body. If it's really cold out, you can even throw some of it over your head.

Work Area. The work area should extend from just above your head to the upper end of the shelter. Here you can store dry wood, fashion survival implements, and hang wet clothes to dry. You can also take refuge here during particularly nasty days and still have a sense of connection with the outer world.

Sealing the Entryway. If you have an outside fire providing heat, you'll want to leave your entryway at least partly open. If not, you can close it up by stuffing it with a door plug similar to your sleeping plug. Better yet, stack up a bunch of bark slabs or logs within easy reach and seal the entryway from the inside after you're tucked away. Best of all, fashion a removable door. To do this, first weave a simple matting large enough to cover the entryway (ten or twelve finger-thick saplings woven together like a mat of popsickle sticks). Stuff this latticework with leaves or debris, lay it on its side, and pile a thick layer of insulation on top of it. Then secure the pile by bending parallel saplings through the top and bottom of the latticework. In fifteen minutes, you can have a door that will open and shut at your convenience without having to knock down a wall or gather a new door plug each time you leave the shelter.

With the sleeping plug and door plugs in place, the interior of the debris hut should be warm and cozy. If the outer insulation is thick enough, you should hear almost no outside sounds and feel well protected from the elements. And you will be. A warm cocoon of insulation under two-and-a-half feet of debris should be enough to protect you to about ten above zero Fahrenheit. Four-foot walls can keep you warm when it's forty below outside.

Variations on the debris hut are endless. Almost any natural shelter, for example, can be made into a serviceable debris hut simply by adding piles of insulation inside and out (see "Natural Shelters," page 26). If materials are available, by all means use debris to beef up your wickiup or lean-to. And don't feel you have to stick to one design. The one I've described stresses warmth rather than comfort. You can arrange the skeletal structure and the interior any way you like, as long as you build a steep dome on the outside and provide a warm cocoon of insulation on the inside.

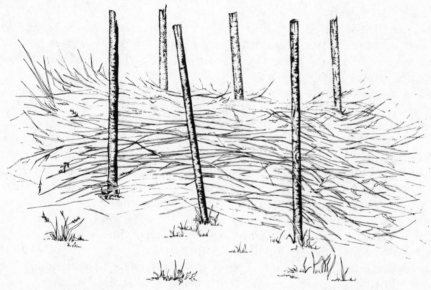

Stacked Debris Wall

Using the same materials, you can build an insulated wall or series of walls to serve many purposes. The stacked debris wall is nothing more than two parallel rows of long stakes with a thick pile of insulating brush in between. For best results, pound these stakes into the ground no more than a foot apart along the length and make the wall a foot and a half to two feet thick. It is also a good idea to interweave the stakes with flexible saplings to help contain the debris. When this is done, fill up the framework with any light, airy material you can find.

Applications of the stacked debris wall are limited only by your imagination. If you first set some sturdy corner posts, you can make an entire
shelter by joining four of these walls and roofing them with a dome-shaped
pile of sticks and brush. For added warmth, you can enclose any shelter
and fire-pit area with a semi-circular debris wall to serve as a massive heat
reflector. Such a wall also makes your shelter an effective blind from
which to observe game in the area. If there are many people in your
group, you can build three or four free-standing debris huts with large
entryways facing a central, well-watched fire and connect them all with a
chin-high wall. This creates a "fireplace" effect. The heat from a single fire
bounces off the walls and warms all the huts to the point where you don't
even need insulation. Even in subfreezing temperatures, this open work
area stays as warm as the beach on a summer afternoon.

Thatched Hut

Rick and I discovered thatching by accident. One day we were trying to
build a pyramid-shaped backrest that we could use for relaxation next to
our shelter. We made a tripod with crossbeams and haphazardly tied bundles of grasses against the slats to cushion our backs. The first thing we
noticed, aside from the comfort of the grasses, was that our backs stayed
unusually warm. After a heavy rain we also noticed that everything beneath the backrest was still dry. The water had run right off.

It was then that Stalking Wolf told us about the beauty and utility of
thatching. He said that hollow grass stems made excellent insulation, and
that if we hung them in skirted bundles, root end up, they would funnel
water to the ground even more effectively than the way we'd tied them.
Using this technique, he said, we could build a roomy shelter to work,
play, and live in for a long period of time.

You have probably noticed by now that each of the shelters described
is a little more difficult to build than the previous one, but that each in
succession offers a little more comfort and convenience. The thatched hut
is the next step up—a semi-permanent dwelling. It involves more work
than the debris hut or the stacked debris wall, but it is tighter, more
energy efficient, and more aesthetically pleasing. Before you begin building, just be sure you have plenty of thatching material, plenty of cordage
(see page 241), and plenty of time.

Framework. The thatched hut framework can be almost any style you
choose. Tipi and lean-to styles are discussed above. You can also make a
cabin framework by pounding in four long, sturdy Y-stakes, then lashing
on connecting beams and steeply slanting roof beams. But an easier way to
get a sloping roof is to build a dome-shaped structure. This can be done by
staking pairs of strong but flexible saplings on opposite sides of an eight-

foot circle, bowing them over, then lashing each pair in the middle to form four or five semi-circular hoops. In an hour or two you can make a dome framework that is strong enough to sit on.

Materials. The best thatching materials are long grasses and reeds. These are both hollow-stemmed (providing dead air space) and often available in great quantities. Materials such as ferns and evergreens will do, but you'll need larger bundles to get the same warmth and protection. Gather the thatching materials into bundles three to four inches thick (even thicker for branched materials such as pine boughs). Tie each bundle a few inches down from the root end, leaving enough cordage to lash it to the crossties later on. The loose ends of the bundles should tend to skirt out. Eventually, these bundles will hang root end up on the walls and roof, easily shedding water and hanging together in the wind.

Crossties. Make the crossties from flexible saplings or sticks. Lash or weave them in parallel rows all the way around the shelter framework. To assure a shingling effect, space the crossties at intervals about two-thirds the length of the thatching material. For example, if you're using grass bundles only a foot long from cordage to tip, this means you'll put in crossties about every eight inches. If you're using cattail stalks, you may only need crossties every two or three feet.

Thatching. Tie the bundles to the crossties beginning with those clos-est to the ground (except for the cabin structure—in which case, do the roof first). Press each bundle firmly against the one next to it and tie it securely to the crosstie. Use this technique with each crosstie, systemati-cally packing, tying, and verifying that each bundle overlaps the crosstie below.

If you have no cordage, you can still secure the thatching. Wrap the first bundle all the way around the crosstie and press it firmly against the supporting pole so that the root end is held in place between the bundle and the supporting pole. (The sheer weight of the bundle should hold it in place.) Slide the second bundle up against the first, and so on, until the entire row of thatching is tightly packed between two supporting poles. Then go on to the next row.

Continue this thatching routine all the way to the top of the struc-ture. With a cabin or dome structure, make sure there is plenty of overlap at the very top to prevent the entry of wind and water. If you're building a tipi structure, the final row will come to a point at the top. To make it watertight, squeeze and tie all the bundles into a single crown. Then cap the crown by lashing several more bundles over the top at different angles.

To weatherproof the final structure, simply spread your fingers and shake all the bundles vigorously. This will make the individual thatching fibers interlock with one another. Secure the thatching further by spiraling cordage around the structure from top to bottom, or by laying brush up against it. Normally, though, you don't need to do much to make a thatched hut more secure. The materials usually interweave so naturally that they seem to have grown there. And as for strength, I once saw a thatched hut withstand a seventy-five-mile-an-hour wind that blew down a silo on an adjoining farm.

Thatched Blanket

The interior of the thatched hut will probably be warm and quiet no matter what the weather. For added warmth, of course, you can fill it with leaves or other insulating material. But since we're talking about thatching, why not make a thatched blanket or a thatched sleeping bag? To do this, gather long bundles of grasses—better yet, cattails or long reeds. Then, using either a simple overhand weave or a figure-eight weave (see "Weaving Clothes and Baskets," page 254), wrap the bundles tightly against each other until you have fashioned a mat about a foot longer than your body. Plug any remaining holes by stuffing them with bundles folded in half.

If the thatching material isn't long enough to accommodate your body width, tie the bundles together lengthwise before rafting them together. (You can even make a blanket by wrapping cordage around handfuls of dried mosses and gradually quilting them together.) To complete the sleeping bag, make a second blanket—this time slightly wider and longer so it can fold over your body and connect with the ground blanket. For maximum warmth, sew these together on the bottom and one side. Then climb in and drift off.

Survival Cement and the Hogan

One day Rick and I were trying to build a makeshift fireplace to smoke some fish. As we started on the domed part, though, we couldn't get the sandstone rocks to stay in place. Stalking Wolf watched us for a while, then said, "What does your father use to build a fireplace?"

We answered, "Cement, of course, but we don't have any."

"Yes," Stalking Wolf said, "Earth Mother also provides cement. The Hopi and Pueblo, the People of the Sun, use it every day." So saying, he mixed together a handful of mud and grasses and secured one of the precarious blocks with it.

Eagerly Rick and I mixed more mud and grasses. Then we systematically plastered this mixture between the rocks on the smoker wall in the same way I had seen my father build a fireplace with bricks and mortar. By the time we were done, we had almost as much mud on our clothes as we did on the smoker, but the unit was strong and sturdy.

This was our introduction to one of the best building materials in nature—a substance I call mud mortar or survival cement. Its basic ingredients are equal amounts of mud and fibrous material such as grasses or ferns. Simply mix the ingredients together in your hands so the fibers are interwoven throughout the mud. As it dries, the mixture sets like cement, and it hardens with a surprisingly strong and water-resistant surface.

You can use survival cement in a variety of ways: to patch holes in a shelter wall, to dome over a brush roof, to build a wall around a cave, or even to enclose a sturdy dome structure with rocks. But the most useful application of this material is in the construction of the classic Southwest Indian shelter called the hogan. The hogan is not a makeshift shelter. It is a warm, durable dwelling that can last for several years. It can be built with logs, rocks, or a combination of the two.

Log Hogan. With logs, the building process is similar to that for the stacked debris wall (see page 33). At each corner, set three strong supporting stakes into the ground so that both logs share the inside stake. Then stack the logs between these supports, plastering each one with survival cement as you go. For best results, overlap the logs at the corners with each successive layer. This will make the structure more airtight and secure. Apply generous amounts of mortar wherever two surfaces meet. When the walls are finished, chink them with mortar both inside and out.

For ease of construction, use small logs no more than six inches in diameter—logs you can easily cut with a crude stone tool or by laying them in a fire. In especially cold surroundings, double the thickness of the walls by adding an inside layer of logs or rocks, or by insulating with stacked debris. Finally, roof the hogan in with a raft of sturdy logs, chinking generously between each one. Cover the roof with a dome-shaped pile of brush, leaves, and grasses. Then add a thick layer of survival cement to keep out the rain. Another way to keep out the rain (and to save on building materials) is to make a structure with triangular sides and a long sloping roof.

Rock Hogan. For a rock hogan, triangular walls will provide a more stable structure. These should be built within a framework of sturdy Y-supports and strong roof beams so the rocks will not take any more weight than necessary. Try to find large, flat rocks. Stack them up a few at a time, plastering each juncture with mud mortar just like you would with cement. Overlap the rocks like bricks, keeping the walls low and thick. Then roof in the structure as described above. The weight of the roof should be supported by the Y-supports and beams, not by the rocks.

The hogan will keep you warm and dry for months. Even under rainy conditions, it should need only minimal upkeep. And once the mortar is dry, you will be hard pressed to knock down a wall even if you try (a two-room log structure that Rick and I built in the Pine Barrens has stood for almost fifteen years). As for warmth, once you've sealed the big cracks and fashioned a log door with lashing and cross bracing, the hogan is so impermeable to weather that it can almost be warmed by candlelight.

Another advantage of the hogan is that you can actually build a small fireplace inside (using rocks and survival cement) with little danger of burning down the shelter. A final word of warning, though. A well sealed hogan is a very airtight structure and could cause severe sickness and even suffocation. (Early pioneers referred to this malaise as "cabin fever.") So be sure to provide some generous openings to keep the fresh air circulating.

Snow Shelters

Snow is problematical because it is wet and cold. But it's an excellent insulator if you can keep your body away from direct contact with it. As an example of its sheltering capacity, the temperature inside a well-made snow cave or igloo typically fluctuates between forty and sixty degrees Fahrenheit, even with outside temperatures as low as fifty below zero!

Keep in mind several important points when making and using snow shelters. One, stay as dry as possible during the construction process. Two, use plenty of insulation between your body and the wet snow. And three, make sure the shelter is well ventilated.

Snow Burrow. Providing you have warm wool clothing and plenty of outer protection, you can wait out a storm for a few hours in a snow burrow not unlike the emergency hollows made by rabbits and other animals. You can make such a shelter in a minute simply by "cannonballing" into a safe snowbank and burrowing in backwards until you're just out of the blast. For maximum heat retention, stay curled up in a ball and create a breathing space before you jump by holding your arms up in front of your chest and face. Don't be too concerned about deepening snow, as long as you have an air hole and can easily climb out. The snow will increase your insulation. When the storm has passed, either climb out or enlarge the burrow into a more comfortable shelter.

Snow Cave. If you take the proper precautions, the snow cave can be a real life saver as an emergency bivouac in exposed mountainous areas above timberline. First, be sure that the temperature is well below freezing so the walls of the cave will stay firm during the night. Next, choose a deep, crusty snow bank that is not subject to slides or drifts. (If no likely bank is available, mound up a dome of snow on level ground.) Dig in about three feet at right angles to the wind to prevent accumulating drifts from blocking the entryway. Then, above the level of the entrance (where most of the warm air collects), hollow out a dome-walled cave large enough to accommodate your body and your gear. Make sure the walls of the cave are smooth and round so that melting water will not drip from the ceiling. Plug the entryway with a snow block. And most important, poke a stick or even an arm through to the outside to provide a vent for fresh air.

The outer wall of a snow cave should be about three feet thick. The vent will usually indicate the thickness. In a snowstorm, of course, the cave walls will be growing thicker by the minute. Since you will be oblivious to even the most raging storms once you're inside, it is especially important to check and re-check the air hole at regular intervals. You may also find it necessary to get up during the night to tunnel out the entryway as the snow accumulates.

Unless you are carrying a stove, it is unlikely that you will have any kind of fire in a snow cave. But if you do, you must then be extra careful to avoid carbon monoxide poisoning by maintaining good ventilation. In any case, a snow cave requires special vigilance. Even the heat from your body can warm the cave walls and cause them to slowly descend when the outside temperature is not cold enough to hold them firm. If you wake up to find the roof sinking in, think about making a safer shelter such as a snow pit (see page 42), while you still can.

A-Frame Trench. A good, safe alternative to the snow cave is the A-frame trench, a very simple variation of the Eskimo igloo. It is quick to construct and can be built either against a hillside or on level ground. First, stomp out a rectangular platform just wide and long enough to accommodate your body. This will outline the shelter area and consolidate the snow. Let it harden for about twenty minutes and don't walk on it.

After the snow has hardened somewhat, dig an entryway about three feet deep. Step into the entry and excavate the rest of the trench by cutting out large blocks of snow for the roof. Most modern igloo builders use a machete-like cutting tool for this purpose, but you can get by with a ski, a flat stick, or even a well-insulated arm if the snow is not too hard. On the other hand, if the snow is too soft, scrape off the top and start cutting the blocks farther down where it's better packed.

To cut the blocks, first smooth the wall of the pit in front of you. Make the first cut parallel to this wall, about six inches back and two or more feet deep. Then cut down along the sides and finally along the bottom of the block. If you've done everything right, the block will settle with a gentle "whump." You should then be able to lift it out easily. When you've made enough blocks, lean them together in pairs from both sides of the trench to form an A-frame roof. Finish the shelter by blocking the ends, punching an air hole through the roof, and chinking the cracks generously with snow.

Once the trench is covered, you can get inside and hollow it out further to make more room. Two people can stomp out a wider pit and roof it in using blocks in groups of three. For greater strength and stability, bevel the blocks. If properly made, most Eskimo shelters are so strong you can walk on them after the snow has consolidated and set.

Natural Shelters. Below timberline, first look for natural shelters that can be converted into warm bivouacs by scooping out snow. Huge tree trunks often accumulate tremendous snowdrifts that may form ready-made depressions or "wells" just below a protective covering of overhanging boughs. Dig these out further—ideally, all the way to the bare ground— and insulate them with a thick matting of evergreen boughs. Another approach is to skirt the trunk with boughs or branches to make an evergreen hut. Such a hut can be made even warmer by packing a thick layer of snow on the walls.

Snow Pit. The snow pit is probably the safest shelter below timberline—especially at temperatures above freezing. To make one, find a well-protected place where you can dig a shoebox-shaped pit. If practical, dig all the way to bare ground. Vary the shape of the pit to suit your needs. You may want to make a triangular or square pit where you can curl up in one corner and perhaps place a fire and various implements in the others.

Dig the pit at least four feet down—deep enough so you can stuff it with insulation and prop yourself up on an elbow for minimal comfort. If you plan to have a small fire, dig even deeper so you will have room to tend the blaze and keep the flames from licking at the roof. Next, line the pit (except for the fire area) with a thick matting of vegetation. Make the bedding at least six inches thick. That way, you will be well suspended above cold snow or accumulating water.

Finally, cover the pit with a large mound of boughs or branches and cap it with a layer of snow. This outer mound can be as thick as you like, as long as you allow for a good air vent through the brush and snow. Tunnel in on the east side after the shelter is completed, pack in a warm cocoon of insulating material, and plug the entry with a block of snow.

Hut Logistics

At first, your shelter may provide only enough space to assure your survival, perhaps with a work area just big enough to get a bow-drill fire going. As your stay continues, however, you can enlarge the shelter to provide a more comfortable sitting and work area, space for storage of dry kindling and firewood, and a place to hang plants and miscellaneous tools. Eventually, you may want to add more rooms or even build additional structures.

As a general rule, though, keep the sleeping area small and gradually expand on living and working space as conditions warrant. If you start with a small leaf hut, for example, later you can build another hut nearby that allows more space for work and storage. For added warmth and protection, you might want to surround your hut with a stacked debris wall and fashion a sturdy door to keep animals out when you're gone.

Personally, I like to maintain a leaf hut for sleeping and build a thatched hut next to it for work and storage. The tipi thatch is particularly good for sitting and kneeling; the angled ridgepoles provide convenient pegs for hanging tools, clothing, and dried plants. The hogan, of course, can be made almost any size. A single room with a sloping roof should meet most of your needs, but as conditions change, you can partition it or add adjoining rooms for a variety of needs. These added spaces can be as personal as a piece of hand-carved wood, but be sure to adapt them carefully to climate, topography, and other relevant conditions.

Arrange your shelter space logically so that needed items are easily accessible. Make sure that wet clothes will not be dripping on tinder or bedding materials, and that your leftover survival stew will not be strewn with leaves when you turn over in bed. Keep plenty of firewood on hand, and organize the shelter so you can toss another piece of wood onto the fire without going out into the cold.

To avoid insect pests, hang up odiferous plants such as skunk cabbage, catnip, or mint. A bed lined with cedar shavings will also help to keep insects to a minimum. (Many Indian tribes burned cedar shavings on rock slabs inside their shelters. This "smudging" was a way of warding off evil and bringing goodness into their lodges. But it also had real survival value, because the burning of the cedar's tannic resins drove away the insects.) As a final precaution against pests, shake out or replace your bedding material every few days.

Internal Heating With Rocks

Once, after a bitter cold night in a poorly made shelter, Rick and I were sitting by the fire trying to warm ourselves with cups of hot tea. When we had finished our third cup, Stalking Wolf sat down and said, "You are sitting in the hands of Brother Cold. Do you think he will warm you?"

We argued that Brother Cold was also inside the shelter, and that we couldn't make it thick enough to keep him away.

Stalking Wolf disagreed, of course, but instead of sending us out to thicken our shelter as we had expected, he began to talk about rocks and lizards. He said, "You ask the rocks to warm your water and food. Why do you not ask them to warm your bodies as your animal brothers do?" It was then we got the idea that we could use hot rocks as internal heaters for our shelters.

None of the shelters mentioned, with the exception of the hogan, can safely accommodate an internal fire. But you can always install a rock heater. Just build up your outdoor fire to a good roar and nestle some football-sized rocks among the coals for an hour or two. (**Caution:** Don't collect these rocks from near a water source or they may explode when heated.) Meanwhile, dig a hole about a foot wide and six inches deep inside your shelter—ideally, in the work area, well away from all flammable materials. When the rocks are glowing red hot, remove them from the coals with sticks or large tongs (see page 253), and drop them into the hole. Then build up the fire with green wood to last the night and seal the door shut. The rocks will keep you warm all night. As long as nothing flammable touches them, they won't start a fire or smoke you out of the shelter.

Once you've tried this method a few times, you will be able to regulate the heat by the number of rocks in the hole. You can even keep rocks cooking all day long, burying them in strategic spots throughout the shelter as you work. Another heating method is to take rocks out of the fire, letting them cool until they are just warm to the touch. You can then use them as hand and footwarmers, or bury them in your bedding like so many heating pads.

Bedwarmers. You can also use rocks to make a heating trough under your bed. To do this, remove the bedding material and dig a body-length trough a foot wide and a foot deep. Fill it with football-sized rocks glowing red from the fire; then cover the rocks with about six inches of dirt. After all the steam has evaporated from the soil, replace the bedding and you will sleep as though warmed by an electric blanket. When you get up the next day, throw the rocks on the fire again in preparation for another night of luxury.

A hot-rock mattress can also be made in the open air by digging an even wider trench, lining it with rocks, and building a fire on top of the rocks. Use the fire for cooking and warmth during the day. Then, about two hours before bedtime, rake out the remaining wood and coals (perhaps placing them into another firepit), and fill in the hole with four to six inches of dirt. (Two precautions when burying hot rocks: Cover the rocks with at least four to six inches of dirt to prevent burns, and wait until the rocks have cooked all the moisture out of the ground so you won't be sleeping in a steam bath half the night.)

Problem Areas

The debris hut, or a variation thereof, will be your mainstay in most parts of the North American continent, with the exception of the open plains, the desert, and tundra or high alpine areas where vegetation is very scarce.

Plains. On relatively featureless, flat terrain, the main problem is finding insulation and protection from the weather. If the bare ground is exposed, this may mean digging a makeshift pit shelter and lining it with little more than sparse grasses. Often rocks can be built up into a coffin shelter that provides an excellent windbreak. If the ground is covered with deep snow and temperatures are subfreezing, by all means tunnel in for the night. But get out early before the sun weakens your shelter. Better yet, build a protective wall with blocks of snow, or mound up enough snow on all sides to make a semi-covered burrow that will see you through the night.

Desert. You can almost always find protective vegetation or rockwork in desert areas. Even a small tree can provide the basis for a sheltered bivouac. Again, rocks can be fashioned into a body-sized shelter, then covered with flat slabs and packed with sand for added protection. If you can't find anything, dig into the sand itself. That is better than lying under the hot sun.

Alpine. High alpine and tundra areas may also be lacking in vegetation. If you are above timberline, make every effort to get down. If this is not possible, search out some variation in the landscape that is out of the wind and pile up whatever is available. Don't make the mistake of saying, "There's nothing here." There is *always* something. In times of scarcity, adjust your expectations. Then your survival instinct and creativity will combine to make best use of the situation.

Exercises

The following exercises will help to solidify the concepts and skills presented in this chapter.

1. Location. Take a trip to the park or the woods with the idea of looking for good shelter sites. As you walk along the trail, point out and discuss likely spots, reviewing their specific advantages and disadvantages. Remember, a good shelter site is out of the weather, away from natural drainages, not too close to the water source, well exposed to the sun, and free from natural hazards such as overhanging boughs and dangerous plants and animals, and offers a good source of fire and building materials.

2. Construction. Pick a spot in the woods and build a shelter from scratch—ideally, a well-insulated debris hut. Stay in it at least one night without a fire and take note of the problems you encounter. Is the insulation adequate to keep you warm? Does the shelter leak? Does it provide enough room for your needs? During the second day, improve on the shelter so that it is more comfortable and convenient.

3. Insulation. On a cold day, experiment with different types of insulation by stuffing your clothing alternately with leaves, grasses, ferns, fir boughs, mosses, and other materials. Those that warm you most effectively will also be the best for shelter insulation.

4. Variations. Experiment with various construction techniques until you are confident that you can build a variety of shelters to suit a number of different conditions and terrains. Those discussed above include natural shelters, wickiups, lean-tos, stacked debris walls, debris huts, thatched huts, hogans, and snow shelters.

5. Heating. Build a shelter and experiment with various heating techniques. First, try a fire six feet from the entryway. Next, try heating hot rocks and placing them in strategic spots. Finally, dig a trench and construct a hot-rock mattress before you turn in for the night. Notice the size of the rocks and how long they provide heat before they cool off. Try to work out the ideal relationship between shelter size and heating needs.

3. WATER

Water is one of the most important elements in wilderness survival, but it is often taken for granted. Few of us stop to consider that the human body itself is three-fourths water, and that water is crucial to every bodily function from digestion to clear thinking. We could not live more than a few days without this precious fluid, for the liquids we drink do not stay with us long. They are constantly being cycled through our bodies as though we were leaky containers that must be kept constantly full.

Even a slight change in the body's water balance can quickly bring on adverse physical and mental effects. Dehydration can cause depression, poor judgment, slowed muscle response, nausea, and a host of other problems that may impair survival ability. In some situations you can become dehydrated without even feeling thirsty. For these reasons, I seriously recommend drinking a plentiful supply of water every day, whether or not you have anything to eat. And in no case should you go more than twenty-four hours without it.

Many early Indian tribes believed that water was the Earth Mother's blood, and that its purpose was to give life to all the world's beings. This, I think, was an especially beautiful attitude. With it, the native Americans acknowledged their brotherhood and interdependence with all living things. In a humble and very direct way, they affirmed the connection between the blood in their own veins, the sap in the trees, and the water of rivers and streams. Feeling such reverence for water, they took great pains to avoid polluting it in any way.

Unfortunately, our feet have become far removed from the earth in these modern times, and much of humankind has lost its respect for water. In fact, so many pollutants have already been dumped into our aquatic reserves that it is hard nowadays to find a lake, river, or stream anywhere in this country that has not been contaminated. As a survivalist in today's world, then, you face even greater difficulties than the native Americans and mountain men of past centuries. Not only must you find the water, but you must also make sure it is drinkable.

Is It Safe to Drink?

Never take chances with drinking water. The possibilities of poisoning, parasitic infestation, dehydration, and the draining of vital energy just aren't worth the risk. A group of my survival students learned this lesson well when one of their instructors drank some questionable water. Within a few hours he was struck by severe gastrointestinal problems. For four days he suffered from diarrhea and upset stomach, which left him dehydrated, weak, and feverish until he was finally treated by a doctor. If he

47

had been in a real survival situation, that sickness could have meant his death.

There are many signs to look for when trying to determine whether a given water source is safe to drink. Fast-flowing water at high elevations and away from human habitation is usually safer than water at low elevations near towns or cities. Wherever the water source, it should be clear, without telltale discolorations or oil slicks on the surface. If you're considering a small, self-contained water source such as a rock depression or a crook in a tree, make sure it is free of algae and animals—indications that it may be stagnant. If the source is large and free-flowing, look for a healthy assortment of plants growing in and around the water. Look for signs of fish, frogs, and insects or other invertebrate life. And look for tracks that might indicate other animals have chosen to drink there. But remember that such tracks don't necessarily mean the water is safe for humans. Wild creatures frequently drink from very polluted water sources—and even eat plants that are deadly poisonous to humans—with no apparent ill effects.

In general, there is no positive proof of drinkability. A water source can contain all the positive indicators and still be unsafe. The Musconetcong River, for example, is one of the most beautiful trout rivers in New Jersey—fast moving, clear, with a healthy assortment of vegetation, fish, and animals. But if you drank from it, you might become deathly ill because it carries a heavy seasonal runoff of chemical sprays from the adjoining farms. And just because a water source is far away from civilization doesn't mean it's safe, either. Timber companies sometimes carry out mass spraying of chemical defoliants in evergreen forests to rid them of broadleaf trees.

Even in the high country where there are no man-made pollutants, you can still get debilitating diseases such as giardia and hepatitis from water contaminated by animals. In fact, you cannot be absolutely sure even of known water sources. One of the cleanest streams in the Pine Barrens—a place where I had drunk freely for years—was suddenly polluted by fuel jettisoned from a passing plane. On another occasion I drank water from a creek I trusted completely, only to find a dead animal farther upstream. Before you drink from any chosen source, then, ask yourself whether you'd be willing to stake your life on that water—because in a survival situation that's exactly what you'll do if you drink it.

Treat It to Be Sure

If you're at all in doubt about the water source, by all means filter and boil it before drinking. Filtering is advisable if the water is muddy or has a lot of suspended particles in it. A piece of cloth will do the job. Or you can simply put clean sand in a hollow log with a grass mesh bottom, rinse the sand until the water comes out clear, then pour the liquid through the clean filter into a container. (Containers can range from natural rock depressions to animal stomachs and hollowed-out stumps. For a detailed discussion, see "Rock Boiling," page 236, "Eating Utensils," page 236, and "Coal-burning Wooden Containers," page 253.) If you have time, of course, you can place the water in a container, wait overnight for the particles to settle, and drink off the top.

As a final step, you should boil any questionable water for twenty minutes to purify it. Many wilderness experts still recommend boiling only five minutes, but such a short processing will not kill some of the spore-stage bacteria that can infest drinking water. You can accomplish this task by either heating the water over a fire or, if you don't have a metal container, dropping red-hot rocks, one by one, into an improvised rock basin, hollow log, or coal-hollowed container. In doing so, however, be sure to use only rocks found on high ground, as stones from lowlands or waterways may contain trapped moisture and explode when heated. It may take a rock or two to heat the water up to boiling, but at that point a single baseball-sized rock can boil a gallon of water for fifteen minutes. (For further information on rock boiling, see page 236.)

This boiling process may take some of the taste out of the water, but you can freshen it by pouring the liquid back and forth between containers a few times before drinking. A final caution: Boiling water will kill bacteria and other living pollutants, but you can't be sure it will get rid of all the chemical contaminants. Some will boil off and some won't. This is all the more reason to take special care in choosing a safe water source.

Finding Water

Observation, awareness, and common sense are the keys to finding water in the wilderness. Water flows downhill. Your job is simply to find where it collects. So survey the landscape and ask yourself where you are likely to discover the troughs, depressions, ravines, and traps that will aid or impede it on its downward journey.

In rugged areas, this may mean river valleys between mountains, stream beds between ridges, or high alpine lakes formed by glaciers. In lowland areas it may mean slightly boggy spots with only a few telltale rushes or reeds. In places of great scarcity, you'll logically look near the bases of sloping cliffs, adjoining hills, and huge dunes—or in dried-up ravines where water often collects beneath the surface. Water-loving plants such as cottonwood, willow, and sedges are invariably good indicators. In the Southwest you can even find water in high places, where it collects in rock depressions called kettles. These may contain from a few ounces to hundreds of gallons of water apiece.

Sometimes the telltale sound of a croaking frog or the warble of a cactus wren will give away a hidden water source. Other times you may actually hear the rush of a distant stream or the gurgle of a spring. All animal trails and tracks must eventually lead to water, if you can follow them. Stalking Wolf told me that the Apaches sometimes found water by watching wild ponies. If the animals were walking in a straight line without grazing, they were walking toward water. If they were grazing, they were moving away from water. The same is true of many other animals. Some birds, such as cliff swallows, can be seen flying in a straight line to an unseen water source and shortly afterwards returning to their nests with beakfuls of mud. In fact, you can learn a great deal by observing any animal (even a pine squirrel or a mouse) and asking yourself where it gets its water.

Natural Catches

Any landscape feature that holds or channels water is considered a natural catch. Finding such a source is usually the easiest way to obtain water. Yet by and large I don't recommend this technique to my survival students. For one thing, it's difficult to locate natural catches that haven't been tainted by chemical sprays or other contaminants. Furthermore, many of our waterways—even those in national parks—are also infected with carriers of amoebic dysentery, heartworm, salmonellosis, and hepatitis. With that word of warning, following are some natural catches that can be viable drinking sources, provided you take the proper precautions and purification measures.

Lakes, Ponds, Rivers, Streams. The safest of these catches by far— and the only ones I advise using except in a dire emergency—are streams. Too often, by the time the water has worked its way into lakes, ponds, and rivers, it has picked up a host of pollutants from animals and humans that cannot always be cleansed away. Streams, on the other hand—especially fast-running water at high elevations—are the closest to being pure because they usually represent the meltwater from untouched snows, glaciers, and recent rains that have not been in contact with the ground long enough to become polluted. So if you've made your shelter near a river, lake, or bog, try to find a stream feeding that larger source for your drinking water.

Examine the water channel carefully before drinking. There should be no sign of man's presence and many signs of healthy plants and animals in and around the water. If you decide to drink, avoid drinking directly from the stream. By doing so, you may stir up the bottom and ingest some debris. It is usually better to improvise a container to collect the fluid.

Remember also, if you decide to camp near any of these natural catch areas, keep all wastes at least fifty yards away from the water source.

Stone and Wood Catches. A depression in a rock (sometimes called a kettle) or a shallow hole in the nook of a tree or stump may contain water. Such pockets are numerous in both forests and deserts, but these are generally undesirable catches because the water doesn't last long before it either evaporates or becomes contaminated by bacteria. If you want to drink from a pocket of water in a stump or a limb cavity, first make sure the tree is not poisonous. Also check to see that no animals live in the water, that a profusion of algae doesn't grow there, and that it hasn't picked up a bad taste from wood tannins and resins. Rock kettles, too, can contain toxins if the collected water has run down over higher poison-containing stones—an occurrence that is especially common in old mining areas. Once you have determined that the water is safe, soak it up with a piece of cloth or some nonpoisonous grasses, wring it out into a container, then filter and boil it as explained above.

Lowland Catches. These are merely areas where the soil is soft and damp—indications of seeps, springs, pockets, or the inside bends of dried creekbeds that may still produce water. To collect the moisture, first dig a hole and wait until water begins to seep into it. (Some of these holes may prove unproductive, but don't be dismayed if water doesn't appear right away. It may take an hour or more for the liquid to seep into the hole, even if you dig down to your armpit.) Gather the liquid with a piece of cloth or dried grasses. Then wring the absorbing material out over a container, repeating the process until you've accumulated all the water you want. Then filter and purify it. The work will go faster if you draw from more than one hole at a time. On the other hand, if you are desperate, you may be able to put a piece of clothing over a shallow depression and manage to suck enough moisture through the material to restore your equilibrium.

In some lowland catch areas, particularly sandy bottomlands, ravines, and dried riverbeds, the water is usually pure and—in an emergency where precautions are impossible—can be drunk as it's gathered. At the opposite extreme, though, I advise completely avoiding catches containing ocean, cave, timberland, or farm water—any of which may contain chemical pollutants.

Solar Still

A build-it-yourself solar distillery is one of the best ways to get drinking water in areas where it is scarce. Developed by two doctors in the U.S. Department of Agriculture, the still is a major survival tool. Unfortunately, you have to carry the necessary equipment with you, since it's all but impossible to find natural substitutes. But the only components are a six-by-six-foot sheet of clear or slightly milky plastic, six feet of surgical tubing, and a container to catch the water. (In a pinch, you can get by with just the plastic sheet, since it's the only non-natural element that is really crucial.) These pieces of gear can be folded into a neat little pack along with other survival necessities and clipped onto your belt for any outing (see "Survival Belt Pack," page 271).

To construct a working still, use a digging stick to make a hole four feet across and three feet deep. Try to locate the excavation in a damp area, gully, or river basin to increase the water catcher's productivity. Place a container in the deepest part of the hole. Then lay the tube in place so that one end is in the bottom of the container and the other end runs up and out the side of the pit.

Next, cover the hole with the plastic sheet, securing the edges of the material with dirt and weighting the center of the sheet with a rock. The plastic should now form a cone with sides sloping at forty-five degrees to the ground. The low point of the sheet must be centered directly over the container and no more than three inches above it.

The solar still works by creating a greenhouse effect under the plastic. Ground water evaporates and collects on the sheet until growing droplets run down the material and drop into the container. When the container is full, you can suck the refreshment out through the tubing without having to break down the still every time you need a drink. And on rainy days or nights you can collect a good deal of water on top of the still as well.

A good solar still, located in a damp area, should keep collecting water for four or five days, after which it should be moved to another area. In drier regions such as deserts, I recommend making the hole four feet deep rather than three, and moving the still every day or two.

You can also place crushed herbaceous plants such as cactus and this-tle in the pit to increase the still's output. I once used such a setup in Death Valley and was able to obtain a half gallon of drinking water a day. Be careful to use only edible plants for such boosters, though, as many poisons will evaporate and drip down into your container even more rapidly than water. For the same reason, I don't recommend using a solar still to treat chemically contaminated water. On the other hand, the still does an excellent job of purifying bacterially polluted water. Just pour the liquid onto the surface soil next to the plastic covering. The water will then filter through the ground and be distilled into a quite safe drinking supply. In fact, you can even purify and recycle urine using this technique.

Water From Plants

Plants can also provide water—and without the pollutants that natural catches can harbor. However, since most vegetation doesn't have enough water to serve as a complete survival source, plants are best used to stay the pains of thirst or to get "quick relief" emergency water. Furthermore, it takes a long time to collect liquid from all but a few plants. Many such sources are good only during certain seasons of the year. And you have to be careful never to utilize vegetation from a sprayed area or roadside.

Hardwoods. In early spring, walnut, maple, birch, and hickory trees can all serve as sources of water. To get the fluid, you simply tap the tree (as Vermont maple syrup makers do) by boring a quarter- to half-inch hole into the trunk with a knife or sharp rock, inserting a hollow reed, and collecting the thin sap in a bark or log cup. Alternatively, you can cut through the bark with diagonal slashes. Make sure that you cut into the sapwood (or cambium) that lies just under the bark—and that you don't kill the tree by cutting all the way around it.

Since water gathered by this method contains a high concentration of sugar, drinking large amounts of it (say, more than a pint or two a day) can cause an upset stomach or cramps. For the same reason, the liquid tends to spoil when it's not drunk soon. Personally, I like to use it to brew a pre-sweetened herbal tea. In a pinch, you can get pure water by evaporating the liquid inside a solar still.

Sycamore Trees. The sycamore can be tapped in the same manner as the hardwoods mentioned above. The water from this tree, however, can be harvested any time of year except the dead of winter; and since it doesn't contain much sugar, it can be consumed in quantity or stored for a few days.

Grape Vines. You can get a surprising amount of water from many grape vines—and it *is* water. After positively identifying the plant, cut the vine at the base and allow it to drip directly into a container. Some vines are inches thick and "bleed" so profusely that you can get a cupful in less than an hour—and many will go on producing liquid for as long as two weeks! But again, be sure to positively identify the vine. Don't confuse grape vine with poisonous plants such as deadly nightshade, Canadian moonseed, or Virginia creeper.

Thistle (see "Plants," page 81). Most common species of North American thistle can provide water. In my experience, the bull thistle yields the greatest and best tasting nourishment. To get the juice, simply peel the thorns off young stems and leaves and chew on the watery food. (My students, who often find thistle a refreshing snack on hot trips, refer to it as "survival celery.") Since thistles supply only a meager amount of liquid, they're best used to quench a burning thirst or to keep you going until you find other water sources. I *did* once get over ten ounces of water during a survival campout by crushing and filtering a dozen thistle plants. But I don't want to use this method again unless my life is on the line. It requires killing too many of my plant brothers.

Cactus (see "Plants," page 81). The cactus is another "edible water" source. My favorite variety is the common prickly pear. It has a high water content and is also a good vitamin-laced food source. Folks who find the flavor or texture or the pulp objectionable can simply crush, squeeze, and strain the plant for its water.

Collecting Dew

Stalking Wolf once told me of a young Indian brave who was sent into arid country as a survival test. He knew how to watch horses and birds for signs of water, and how to listen for frogs and other aquatic animals. But

there were none to be seen or heard. The sun beat down and his thirst increased with each passing hour. He searched the landscape in vain for kettles, rock clefts, and other natural catch areas. He passed the entire day without water under the sweltering sun.

That evening, the brave built a makeshift shelter and bedded down for the night. He slept fitfully, because of his burning thirst. The next morning, just before sunup, he poked his head out of the shelter. It was going to be another hot day. As he was preparing to search further in the cool of the morning, however, he happened to notice a mouse apparently chewing on a large boulder.

The brave had been taught to be curious and to learn from even the smallest of his animal friends. So he thought, "I wonder why my mouse brother is eating that rock."

He stalked closer to find out. When he had inched himself to within a few feet, he could see that the mouse was not eating the rock at all, but was lapping up dewdrops from the boulder to quench its thirst.

The young Indian needed no more invitation than that. He, too, knelt down and began licking the boulder. After some time he noticed that his thirst began to break, but he could not seem to get enough of the precious liquid. It was then, as he continued scraping his tongue over the boulder, that he happened to look right into a packrat nest lined with grasses. Taking some of the grasses, he used them as a sponge to wipe dew off the boulder. As he wrung the liquid from the grasses into his mouth, he knew he would never have to go thirsty again.

Believe it or not, collecting dew is probably the simplest and safest way to get drinkable water in a survival situation. Unlike the water found in natural catches, dew is recently condensed, distilled water. Unless it forms on a surface contaminated by chemical sprays or other pollutants, it is as pure as the atmosphere and need not be filtered or boiled before drinking.

The only equipment needed to gather dew is a rag, a piece of clothing, or a handful of dried, nontoxic grasses. Just wipe the moisture from the landscape and wring the liquid into a container or directly into your mouth. Collect the condensed droplets from grass, rocks, leaves, and even sand. Do not, of course, gather moisture from poisonous plants, near a highway or city, or in any area that might have been sprayed by chemicals.

You'll have to get up early and work hard (dew doesn't stay around long!), but don't let the simplicity of this method lead you to believe that it's ineffective. Students of mine have collected more than a quart a day in some of the hottest Southwest deserts. At my farm in New Jersey, two students once used this technique (with the aid of large sponges) to fill a twenty-gallon garbage can with water in less than two hours.

Water in Winter

In the wintertime, collecting frost is just as easy as collecting dew—and there's more of it. Just be sure to wipe it vigorously so it melts and soaks into the cloth or grass. A solar still will also work well in the winter, as long as there is enough daytime heat for water to evaporate. An added advantage of the still is that the topside acts as a catch for rain, which can be drunk without purification.

Don't Eat Snow or Ice. It takes a lot of energy to melt snow and ice when you eat it, and in cold weather you can't afford any extra drain on your stamina. Therefore, it's best to melt these substances and to warm the water slightly before ingesting it. (While snow is usually pure and probably won't need further treatment, bacteria might have encysted in the ice—so boil it to be on the safe side.)

You can melt and warm snow in several ways. One is by building a fire and digging depressions in the snow nearby to collect the water. Another is by dropping a heated rock into a container of snow. You can also get fair quantities of water by putting a snow-filled container in a snow pit, covering it with evergreen boughs, and letting sunlight gradually melt the snow beneath the heat-absorbent greenery. Finally, the simplest snow-melting technique of all is to drop a red-hot rock into fresh snow and push more snow in on top of it. As the rock burns its way to the bottom, it creates a column of water that is already warm and ready to drink. When you need to replenish the water supply in the column, simply drop in another hot rock and dump in more snow.

Conserving Water

If you find yourself in a situation where you have a limited reserve of water, conserve your supply to the utmost by following a few simple rules. (1) Don't eat anything if you don't have water to drink with it. By consuming food, you'll burn up your body's fluid supply all the faster. (2) Travel only during the coolest hours. In the desert, sleep during the day and travel at night. (3) Walk at an easy pace so that precious moisture doesn't get used up through perspiration. (4) Wear light-colored clothing, if you have it, and don't expose your skin to the hot sun. (5) Don't drink urine unless you've first purified it in a solar still. Doing so will increase your body's rate of dehydration. (6) Store as much water as you can in your stomach by drinking as much and as often as possible. People have died with full canteens as a result of trying too hard to conserve their water supplies!

There are also some situations in which you may not feel much thirst before serious dehydration sets in. One of these is during travel at high altitudes, where body moisture often evaporates very quickly. Another is in cold or wet weather. In such cases, force yourself to drink regularly.

Exercises

By now you're probably beginning to realize that it's easy to collect water on almost any landscape, and that a few simple precautions will assure that it's drinkable. To solidify the information in this chapter, practice the exercises below and you'll never be without this most precious resource.

1. Safety. When passing a potential water source, get into the habit of determining whether it's safe to drink. Ask yourself, "Is it fast-moving? Is it clear? Is there a healthy assortment of plants and animals nearby? Could it have been polluted with chemicals? Are there any signs of stagnation?" Gradually you will get into the habit of looking at every water source with a much more critical eye.

2. Filtering. Practice filtering muddy water into a container. Try a variety of materials, including grasses, fibers, and different kinds of clothing to see what works best.

3. Boiling. Heat up a quart of cold water with red-hot rocks of different sizes and see how many it takes to get the water to the boiling point. Start with rocks the size of a marble, then go to golfball size, and finally to baseball-sized rocks. Once you've done this, time the rocks to see how long each one keeps the water boiling.

4. Sources. Practice locating logical water sources, even though you can't see them. When traveling the backcountry, try to detect hidden streams, seeps, and springs by listening for the sounds and looking for the life forms or geologic formations that suggest their presence. (What are these?)

5. Collecting. Collect water in as many ways as you can think of. Try taking it straight from natural catches with a rag or piece of clothing. Make a solar still. Wipe dew off the ground. Melt snow or ice. Compare the ease and effectiveness of these various techniques.

4. FIRE

To the first human beings, fire must have seemed even more magical than it does now. Here was form without substance, light without sun—a potential source of warmth, comfort, pain, and destruction all in one. For thousands of years, primitive humans probably fled from fires. Yet at some point, their innate curiosity must have prompted them to examine a hot, smoldering coal, and hunger must have urged them to taste the flesh of a charred animal. Gradually, humans learned to control fire, but they never completely lost their reverence for it. Even today, fire works its magic on us as we warm our hands near glowing coals or sit captivated by the dance of the flames.

Our natural attraction to fire is well founded. Although it is not usually as critical as shelter or water, there are certainly times when we could not live without it. Jack London's short story, "To Build a Fire," describes the desperate firebuilding efforts of a man who broke through the ice in the far north at fifty below zero. In such cases, life literally hinges on the ability to make a fire quickly. In less severe situations, fire is still a critical necessity in preventing and treating hypothermia and in sterilizing water. It is also the heart of any cooking endeavor, a great aid in toolmaking, and in the long run a wonderful source of warmth and cheer.

If you doubt the importance of fire, I highly recommend trying to go without it for a while. In the Pine Barrens one summer, Rick and I got pretty sloppy with fire, taking it for granted by wasting fuel and neglecting to show our thanks to the Great Spirit. So Stalking Wolf made us go for two weeks without it. He said that being without Warm Fire for a period of time would teach us how sacred it really was.

Rick and I spent a long and debilitating two weeks without Warm Fire's wisdom in our camp. First we missed its warming flames near our bodies. Next we missed its dancing light by our shelter, then the glow of its coals and hot rocks. It was disheartening not to have a fire to dry out our wet clothes and cook our food. Instead of hot teas, we drank cold water. Instead of delicious stews, we ate raw vegetables. Without Warm Fire's touch, animal foods were not safe to eat. Finally, we missed its ability to burn and soften wood for the construction of tools. When that two weeks was over, Rick and I fully appreciated the gifts Warm Fire had to offer, and thereafter we always treated it with the respect and reverence it deserves.

Firemaking seems simple once you know how. But it is one of the most difficult of the survival skills to learn—especially without the aid of matches. There are a great many important things to know: where to put the fire, how to protect it from the elements, where to find tinder and fuel, how to start and maintain the fire, and a host of other skills that will add to your comfort and convenience. It will take a lot of practice to learn these skills; but once you have mastered them, you will gain a sense of security you may never have known in the wilderness.

Building the Fire

Precautions

Before you begin building your fire, think about its proper location. It should be placed for maximum warmth and convenience without sacrificing safety. If you have built a shelter, chances are you have already chosen an area that is high and dry, well protected from the weather, and free from flammable materials such as overhanging boughs or dry leaves. If such materials have accumulated on the ground, sweep them from the area, leaving a radius of at least four feet clear around the fire area.

It is not enough just to find bare ground. Look for the possibility of hidden materials that may be set smoldering by a hot coal. Every year, some of the most devastating forest fires are started in layers of thick, dry humus, dried-up peat bogs, and underground root systems. Such fires may smolder for months and travel for miles before bursting into full flame.

Also insure that the shelter itself does not catch fire. Unless you have built a hogan or a snow shelter, the fire should be located from four to six feet from the shelter entryway. This is usually far enough to guard against flying sparks and to keep you from getting smoked out when the wind changes. To further protect your shelter, put slabs of bark or damp wood around the entryway and other areas that are exposed to flying sparks. This is especially advisable if you're using shelter materials such as dry leaves or grasses. In this case, you may decide to locate the fire even farther than six feet from the shelter.

Watch the fire carefully and continuously. Whether you are cooking or just lounging in your shelter, part of your attention should be riveted on the fire, alert to shifts in the wind or other hazards. At times when it is not possible to keep an eye on the blaze (such as when you drift off for a few hours), make sure it is burning low and not producing any heavy sparks.

Finally, make the fire only as large as necessary for warmth and cooking. A small fire is much easier to control. It also saves fuel. If it is recessed and walled properly, it can produce as much heat as a large one.

Fire Pit and Reflector

The proficiency of a person in the woods can often be judged by what I call the "spin indicator." In cold weather, for example, it is common to see campers huddled around a completely unbordered fire, alternately baking on one side and freezing on the other without ever getting comfortable. The experienced woodsperson, however, plans ahead by choosing a spot that offers a natural heat reflector (such as a large boulder or stump) on one side of the fire, then builds a fire pit with another reflector on the opposite side. This way, both sides of the body are warmed at the same time.

In the long run, the fire pit and reflector are just as important to your well-being as the flames. The pit provides a safe, efficient base for the fire, and the reflector completes the "fireplace," catching and directing two-thirds of the heat that would normally be lost to you and your companions. So even if you are initially forced to build a fire on unprotected, flat ground, you should transfer it to a pit-with-reflector as soon as possible.

The fire pit is a dish-shaped hole with gently sloping sides, from six to twelve inches deep, depending on the width of the fire. This depression cradles the fire, grouping its coals toward the center to help them burn longer and hotter. Don't make the hole so deep that the pit keeps the heat from reaching you. And if you're digging in rich, loamy earth or soil that's

full of root stems, line the bed with rocks to avoid starting an underground fire. (**Caution:** For this or any fireplace job, use only rocks gathered from a high, dry area, since waterlogged rocks may explode when heated. At my farm, an exploding rock once blew out of a concrete fire pit and sent a chunk of rock burrowing into a solid oak beam about sixty feet away.)

The reflector is a horseshoe-shaped wall built around the fire. Ideally, it is built by stacking large rocks in a semicircle about the fire. The actual size of the reflector will vary with the size of your fire and your heating needs. But generally it should be about two feet high and three feet wide.

The smoother the wall, the better the heat reflection. Use dirt or other materials to fill any holes between rocks. If you can't find rocks, many other materials will do. You can use mud, dirt, sand—anything that will block the wind and provide a good reflecting surface. By pounding supporting stakes into the ground, you can even stack wet or green firewood into a horseshoe shape, periodically feeding a dried log into the fire and replacing it with another wet one.

You may find other uses for the fire pit and reflector. For example, the hot rocks can be used for cooking (see "Rock Boiling," page 236). When they have cooled somewhat, they can also be used to line the sleeping area—or dropped into your bedding as heating pads on especially cold nights (see "Bedwarmers," page 44).

Gathering Fuel

There is a simple rule for selecting tinder and firewood in a survival situation: *it must be dry*. The driest wood is found high up, away from water sources such as streams and lakes, on south-facing hillsides with an open exposure to the sun, and on the lee sides of incoming storms. In general, use the same criteria as for selecting a good shelter site.

Don't collect your fire-starting fuel from the ground—especially in wet weather. Instead, gather dead, dry vegetation from standing trees and plants. Look under low evergreen boughs or on the undersides of shrubs where dead branches have been protected from the rain. Such fuel does not absorb ground moisture and dries quickly. Even in a downpour, you can usually carve off the outer wet fraction of an inch to find dry wood below.

You can usually determine the dryness of a potential fuel source by breaking it. If a stick snaps cleanly and audibly, it's probably good firewood. In most weather conditions, you can also find reasonably dry wood by touch. And when your hands are too cold to be sensitive, you can do a "face test" by pressing the fuel against your lower lip or cheek to feel for dampness.

In areas of great scarcity, you can often find dead patches of vegetation—clumps of matted grasses and plants—that are combustible. In desert areas, follow the rules for finding water (see page 49), and there you will also find the greatest amount of potential fuel. But remember that wild places all over the world today are becoming depleted at an alarming rate. In fragile areas where fuel is scarce or grows very slowly, it is even best not to build a fire if you can avoid it.

Tinder is the first of the four necessary grades of fuel. This is the light, airy material that catches and spreads a spark into flame. There are literally scores of natural materials that make good tinder. The dried inner bark of certain trees—basswood, elm, cottonwood, aspen, willow, sage, cedar, walnut, and cherry, to name some of the best—makes excellent tinder. Dry reeds and grasses are likely candidates. Many plants such as dogbane, velvetleaf, yucca, primrose, fireweed, bulrush, milkweed, cattail, and thistle (and the down from these last three) are also good. As a rule, almost any dry, fibrous plant material can be used for tinder. Even some mosses and lichens can be used if properly prepared. The important thing is not to memorize a list, but to experiment with the materials in your area to see what works best.

To prepare the tinder, remove all hard, crumbly bark or inner pith from the gathered fuel. Then systematically twist, turn, and push the material between your fingers to loosen and separate the fibers. Finally, rub the fibers back and forth in your hands until you've created a fluffy bundle made up of filaments as small as thread. You can soften stubborn fibers by pounding them between two rocks. Do a thorough job, since the tinder must be light and airy to nourish a coal. Once it is well buffed, try the "face test" to make sure it is dry. If not, buff and fluff it some more.

As you experiment, you may find that some materials will crumble in your hands. These are either too decayed or lacking in fiber. Materials such as cattail and thistle down are so fine they can be used without any preparation to catch and spread a coal, but they must be laced with other fibrous materials to produce a flame. On the other hand, if you have a commercial firestarter, you may not have to take such great care with the tinder bundle. Many materials that will not hold and carry a spark will easily catch the flame from a match or lighter.

Kindling is the next type of fuel you will need. It is composed of tiny twigs or slivers that range from the thickness of a pencil lead to that of a pencil itself. You can either break it off sheltered, dead branches such as the undersides of evergreen boughs, or carve the fuel from larger pieces of wood. In wet weather, you can even make "fuzz sticks," carving down to dry wood and shaving thin strips into curled branches that will more easily burst into flame.

Be sure to keep both kindling and tinder absolutely dry. In wet weather, this can be done by placing the fuel between your outer shirt and your undershirt as it's gathered. Do not place it next to the skin, where it will absorb body moisture.

"Squaw Wood" is thicker and longer than kindling, from pencil to wrist size in diameter. It is named for the Indian squaws who, along with the children and elders of the tribe, collected large quantities of these sticks as a part of their daily routine. Rather than cutting huge trees for firewood, Indians burned these small and easy-to-gather sticks as often as possible—and so should you.

Bulk Firewood is too-big-to-break fuel that's added to a fire only after the blaze is going strong. You don't usually have to be careful about keeping it dry. By the time the kindling and squaw wood are burning well, your fire should be hot enough to burn even green and damp wood.

Conserve your energy when gathering firewood. Many campers make ten trips when they could make two. Instead of walking back and forth with small loads, bundle larger amounts with cordage or rig a "travois"—a platform made of two long poles rigged with crossbeams—and drag the wood back in a single load. Also, don't try to drag in a log the size of a bed. Nor should you waste energy trying to cut or split bulk firewood. Instead, let the fire do the work. Either place the ends of these pieces in the coals or let the fire cut them in two.

Don't take shortcuts when gathering any of the four types of fuel. Take enough time to get the best materials. That way, your fire will be easy to start, and it will keep burning no matter what the weather. Finally, be sure to gather enough firewood to last through the night. There are few worse tasks than having to leave a snug shelter and stumble around in the dark to replace a dwindling fuel supply.

Making the Tipi Fire

There are many different structural forms for a fire, but the tipi shape is by far the best for survival purposes. It starts easily, burns efficiently, and throws out large quantities of heat and light. Furthermore, most of the smoke and sparks are channeled straight up; and the slanting walls and resulting high flames help the blaze hold up even in rain and snowstorms.

To build the tipi fire, first line the ground or fire pit with dried bark or grasses to prevent moisture from wicking into the fuel. Then make a small cone out of the kindling by propping the smallest sticks against one another, tipi-fashion. Leave enough room between the twigs for air to get

through, and leave an opening so you'll be able to place the tinder bundle inside. Face the entrance toward the wind to help drive the flames up through the fuel.

Next, encircle the tipi with a row of slightly larger sticks, lacing the kindling with dried grasses, pine needles, or other easily combustible material. Finally, expand the size of the tipi by placing squaw wood around the kindling. Work carefully from the thinnest to the thickest pieces until the tipi is eight to ten inches across and a foot or more in height. If it's raining, lay small slabs of bark around the cone to help keep the interior dry until you're ready to start the fire. Once you have a good, dry layer of thumb-sized wood in place, you will be able to light the fire with some assurance that it won't go out.

Another source of insurance, if you can find it, is the highly flammable pitch from evergreen trees. Pitch globules, which often seep from the bark of pines and firs, can be gathered with sticks and dabbed onto pieces of kindling to make them more combustible. Better still are pitch sticks— sections of wood literally soaked with pitch that are found in the heartwood of dead and rotting evergreens. Such wood is often identified by mottled white streaks on the decaying timber. Simply strip such pieces into small sticks with your fingers or a knife and add them to your kindling. When ignited, they burn furiously with a spitting flame, even when they're wet.

Firemaking Techniques

Important as it is to carry a lighter or a good supply of matches in the wilderness, it is best not to have to rely on such aids. You never know when you might lose your lighter or soak your matches, and you can never carry enough of these firestarters to last indefinitely. On the other hand, if you know how to make a fire using only natural materials, you will feel secure whatever the situation.

The Bow Drill
There are more than thirty different ways of starting a fire with natural materials. Of these, the easiest is the bow drill. Also called the "bow and spindle" and "fire by friction," this technique was used for centuries by primitive peoples everywhere. The essential parts are a bow, a spindle, a handhold, and a notched fireboard. The coal is produced through friction as the wooden spindle whirls against the fireboard, dropping hot powder into the notch. The coal is then dropped onto the tinder and blown into flame.

Like most of the Indians' survival tools, the bow drill was personified and regarded as a gift from the Creator. One legend tells how the Great Spirit passed on the "wisdom of the whirling wood." The spindle was considered the male entity—the active, aggressive component—while the fireboard symbolized the receptive, nurturing female. The union of the two was like a meeting of lovers whose warmth and passion ultimately gave birth to the coal. Beneath the fireboard, the tinder bundle represented the earth and all of creation nurturing the newborn into the fullness of life.

Like any new skill that involves timing and coordination, bow-drill firemaking may be awkward and frustrating at first. It requires proper materials, carefully shaped to the right specifications, as well as patient practice of form and technique. It will probably take many trials before you finally blow the coal into flame. But once you have been successful, it will stay with you the rest of your life.

Wood Selection. Selecting wood for the spindle and fireboard is one of the most critical aspects of bow-drill firemaking. Both components should be made from the same type of wood, or from different woods of approximately the same hardness. Otherwise, one or the other will be consumed without producing a coal.

In general, select a branch of dead wood that's very dry but not rotten. Ideally, it should also be a wood of medium hardness. Cottonwood, willow, aspen, tamarack, cedar, sassafras, sycamore, and poplar are best. Yucca and sage can be used, though they are a little on the hard side. The dried pithy stems of mullein and burdock also make serviceable spindles and fireboards if properly prepared. But stay away from the very hard species like oak, hickory, and walnut. Also try to avoid the very soft, resinous types like pine, fir, and spruce.

On the other hand, almost any wood can be used to get a fire going provided it is dry enough. The key is to get a dead wood that is dry but not so far gone that it's punky or crumbly. You can determine the wood quality with a simple "thumbnail test." Push your thumbnail into the wood. If it crushes into the wood easily, it's too far gone. If it takes an effort to make any mark at all, the wood is probably too hard. If it makes a nice clean dent without cutting in, it's just right.

Interestingly enough, the more unsuitable the wood you use for practice, the better you will master this art. When Rick and I were learning the bow drill, for example, Stalking Wolf first gave us a chunk of green oak to work with. We tried for two weeks, five hours a day, and never got a fire going. Then he gave us a piece of damp cedar and we fired it up in a few minutes. We succeeded mainly because the oak had forced us to perfect our skills. Conditions are rarely perfect for firebuilding in the wilderness. If you practice only with the easy woods, you may find that you cannot get a fire going under adverse conditions even with cottonwood or willow. For this reason, I recommend beginning with cedar. It is one of the softest of the medium-grade woods, and it will demand that your form be just right.

To begin with, you may want to get a foot-long chunk of four-by-four cedar at your local builder's supply and cut it into the proper implements. But in the bush you can get your bow-drill materials just as you would gather firewood—from a standing dead tree.

Again, never gather firestarting materials near lakes, streambeds, or any other place where moisture collects. A group of my advanced survival students (all of whom had successfully made many bow-drill fires before) spent an entire week without fire because they did not think to search above the river valley. Go up high to gather your materials. Look on south-sloping hillsides that are well exposed to the sun. Knock dead branches out of tall trees. Before you decide to use a piece of wood, give it the "thumbnail test" and heft it in your hand, feeling for the lightness that indicates it is free of moisture.

The spindle is a smooth cylinder about three-fourths to an inch thick and about eight inches long. You can carve it from a rough chunk of wood any size, but you'll save time and energy if you can find a straight branch about the right diameter and shape it with your knife or a rock. Whittle or abrade the spindle until it's almost as round and straight as a dowel. Then taper both ends into blunt points. Eventually, one end will turn freely in the greased socket of the handhold, while the other creates friction and hot dust against the fireboard.

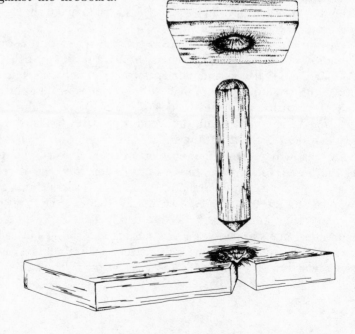

The fireboard should be about half an inch to three-fourths of an inch thick, eight to twelve inches long, and at least twice the width of the spindle. This makes it thick enough so it won't split or burn through easily, and long enough to be stabilized under your shoe. If you like, make the fireboard even wider and longer to allow room for more sockets as the spindle works through the wood. If you use a branch, be sure to split and smooth it so the fireboard is flat on both sides and will not wobble under your foot.

The handhold—the object that fits in your palm and holds the drill in place—can be made from a small section of branch, a rock with a depression in it, or a piece of bone. Almost any type of wood will do, but it's best to use one that's harder than the spindle and fireboard material. Shape the handhold so you can grasp it firmly but comfortably in one hand. It should be small enough so you can get a good grip on it, but large enough so your fingertips stay away from the whirling wood. (It gets *hot* down there!)

The bow is a two- to three-foot stick that is strung loosely with a length of shoelace, leather thong, sinew, or braided cord (see "Cordage," page 241). It can be made from a stout, slightly curved branch (either green or seasoned) about half an inch to an inch in diameter. Choose one that is strong enough so the cord will not slip on the spindle when you begin to drill. Since the cord may need frequent tightening, tie a fairly permanent knot on one end of the bow and an easily adjustable knot around the other (see "Knots," page 244).

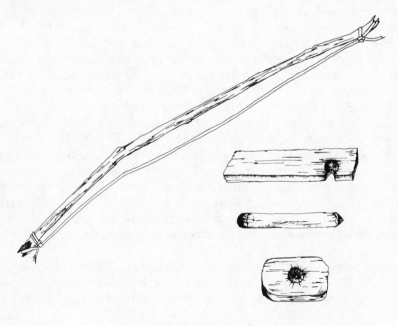

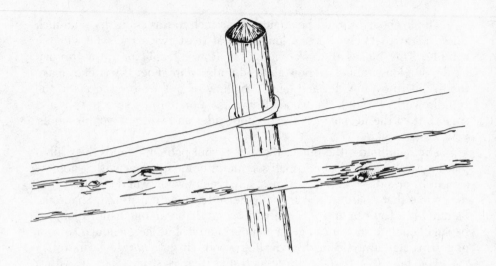

Drilling the Sockets. Now that the apparatus is made, you are ready to drill spindle sockets into the fireboard and handhold. First, measure in from the edge of the fireboard a little more than half the diameter of the spindle and twist your knifepoint or some sharp object there to get the socket started. Do the same for the center of the handhold. Next, twist the spindle onto the outside of the bowstring. (It should feel like it wants to flip out of your hand.) Then set up the components as shown.

Take careful note of the proper form. If you are right handed, rest your right knee on the ground while placing your left foot across the fireboard. The socket mark should be just beside your instep. Your chest should be set firmly on your left knee. Your left hand, braced tightly against the shin, should grasp the handhold and keep the spindle perpendicular to the fireboard. The bow is then held in your right hand and moved in line with your body. From this position you can easily spin the drill and press down on it from above. In addition, your body will overshadow the apparatus to create a meager but valuable weatherbreak.

Once everything is in the right position, begin vigorously moving the bow back and forth with long strokes while gradually increasing downward pressure on the handhold. This will probably seem quite awkward at first. But after you've gotten the hang of it, you'll soon have the apparatus smoking. Stop drilling after the spindle has made a good, round impression in both the fireboard and the handhold. Now you're ready to cut the all-important notch.

The notch is cut from the edge of the fireboard almost (but not quite) to the center of the socket. It should be a wedge-shaped slice, a little smaller than an eighth of a pie, through the entire thickness of the board.

You can saw or chip out this notch with a knife or other instrument, but it should be a clean, well-manicured cut.

Greasing the Handhold. Finally, grease the handhold socket and the upper end of the spindle. This will help the drill to rotate smoothly and prevent the handhold from smoking. You can use natural body oils by simply rubbing the end of the spindle along the sides of your nose or in your hair. Pine pitch, animal fat, and slime molds will also work. But don't use water. It will make the wood swell up and bind in the handhold. Also, never put the greased end of the spindle in the fireboard socket. Otherwise, you'll have to sand or recarve both spindle and socket before you can get enough friction to make a coal.

Starting the Fire. Before you start the fire, check to see if the ground you're working on is damp. If it's moist, use a plate of dry bark to give yourself a decent work surface. Next, lay down your tinder and position your fireboard directly over it (the notch opening toward you) so the very center of the bundle is directly beneath the notch.

Now, taking the same position you used for making the spindle sockets, set up the rest of the apparatus. Be sure your form is correct, with the handhold firmly braced against your shin and the drill held straight up and down. Holding the bow at the end and keeping the arm straight, begin making slow, steady strokes with very little downward pressure. When you feel comfortable with it, gradually increase speed and pressure. Soon

the board will begin smoking and you'll see dark powder forming in the notch. When this happens, apply even more pressure and drill faster until the board is smoking violently. (Don't push too hard, though, or the drill will slow, the string will slip, and the smoke will diminish.) When burning dust begins to pour into the notch and onto the tinder bundle, take ten more double strokes and carefully lift the spindle from the board.

Now, place your knifepoint or the sharpened end of a stick at the top of the notch and gently lift the whole board with the other hand until the coal drops into the tinder bundle. If the coal is smoking, pick up the bundle in both hands, gently "bird-nesting" it around the coal. Lift it up high to keep your face out of the smoke, and blow a thin jet of air toward the coal. If it is alive, it will start to glow and smoke. Keep blowing calmly but steadily. As the coal brightens and begins to spread, blow harder and pack the tinder around it more tightly. Be careful not to squeeze the coal to death. Also take care not to drop it or blow it out the far side of the bundle. When you can see the coal spreading and feel the tinder heating up, blow even harder until it bursts into flame. Then place the flaming bundle quickly inside the tipi structure. (Take care not to burn your face, hands or hair.)

Sometimes the sheer act of placing the bundle inside the tipi makes the flame die down. If this happens, don't remove the tinder—just keep blowing and it will catch flame again. If you feel your fingers burning even before the tinder catches flame, place the bundle under the kindling and manipulate it with a stick as you continue to blow.

Most likely, you will not produce a coal on your first few tries. After each attempt, clean out the notch and dust off the tinder bundle. Before long, you may find that you have drilled through the fireboard and will have to make a new socket and notch. Eventually, you will have to replace the drill, too.

Troubleshooting. Don't be discouraged if you can't get a fire going, even after repeated attempts. Instead, try to learn something from each failure. Following are some common problems and how to solve them.

• **Cord slips around spindle.** Either the cord is too loose and needs to be tightened, or the spindle has been over-smoothed by friction and should be roughened slightly by abrasion or a few knife strokes. It is also possible that you are applying too much pressure on the handhold.

• **Cord rides up or down on spindle.** The cord should be in the middle of the spindle as you drill. Keep your arm straight and take long, level strokes with the bow. Avoid dragging the bowtip.

• **Spindle pops out of socket.** Usually this is because the handhold or fireboard socket (or both) are not deep enough. Carve or sand the grease from the spindle and drill the socket deeper.

• **Handhold smokes and heats up.** There is too much friction on the handhold. It needs more lubrication. If you are using different woods for the handhold and spindle, this may also mean the handhold is too soft.

• **Drilling at an angle.** Check the fireboard to see that your socket is vertical. If not, take more care to hold the spindle upright. Brace your wrist on your shin and adjust your position by rocking forward or backward over the board.

• **Spindle wobbles as you drill.** Brace your wrist and forearm more firmly against your shin and leg, and take care to hold the spindle straight.

• **Coal falls apart.** Ideally, the coal should hold together in a dark, brown, powdery mass. If it falls apart, it usually means either that the wood is too damp or that you have not been pushing hard enough.

• **Coal goes out immediately.** Examine the color and consistency of the coal. If it is soft, powdery, and light brown, you are probably not drilling long or hard enough. If it is black or striated, you may be pushing too hard, slowing the spindle and scraping off larger chunks than you want.

• **Coal goes out in tinder.** If you had a good, glowing coal that went out while you were blowing on it, either your tinder is too damp or you are not using the proper technique. You may be packing the tinder too close and smothering the coal, holding it too loosely to allow the coal to spread into the fibers, or blowing with the wrong force at the wrong time. You may also be blowing so close to the bundle that the moisture from your breath is putting out the coal.

• **Coal burns through tinder without flaming.** This usually means your tinder is packed too tightly to allow air to circulate among the fibers. Fluff up the bundle and try again. For added insurance, dig a small hole under the fireboard to prevent the board from crushing the tinder. Then line the hole with dry material to keep ground moisture away.

All this troubleshooting, not to mention the cutting, burning, greasing, and stroking involved in using a bow drill may seem troublesome. But with practice, a survivalist can proceed from start to finish—including making the entire apparatus—in as little as fifteen minutes. The task doesn't require a lot of strength, either. Form and coordination are much more important. Indeed, I have seen children make fires using this method.

The Mouth Drill

The mouth drill works on the same principles as the bow drill. The main difference is that friction is produced by rubbing the spindle between the hands, and downward pressure is produced by the head and neck pushing against a mouthpiece held between the teeth. The beauty of this system is

that it doesn't require any cordage. However, it is more difficult than the bow drill, and both equipment and form must be perfect. Since both methods require mastery of similar skills, I strongly recommend learning the bow drill first.

The spindle should be from two to two-and-a-half feet long, about half an inch thick, and as straight as possible. Some of the best materials are cottonwood, willow, yucca, mullein, and burdock. Mullein and burdock stems are especially convenient because they do not require any carving. Friction is produced by the hard outer shell, and the inner pith immediately turns to coal.

The fireboard should be large enough to kneel on as you bend over it. Again, it can be made from any dry, medium-hard wood—preferably the same kind used for the spindle. You may want to make a solid fireboard out of willow or cottonwood for use with pithy spindles. But you can even make an effective fireboard from mullein or burdock. Just twirl the spindle until it burns down to the pith, then carve the pith out at an angle just beneath the hole. The hot dust then rolls down inside and collects in the hollowed receptacle near one end. Finally, the stalk is turned upside down and the coal tapped onto the tinder.

The mouthpiece is all-important. Make it sturdy and large enough so the spindle does not slip out and hit you in the face. A section from a two-inch-thick branch should work well enough. Carve a bite plate into the branch so it fits well back into your mouth. The more teeth you can sink into it, the better.

To start the coal, first stabilize the fireboard under one or both knees. (The notch will probably be facing away from you this time.) Hunch over the board and clamp the long spindle between the fireboard and the mouthpiece. With stiff fingers, rub the spindle smoothly between your palms until the board begins to smoke. Then apply more pressure and rub even faster. When the board is smoking well, drop the coal onto the tinder and blow it into flame.

If you did not fully realize the importance of craftsmanship with the bow drill, you will certainly appreciate it with the mouth drill. The spindle must be straight, or every crook will register as a vibration until you feel like your head has been pressing on a jackhammer. The mouthpiece socket must also be deep enough so that the spindle does not slip out. Cracked teeth and flared nostrils are not uncommon injuries among the careless!

The Hand Drill

The hand drill is very similar to the mouth drill except that there is no mouthpiece. Both friction and pressure are produced entirely by the hands and arms. For this reason, the method is very difficult to master, and you should become an expert with the two already described before you seriously try to learn it.

You will also have to prepare the best possible materials—preferably well-cured willow shoots or long, straight shoots of mullein or burdock packed with cattail down for added combustion. Since this method uses no handhold, the spindle must be even longer than that of the mouth drill—from three to four feet—and as straight as an arrow shaft. A plug of soft, pithy wood lashed to the business end of the spindle also improves the apparatus greatly.

The hand drill can be used either kneeling or sitting. Start rubbing the spindle at the top, using the same technique as for the mouth drill. As you apply pressure, your hands will work toward the bottom of the spindle. Then you must quickly slide them back up. This is best done by moving one hand up while briefly holding the spindle in place with the other. Repeat the spinning movement until the coal has formed. If you have a partner, the process can be made easier. One person spins until he or she has reached the bottom, then the other immediately takes over at the top. This way, each person gets a brief rest and the spinning goes on without interruption.

Flint and Steel

The early pioneers often started fires by striking the sharp edge of a piece of flint or silica-rich rock (such as quartzite, chert, agate, or jasper) with the back of a knifeblade or other steel implement. On impact, the rock throws sparks of steel onto the tinder bundle, where they are quickly blown into flame. As a matter of fact, cigarette lighters are nothing more than updated versions of this old method, using pressurized gas or gas-soaked wicks as tinder.

There are numerous difficulties with flint and steel, the main one being that steel is hard to find in the wilderness. Unless you have a knife or chance to find some castoff steel implement, you might as well forget it. Also, since the spark is small and goes out quickly, your tinder bundle must be made of the finest, driest material you can find. Charred cotton is ideal but is not readily available in the bush. Lacking this, you can successfully use a handful of cattail down or the finely worked outer bark from plants such as sagebrush and cliffrose.

Striking the Spark. Make a large tinder bundle, line it with very soft material, and place it on a piece of dried bark. Then, holding the rock just above the tinder, strike a sharp edge of it with the back of your knifeblade until a spark falls onto the tinder. Getting this down will take some practice. You should hit the rock with a sharp, glancing blow—just enough to shave off a spark. When you become adept at it, you may be able to strike a spark while holding the rock and tinder in one hand.

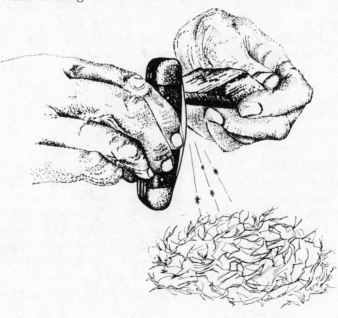

If the spark does not spread after repeated tries, it may be that the tinder is not fine or dry enough. In that case, you can line the "nest" by charring and powdering such things as manure, dry rot from stumps, or the pith from various plants. But here again, you need fire to produce most of these materials in the first place. For obvious reasons, I don't recommend flint and steel as a survival fire starter unless you have a piece of steel and some charred cotton in your survival belt pack (see page 271) with you.

Other Fire Starters

There are many other ways of starting fires with natural materials. The fire saw is a method that involves rubbing the beveled edge of a stick in the notch of a fireboard. The fire thong is a length of cordage that is twisted around a dead branch and pulled back and forth until it bursts into flame. Rick and I figured out a variation on the bow drill using a log with a crank to weight and turn the spindle. We also learned how to use waves to create friction between floating logs so we could have hot coals any time we wanted. If you remember that almost all firestarting techniques involve friction to produce a coal, you may be able to invent some new methods of your own.

Maintaining the Fire

One of the last things you'll want to do when you wake up on a wet, snowy, or frosty morning is get up and crank out another bow-drill fire. You can avoid this if you insure that your fire will last through the night. Before you go to bed, build up the fire with regular firewood—preferably hardwoods. Then add a layer of wet wood. Finally, adorn the fire with a layer of green wood. The wet wood will take a while to dry out before it burns. The green wood will burn slowly and evenly for hours, leaving coals that should last until morning. Then all you'll have to do is toss on a handful of tinder and a couple of logs and wait for the fire to flare up again.

If you can't attend the fire for even longer periods, there are numerous devices you can make to feed it automatically. One is the log ramp—a row of smooth, rounded logs on an inclined scaffolding made with two pairs of Y-sticks with cross beams. Theoretically, when the fire consumes the bottom log, the one just above it falls down and holds up the others. The apparatus doesn't work quite as well as theory suggests, but if you prepare it carefully, you can keep the fire going for many extra hours with very little trouble.

Another method of prolonging a fire is the pedestal mount, in which a fresh stack of wood is held high above the flames on three logs. When the pedestal logs are consumed, they collapse and drop a fresh load of wood onto the fire. A similar contraption is a pile of wood set on a thin platform just above the flames. The platform finally burns through and drops a new load of wood on the fire.

If you don't want to go to all this trouble and won't be needing the flames, I've found that simply burying the fire under a couple of inches of dirt or sand in a fire pit at least six inches deep keeps the coals alive through the night. In the morning all you have to do is scrape off the dirt and you have a pit of coals ready to blow into flame.

Best Firewoods

The value of different firewoods depends on your needs. Following is a brief discussion of various types of wood and their best uses.

Softwoods such as pine, fir, hemlock, tamarack, cedar, and other evergreens burn quickly, generating lots of heat and light for a short time. They make excellent kindling and are especially useful for emergencies when you need immediate warmth. They are also fine for doing detail work or reading at night. But they are not good for maintaining a fire because they have to be replaced so frequently. (**Caution:** Do not burn pine unless absolutely necessary. It produces a resinous, toxic smoke that can be harmful when inhaled.)

Medium hardwoods such as cottonwood, poplar, aspen, willow, maple, sage, and alder burn somewhat more slowly and give off moderate heat and light. For these reasons, they make very good squaw wood. They are also convenient for quick cooking methods such as frying and boiling, and for working or reading at night. In addition, they burn slowly enough so you won't have to feed the fire every few minutes.

Hardwoods such as oak, hickory, walnut, and other dense deciduous trees burn much longer with good heat and poor light. Consequently, they make the best long-term cooking and bulk firewoods. They maintain an even temperature and leave long-lasting coals that can often be left unattended for hours.

Remember that the above are only general guidelines. The woods within these categories may vary greatly. Osage orange, for example (one of the hardest of the hardwoods), burns so hotly that manufacturers of certain stoves warn not to use it with their products. The quality and duration of the fire also varies with the wetness or greenness of the wood. Generally, wet wood burns three to four times longer than dry wood, and green wood may burn up to eight times longer than dry wood.

Exercises

Following are some exercises that will help you to learn the skills presented in this chapter.

1. Tinder. Gather as many different tinder materials as you can find in your area and experiment to see which are best. This may include leaves, mosses, lichens, plant stalks, bark—anything that you think might burn easily. Prepare tinder bundles with each of them, observe how they burn, and make mental note of the differences.

2. Tipi Fire. Try starting a tipi fire from scratch in sixty seconds. This is an exercise I frequently spring on my survival students without warning. The first time, they usually fumble around for several minutes. But on subsequent tries, they are much faster because they have become more aware of what materials they need, where to get them, and how to build a quick-flaming fire.

3. Bow Drill. After you have thoroughly learned the bow drill in your basement or back yard, go camping and leave your matches at home. This will provide a greater sense of urgency and force you to master fire-starting with natural materials before you get caught in a survival situation.

4. Woods. Observe the burning of many different kinds of wood—soft, hard, dry, wet, and green. Watch each wood closely, noting the color and duration of the flame, as well as the quantity of heat and light produced. (Cedar burns almost white hot, oak a deep yellow or even red.) This exercise will familiarize you with the heating and lighting capacities of various woods in your area.

5. PLANTS

Think of the greenery that enfolds the earth: leaves and algae cells releasing oxygen to the air; jungles and forests teeming with wildlife; farms and gardens growing fruits and vegetables; rangelands supporting billions of domesticated animals. It is a panorama that staggers the imagination. Yet the importance of plants is often taken for granted by those who live among the world's great islands of concrete and steel. In an environment of synthetics, it is easy to forget the dance of radiant energy. Endlessly it flows from sun to leaf, leaf to insect, insect to frog, and frog to fox along the great chain of being. Every member of the human family is attached to that chain, and to the green foundation strands in the web of life. Indeed, the most advanced societies on earth are based on the metabolic processes that go on inside a blade of grass. In a survival situation, where grasses, herbs, shrubs, and trees are the primary source of almost every necessity, it is easy to see this connection.

Edibility and Identification
When it comes to wild edibles, there is no shortcut to positive identification. Some publications mistakenly suggest that if you don't know a plant, you can eat a small quantity and wait for a specified time to see whether it has any adverse effects. This is a serious error. With some plants, even a single bite is enough to cause discomfort or death.

I usually require my survival students to identify and study new plants on their own. Rarely do I give them the names of unidentified wild edibles because they often look no farther than the name. In one of my weaker moments, I remember, a student came to me asking the name of a particular plant and I said, "That's cow parsnip." About two hours later, it dawned on me that I now had a responsibility to tell him more.

I found the student near a swamp and began by warning him that the leaves of the cow parsnip can raise a rash on a person's hands. He turned to me and said, "Oh, that's all right. I've found another one and I'm holding it by the stem this time."

This time he was holding a poison water hemlock, which looks much like cow parsnip, but which is fatal to most people who mistakenly take a bite of it. Needless to say, I sat that person down with good references and made him read everything he could find on both plants before he did any more foraging. The experience impressed upon him the importance of a thorough study with reputable guidebooks.

Identification, of course, is most critical with food plants. In some cases, this may take careful study of the plant's stalks, leaves, flowers, seeds, and roots, since some poisonous plants closely resemble edible species. Furthermore, you should be familiar with the usual methods of preparing and eating various plants, since many can cause illness if not boiled, or if eaten in too large a quantity.

Even if you're not going to eat the plant, take pains to positively identify it. Poisonous plants used to filter your water will poison the water. Those used for tools may cause skin rashes. And those used for trap parts or bait may repel the very animals you want to attract.

Knowing a plant's properties will also make them much more useful to you. For example, medium-hard woods such as willow and cottonwood are best for starting fires. The inner barks of certain trees and fibrous plants make better cordage than others. And many plants have powerful medicinal qualities. (Most of these uses are listed with each species in the section entitled, "One Hundred Edible Plants," beginning on page 87.)

Regardless of the plant, then, follow a few simple rules to assure your health and safety. Here is a quick summary: (1) Positively identify the plant. Be able to do this at any season of the year. (2) Learn what parts are edible and at what times they are in season. (3) Find out how the plant should be eaten. Some can be eaten raw, while others require cooking or treating. (4) Eat only a small portion at first. Some people are more sensitive to certain plants than others. (5) Heed written warnings about specific plants. That way you'll avoid stomach aches and skin rashes.

Seasonal Fare

The availability of plants and plant parts fluctuates greatly with the seasons. Plant parts with high nutritional value in the summer may be shriveled or nonexistent in the winter. But if you know your plants well, you'll still be able to identify them and utilize the sources of greatest food value.

In the springtime, look primarily for tender green leaves and shoots. Many of these can be eaten raw. The roots still contain a great amount of food value in early spring, but as the season wears on, more and more of this energy is transferred to the stems, leaves, and flowers.

Summer is the time of full development for most plants. Leaves, shoots, and flowers are so abundant and so rich in nutrients that you may be able to maintain yourself on a primary diet of plants with very little animal food at all. However, make sure you're getting plenty of proteins by supplementing your greens with nuts and seeds where you can find them. Roots are a poor source of nutrients in the summer, since most of the energy is going into plant growth and reproduction.

During the autumn months, you can often find large numbers of nuts and berries to supplement your greens. These are very high in protein. As annual plants disappear and leaves begin to fall, plant energies return once again to the roots.

The cold winter months can be a rather bleak time for survivalists, though being caught out at such a time is no reason for despair. You'll just have to use more of your knowledge and ingenuity. A few plants, such as miner's lettuce, can still be found with green, leafy rosettes—even under the snow. If you can identify leafless plants, you'll still be able to dig up the energy-rich roots. And in many places you'll find evergreen trees whose needles make excellent and restoring teas.

It might seem at first that tea is meager fare, but don't discount its food value. In the Pine Barrens I often make a winter tea by steeping a mixture of pine needles, oak buds, and sassafras roots. It doesn't fill my stomach, but it maintains my health and energy while I'm looking for an animal. And that is much better than gorging yourself on something that has very little food value. If you can find a few torpid insects or a small bird or mammal to add to such teas, you'll have a nutritious and sustaining stew.

The Big Four

There are four general categories of plants you can eat almost anytime and anywhere, as long as you take the proper precautions. Even if you can identify no other plants, knowing these four types can provide you with enough nutrients to keep you alive in most areas of North America at almost any time of the year.

Grasses. Almost all bladed grasses—from the wild meadow varieties to wheat, oats, and bamboo—are edible. That includes stems, leaves, roots, and seeds. Grasses are so rich in vitamins and minerals that animals often chew on them to get nutrients they can't get anywhere else. The young shoots up to about six inches tall can usually be eaten raw. Most mature grasses are quite fibrous, containing large amounts of cellulose that is difficult to digest. For this reason, it is best to chew them thoroughly and spit them out after swallowing the juices. Alternatively, you can steep the green or dried leaves to make a refreshing tea.

Grass seeds are very rich in protein. They can be eaten raw, roasted and ground into flour, or boiled into mush. **Warning:** Although about ninety-nine percent of all grass seeds are edible, there are a few species whose seeds are toxic if eaten raw. For this reason, I recommend roasting the seeds of unfamiliar grasses before eating. Also make sure the seeds are either green or brown. Purple or blackish seeds may indicate the presence of a toxic fungus.

Cattails (see illustration page 97). This remarkable plant grows in swamps, marshes, and wet ground throughout most of North America and is easily identified by its swordlike leaves, long, stiff stalks, and sausage-shaped seed heads. It sometimes reaches a height of nine feet. In the spring, two green flower heads form at the top of the stalk—the male above and the female below. The male flowers become a golden pollen mass, while the female flowers eventually transform themselves into the characteristic downy seed head.

The cattail is an edible for all seasons. In fact, it has so many edible parts that it's like a wilderness supermarket. In early spring the young shoots and stalks (up to two feet) can be peeled and eaten raw or boiled. In late spring, the green flower heads can be husked and boiled. In early summer, the pollen heads can be picked and eaten raw, or dried into flour. The root is also a cornucopia of edibles. Any time from late summer through winter, look for horn-shaped sprouts growing from the tangled rootstocks at the base of the plant. These can be eaten raw or boiled for a few minutes. The rootstocks themselves are also an excellent source of starch. They can be crushed, dissolved in cold water, and made into flour after draining and drying.

Not only is the cattail a supermarket, but also a pharmacy. Ripe cattail flowers, for example, can be mashed and used as a salve for cuts and burns. Between the young leaves you'll also find a most remarkable drug in the form of a sticky juice. It makes an excellent styptic, antiseptic, and anaesthetic. It will even numb an aching tooth if you rub it on the gums. In fact, my dentist expressed some amazement when I once used it in place of novocaine to have a tooth extracted.

As if all this were not enough, the cattail is also a department store—a repository of tools, clothing, furniture, and building materials. The downy seed heads make excellent tinder and insulating material. The leaves can be used for insulation and weaving. And the versatile stalks make serviceable hand drills, arrow shafts, and thatching materials.

Pine Trees (see illustration page 120). The pines are tall multi-branched trees with scaly bark and sharp evergreen needles arranged in bundles of two to five. The female cone is a large, egg-shaped structure with many scales (sometimes pointed). Under each scale are two winged seeds.

You can eat several different parts of any pine tree, no matter what the species. For example, you can chop and boil the needles into a tea that contains more vitamin C than fresh-squeezed oranges. (Dice them as finely as you can and let them steep for five minutes in boiling water.) In spring, the male pollen anthers can also be eaten and are very high in protein. And the seeds from the mature cones are as great a delight to a survivalist as they are to a squirrel. (Open them by the heat of the fire.) If you're desperate, you can even eat the tree's inner bark.

As for other uses, the pine is a source of pitch for glue and fire. Its needles also serve as survival baskets, shelter coverings, and emergency "feathers" for arrows.

Acorns (see "Oak Trees," page 117). Oak trees are common in most parts of the country. Even when green, all acorns are edible and very nutritious if properly prepared. Just a handful of these tasty nuts has as much nutritional value as a pound of hamburger. Acorns from the white oak and the pin oak can be eaten raw. All others, though, either have to be leached in running water for several hours or boiled in several changes of water to get rid of their harsh, bitter taste. Don't throw the water out, though, since it makes a powerful antiseptic for skin diseases, cuts, sore throats, and toothaches (gargle only, please).

Guidelines for Gathering

The first rule for gathering plants is to harvest with wisdom and respect. Plants, too, are living organisms with a right to express their unique energies. If you find an endangered species or a plant that grows only sparsely in your area, kindly leave it alone and try to find other edibles first. If you're not in a survival situation, be even more frugal and thoughtful. Of course, you should also be mindful of your own safety when gathering wild edibles. Avoid gathering plants in any areas that might have been sprayed with toxic chemicals or affected by pollutants.

There are many ways of gathering wild edibles. Tender green leaves, shoots and ripe nuts and berries can simply be picked and dropped into your shirt or a deep basket (see "Survival Baskets," page 256). Cones can be brought back whole in baskets and the seeds extracted by heating the cones over the fire until they open wide. When grass seeds are ripe, they can be separated from their stalks by thrashing the grass against a shallow basket. If this method doesn't work, strip the stems from the stalks and pound the seeds free in a shallow rock bowl. After you've blown off the chaff, you can eat the seeds raw, pound them into flour, or boil them into mush.

Finally, roots are best gathered with a digging stick—a sturdy, three-foot sapling that is beveled like a crowbar and firehardened at one end (see "Firehardening," page 252). Thrust the stick into the ground beside the plant and pry upward while pulling on the plant from above. (This digging stick, by the way, can also serve many other purposes. See "Throwing Sticks," page 213.)

Other Plant Uses

Plants have literally hundreds of uses in a survival situation. Some of these, such as shelter, cordage, baskets, containers, and tools, are treated in separate sections (see the index at the back of the book). Many specific construction and medicinal uses for plants are dealt with under each species description. However, I would like to outline here some general plant uses—especially those for health and body care—that will make your wilderness stay more comfortable.

Toothbrushes. A person in a survival situation is not generally blessed with a toothbrush, but there are a number of good substitutes. The ends of cattail stalks, for instance. Once you remove the downy head, you're left with a fuzzy stick that's just right for cleaning teeth. You can also brush your teeth with a cedar-bark tinder bundle tied to a stick and dipped in water. The cedar is slightly abrasive and contains tannic acid, which is an effective fighter of tooth decay.

Toothpaste can be made by stripping and pounding the inner bark of such plants as birch, sassafras, and spicebush twigs. Just add a little water and mix them into a paste. Other plants that make a good tooth poultice are plantain leaves and the inner barks or buds of cedar and alder trees. If you want to soften the taste of these, mix them with a little pine oil, produced by boiling the needles or inner bark of the pine tree and skimming the oil off the top. Finally, charcoal or wood ash make an excellent toothpaste when mixed with a little water.

Mouthwashes can also be made from any oak or cedar tree. You can boil the inner bark of the cedar until it's a reddish brown, then let the liquid cool down and gargle with it. These mouthwashes are good for toothaches and cuts in your mouth. I don't advise swallowing them, though, because they tend to cause diarrhea.

Soaps, Cleansers, and Insect Repellents. The liquid extracted from the bark of tannic trees can also be used for bathing, washing clothes, and warding off insects. These solutions will not lather much, but don't let that deceive you. The tannic acid they contain is very powerful. Make the solution stronger or weaker by adding more bark or less water. If you use it for soaps, don't make it so strong that it singes or discolors your skin—unless you want an instant California tan! Too much tannin will also streak your clothes.

You can make a cleanser much like Pine Sol by crushing and steeping pine needles in boiled water. For best results, crush the needles and press the liquid into a small container. Then steep the needles and skim more oily film from the surface. Four good-sized handfuls of pine needles yields about a thimbleful of powerful cleanser.

Soaps can also be made from the leaves, flowers, and roots of any plant containing a substance called saponin. A few such plants are yucca, spirea, bouncing bet, meadow sweet, and phlox. Produce a mild lather by mashing the plant and mixing the juice with a little water. For stronger soaps, use the juice without water.

Oils. Nuts and seeds usually contain lots of oils. These are excellent aids to digestion and other bodily functions, but they can also be used as waterproofing and fuels for makeshift lamps. Collect the oil by mashing the nuts or seeds and draining the liquid into a small container.

Lamps. One way to make a lamp is to soak some thick cordage material in oil or pitch and place it in a non-flammable container such as a shallow rock depression before lighting. Long-lasting torches can also be made by soaking cattail heads in oils, pitch, or tallow. Pitch is a particularly good fuel. It can be gathered from the barks of trees and heated until liquid, or attached to a stick and lit in solid form. (For more information on pitch, see "Making the Tipi Fire,"page 65, and "Glues and Oils," page 263.)

Toilet Paper Substitutes. In the bush, many things can substitute for toilet paper. For softness and absorbency, buff up some tinder material (see page 63). In most cases, though, nontoxic leaves will do just fine. And if you have no choice, you will find (as in most survival situations) that you can get by with almost anything.

One Hundred Edible Plants

This section includes an alphabetical listing (including descriptions, illustrations, and uses) for one hundred of the most common and widespread wild edible plants found in North America. Included also are illustrations of some poisonous plants with which they may be confused. The chart on pages 88-90 lists plant names and their general habitats. Definitions and illustrations of plant terminology are included in the Plant Glossary, page. 275.

One of the best ways to study plants is to go to a particular habitat and familiarize yourself with the edible species found in that area. Concentrate on a few plants at a time and get to know them well. But don't be satisfied just to learn their names. Study their qualities and uses, both as described here and in other references. One of the most useful references for the beginner is Lee Peterson's *A Field Guide to Edible Wild Plants*, published by Houghton Mifflin. Many other excellent guides are listed on page 277.

GENERAL PLANT HABITATS

PLANT	Page	Waste Ground, Disturbed Soils	Fields, Meadows	Dry, Open Woodlands	Wet, Shady Woodlands	Streamsides, Lakeshores	Bogs, Marshes, Swamps	Deserts, Plains
AMARANTH	91	•						
BALSAM FIR	91				•			
BARBERRIES	92		•	•	•			
BIRCHES	92				•		•	
BLACKBERRIES, etc.	93	•		•	•			
BLUEBERRIES, HUCKLEBERRIES	93			•	•		•	
BRACKEN FERN	94	•		•				
BUFFALO BERRY	94					•		
BUGLEWEED	95		•			•	•	
BULRUSHES	95					•	•	
BUNCHBERRY	96				•			
BURDOCK	96	•						
CATNIP	97	•						
CATTAILS	97					•	•	
CHIA	98							•
CHICKWEED	98	•	•	•				
CHICORY	99	•	•					
CLEAVERS	99				•			
CLOVERS	100	•	•	•				•
COLTSFOOT	100	•			•	•		
COMFREY	101	•						
COTTONWOODS	101	•			•	•		
CRANBERRIES	102						•	
CURRANTS, GOOSEBERRIES	102		•		•			
DANDELION	103	•						
DOCK	103	•						
DWARF GINSENG	104				•			
ELDERBERRIES	104			•	•			
EVENING PRIMROSE	105	•						
FIREWEED	105	•	•					
FLY-HONEYSUCKLE	106				•		•	
GILL-OVER-THE-GROUND	106	•	•		•	•	•	
GOLDENROD	107	•	•	•				
GRASSES	107	•	•	•	•	•	•	•
GREENBRIERS	108				•		•	
GROUNDNUT	108			•		•		

GENERAL PLANT HABITATS

PLANT	Page	Waste Ground, Disturbed Soils	Fields, Meadows	Dry, Open Woodlands	Wet, Shady Woodlands	Streamsides, Lakeshores	Bogs, Marshes, Swamps	Deserts, Plains
HEMLOCK TREES	109			•	•			
HOG-PEANUT	109		•		•	•		
JERUSALEM ARTICHOKE	110	•	•					
JEWELWEED	110				•	•	•	
KINNIKINNIK	111			•				
LABRADOR TEA	111				•		•	
LAMB'S-QUARTERS	112	•						
LETTUCES	112	•						
LIVE-FOREVER	113	•	•					
MALLOWS	113	•	•					
MAPLE TREES	114				•			
MILKWEED	114	•	•					
MINER'S LETTUCE	115				•	•		
MULLEIN	115	•						
NETTLES	116				•	•	•	
NEW JERSEY TEA	116		•	•				
OAK TREES	117			•				
OYSTERPLANT	117	•	•					
PARTRIDGEBERRY	118	•	•			•		
PASSION-FLOWER	118		•	•				
PENNYROYAL	119	•	•	•				
PEPPERGRASSES	119	•	•					
PEPPERMINT	120	•	•			•		
PINE TREES	120			•	•			
PINEAPPLE-WEED	121	•						
PLANTAIN	121	•						
POND LILY	122						•	
PRICKLY PEARS	122							•
PURSLANE	123	•						
REED	123					•	•	
ROSES	124		•	•	•	•	•	
SALAL	124				•			
SASSAFRAS	125				•			
SAW PALMETTO	125			•				
SERVICEBERRIES	126			•	•			

GENERAL PLANT HABITATS

PLANT	Page	Waste Ground, Disturbed Soils	Fields, Meadows	Dry, Open Woodlands	Wet, Shady Woodlands	Streamsides, Lakeshores	Bogs, Marshes, Swamps	Deserts, Plains
SHEEP SORREL	126	•						
SHEPHERD'S PURSE	127	•						
SOLOMON'S SEALS	127			•	•			
SPICEBUSH	128				•	•	•	
SPRING BEAUTY	128		•		•			
SPRUCE TREES	129				•			
SPURGE NETTLE	129		•	•				
STORKSBILL	130	•						•
SUMAC	130		•	•				
SUNFLOWER	131	•	•					•
SWEET CICELY	131				•			
SWEETFERN	132		•	•				
SWEETGALE	132					•	•	
TAMARACK	133			•			•	
THISTLES	133	•	•					
TOOTHWORT	134				•	•		
VIOLETS	134		•	•	•		•	
WALNUTS	135			•		•		
WATERCRESS	135					•		
WILD ASPARAGUS	136	•	•					
WILD CARROT	136	•	•					
WILD GINGER	137				•			
WILD GRAPES	137			•	•	•		
WILD ONIONS	138		•	•				
WILD PARSNIP	138	•						
WILD POTATO VINE	139			•				
WILD RAISINS	139				•	•		
WILD STRAWBERRIES	140		•	•	•			
WILLOWS	140				•	•	•	
WINTER CRESS	141		•			•		
WINTERGREEN	141			•				
WOOD SORRELS	142		•		•			
YARROW	142	•	•					
YUCCAS	143	•						•

AMARANTH
Amaranthus spp.
Amaranth family
Leaves: Late spring
to early fall
Seeds: Late summer
to late fall

Description: A stout, weedlike, annual herb, 6 inches to 6 feet tall. Stems rough, hairy, freely branching. Leaves usually 3 to 6 inches long, alternate, toothless, rough and veiny, ovate to lanceolate. Undersides of young and lower leaves purple. Flowers in green axillary clusters up to 2½ inches long. Seeds abundant, shiny black, in chaffy bracts at the ends of stems and branches. Roots red. **Habitat:** Waste ground and disturbed soils. **Range:** Throughout U.S.A. and Canada, except alpine and desert areas.

Food: Young leaves can be eaten raw, while mature leaves can be boiled as potherbs. Seeds can be parched and ground into flour or boiled into cereal. **Warning:** Amaranth sometimes accumulates high levels of nitrates and can cause discomfort if eaten in large quantities. **Medicine:** Tea from the leaves is effective in treating diarrhea and excessive menstruation. **Other Uses:** The long, straight stem serves as a fair hand drill for firestarting, and stem fibers make good tinder.

BALSAM FIR
Abies balsamea
Pine family
Inner Bark: Spring
Pitch: All year

Description: Slender, steeple-shaped tree, 50 to 70 feet tall, 1 to 2 feet in diameter. Needles ⅜ to 1¼ inches long, flat, stalkless, with broad circular bases, dark green above, two pale white lines below. Cones 1 to 4 inches long, fleshy, purplish to green, growing erect on upper branches. **Habitat:** Cool, damp woods and mountains tops. **Range:** North central to northeastern U.S.A. and adjoining Canada.

Food: Inner bark can be stripped, dried, and ground into flour. The pitch is a highly concentrated food and should be eaten only in small quantities. **Medicine:** Bark and twigs can be brewed as a tea for rheumatism and for kidney and bladder disorders. The pitch, applied externally, also helps to heal wounds. **Other Uses:** The pitch can be boiled down into glue.

BARBERRIES
Berberis spp.
Barberry family
Berries: Fall

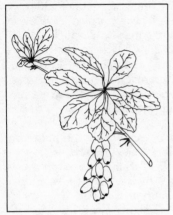

Description: Thorny shrubs, 2 to 10 feet tall. Leaves 2 to 3 inches long, leathery, bristle-toothed, alternate or in whorled clusters. Leaves of some species such as Oregon grape (*B. nervosa*) evergreen, pinnately compound, with 5 to 19 thorny, holly-like leaflets. Flowers ¼-inch wide, yellow, in elongate clusters. Berries tart, juicy, orange to red, in hanging clusters (fruit of Oregon grape deep blue with waxy coating). **Habitat:** Dry open woods, fields, and thickets to shaded forests. **Range:** Throughout most of U.S.A. and southern Canada.

Food: Berries make an excellent cooked fruit or cold drink when mixed with water.

BIRCHES
Betula spp.
Birch family
Inner Bark: Spring
Sap: Spring
Twigs: All year

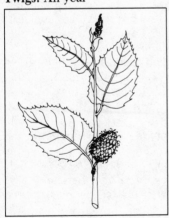

Description: Trees and shrubs up to 80 feet tall, with trunks to 3 feet in diameter. Leaves double-toothed, ovate to heart-shaped, with many pairs of prominent veins, and with wintergreen odor. Bark dark brown to yellowish-gray to white, with narrow horizontal scars, usually in papery sheets and sometimes with shaggy horizontal curls. **Habitat:** Wet areas, mature forests in hilly or mountainous regions. **Range:** Throughout northern U.S.A. and Canada.

Food: Inner bark can be dried and ground into flour. Bark, buds, twigs, and leaves make very good tea. The sap can either be drunk like water or boiled down into syrup. **Medicine:** A strong tea made from the leaves, bark, or sap is a good remedy for flu and skin disorders. It can also be gargled to heal mouth sores. **Other Uses:** The tea can be used as a wash for de-scenting the body before hunting or trapping. Birch bark makes a tinder that burns even when soaking wet. It is also useful for making torches, shingles, and containers.

BLACKBERRIES, etc.
Rubus spp.
Rose family
**Young shoots
(blackberry):** Spring
Leaves: Summer
Berries: Summer

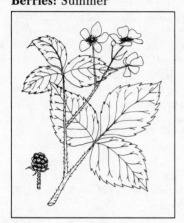

Description: Thorny or prickly shrubs, often vinelike, 1 to 6 feet high. Genus includes blackberries, raspberries, and dewberries. Stems usually green or red. Blackberry stems angular; raspberries round-stemmed; dewberries with low, trailing stems. Leaves 2 to 10 inches long, compound, with 3 to 7 leaflets. Flowers 5-petaled, white (occasionally reddish), conspicuous. Berries juicy, red, black, or salmon-colored. **Habitat:** Open woods and thickets. **Range:** Throughout U.S.A. and Canada.

Food: Berries and young blackberry shoots can be eaten raw. The dried leaves can also be steeped as a tea. **Other Uses:** Straight, dry sections of blackberry stems make effective hand drills for firemaking (see page 75).

BLUEBERRIES, HUCKLEBERRIES
*Vaccinium spp.,
Gaylussacia spp.*
Heath family
Berries: Summer to fall

Description: Shrubs, 2 to 10 feet tall. Stems delicate, many-branched, greenish or reddish. Leaves 1½ to 3 inches long, alternate, usually deciduous, elliptic, toothless or minutely toothed. Flowers ¼- to ½-inch long, urn-shaped, whitish to greenish. Berries usually blue (some black or red), glossy or powdered with white, with starlike pattern formed by calyx. **Habitat:** Acid soils in swamps, woods, forests, and thickets. **Range:** Throughout U.S.A. and Canada, except Great Plains and western desert areas.

Food: The fruit can be eaten fresh, cooked, or dried. **Warning:** Do not confuse blueberries and huckleberries with the poisonous buckthorns (*Rhamnus spp.*). Buckthorn berries do not have the five-lobed calyx, and the stems often have sharp thorns. **Other Uses:** The straight stems of some of these species make excellent arrow shafts.

BRACKEN FERN
Pteridium aquilinum
Fern family
Fiddleheads: Spring
Rootstocks: Fall to spring

Description: Large, many-branched fern, 1 to 6 feet tall. Mature stems smooth, rigid, light green, oppositely branched. Fiddleheads soft, hairy, clawlike at tips. Fronds pinnately compound, roughly triangular, with many narrow leathery leaflets, arising singly from rootstocks. Rootstocks ¾-inch thick, up to 8 inches deep, running horizontally; black outside, white inside. **Habitat:** Dry, open woods, disturbed soils. **Range:** Throughout U.S.A. and southern Canada.

Food: The young fiddleheads (up to 8 inches tall) can be eaten raw in small amounts or cooked like asparagus. The rootstock can be roasted and the inner starchy part eaten or pounded into flour. **Warning:** Do not mistake young bracken fern shoots for poison hemlock or water hemlock. Also, eat this plant sparingly and with caution at first. Some people have an allergic reaction to it, and too much can cause diarrhea.

BUFFALO BERRY
Shepherdia spp.
Oleaster family
Berries: Late summer
    to winter

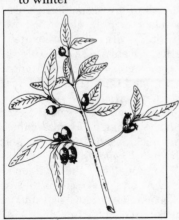

Description: Low-growing shrub, 3 to 6 feet high. Stems with silvery or rusty scales. Leaves 1 to 2 inches long, ½-inch wide, elliptic to ovate, opposite, toothless. Flowers bell-like, greenish-yellow, in small clusters. Berries orange-red, about ¼-inch in diameter. **Habitat:** Sandy soils on slopes and stream banks. **Range:** Throughout northern U.S.A. and Canada.

Food: Berries can be eaten raw, crushed and mixed with water for a refreshing drink or beaten and mixed with sweetener to make a frothy confection. **Warning:** Eat the berries sparingly. Too many may cause diarrhea. **Other Uses:** Roots and flowers can be mashed and used as a soap substitute.

BUGLEWEED
Lycopus spp.
Mint family
Tubers: Fall to early spring

Description: Herb, 6 inches to 2 feet tall. Stems square, slender, and hairless. Leaves 1 to 3 inches long, lanceolate, opposite, sharply toothed or lobed, light green. Flowers tiny, white, clustered in uppermost leaf axils. Tubers white, knobby, finger-like projections ½ to 3 inches long with fine hair-like rootlets. **Habitat:** Low, wet, sandy ground; in meadows and at the edges of lakes and bogs. **Range:** Throughout U.S.A. and Canada.

Food: Tubers can be eaten raw or boiled.

BULRUSHES
Scirpus spp.
Sedge family
Young shoots: Spring
Pollen: Summer
Seeds: Fall
Rootstocks: Fall to early
    spring
Sprouts: Early spring

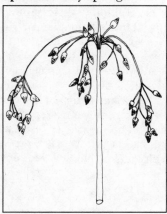

Description: Stems 3 to 10 feet tall, dark green, usually leafless, smooth, round or triangular, flexible and pithy. Leaves when present 2 to 24 inches long, about ½-inch wide, dark green. Flowers at ends of stems, in loose or dense clusters of brown, bristly spikelets ½ to 1 inch long. Roots composed of stout, scaly, ropelike rootstocks, growing horizontally. **Habitat:** Edges of swamps, marshes, shallow water, and muddy ground. **Range:** Throughout U.S.A. and Canada.

Food: Shoots and sprouts can be eaten raw or boiled. Pollen, seeds, and rootstocks can be dried and ground into flour (peel rootstocks first). Seeds can also be boiled into cereal. **Other Uses:** Mature stems can be dipped in fat to make candles.

BUNCHBERRY
Cornus canadensis
Dogwood family
Berries: Early fall

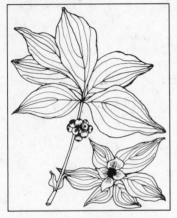

Description: Low, perennial herb, 2 to 8 inches tall, forming dense mats. Leaves 1½ to 3½ inches long, elliptic, with curving longitudinal veins, usually in whorls of 5 to 7. Flowers in greenish-white clusters surrounded by 4 white bracts. Berries pea-size, bright orange-red, in central clusters; soft when ripe, slightly pulpy. Rootstocks creeping. **Habitat:** Moist coniferous woods, often on or near rotting logs and stumps. **Range:** Northern U.S.A. and Canada.

Food: Ripe berries can be eaten raw or preserved by drying.

BURDOCK
Arctium spp.
Sunflower family
Stems: Spring to summer
Leaves: Spring
   (first year only)
Roots: Summer
   (first year only)

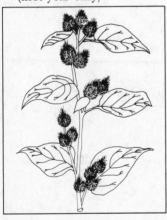

Description: Large, brushy, biennial herb, 1 to 5 feet tall. Stems coarse, stiff, many-branched. Leaves ovate (lower ones heart-shaped), toothless, densely hairy beneath, with wavy edges. First year leaves in rosettes, second year leaves alternate. Flowers red to purple, composite, on spiny seedpod. Seeds in roundish clusters, with many-hooked spurs. **Habitat:** Waste ground and disturbed soils. **Range:** Throughout Canada and U.S.A. except in the extreme south and southwest.

Food: Stems and roots can be peeled and boiled like vegetables. Leaves should be boiled in several changes of water. Seeds can also be dampened and grown as sprouts. **Other Uses:** Tall rigid stems can be used as drills for firestarting. The burrs make excellent survival "Velcro" for holding clothing together.

CATNIP
Nepeta cataria
Mint family
Leaves: Early spring

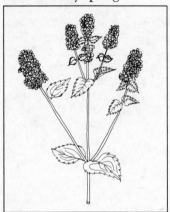

Description: Aromatic herb, up to 3 feet tall. Stems square, erect, branching, covered with dense whitish hairs. Leaves 2½ inches long, opposite, arrowhead-shaped, coarsely toothed, covered with whitish hairs—especially on lower surfaces. Flowers ½-inch long, two-lipped corollas, pale pink spotted with bright purple; borne in dense whorls near top of stem. Fruits 4-sided nutlets. **Habitat:** Roadsides and waste ground. **Range:** Throughout U.S.A. and Canada.

Food: The dried leaves make a soothing tea. However, the aroma of catnip is very volatile, so the plant should never be boiled.

CATTAILS (See page 83)
Typha spp.
Cattail family

CHIA
Salvia columbarae
Mint family
Seeds: Early summer

Description: Annual winter herb, 6 to 16 inches tall. Stems low, rigid, square, one or more per root. Leaves dark green, deeply cut, rough or hairy, nearly all at base, with 1 or 2 pairs on stems. Flowers characteristic of mint family (two-lipped corollas), blue, borne in 1 or 2 dense whorls. Nutlets or fruits shiny brown, oily, borne within a calyx. **Habitat:** Deserts, plains, and prairies. **Range:** Southwestern U.S.A.

Food: Seeds can be parched and ground into flour or swallowed with water. They make a very nutritious traveling food.

CHICKWEED
Stellaria media
Pink family
Stems: All year
Leaves: All year

Description: Low-growing annual or winter annual, 3 to 8 inches tall, with trailing stem to 16 inches. Stem loosely ascending, finely-haired, many-branched. Leaves to 1 inch long, opposite, ovate, pointed at the tip. Flowers with 5 small bilobed white petals, each deeply cleft. **Habitat:** Woodlands, thickets, meadows, fields, waste ground, and disturbed soils. **Range:** Throughout U.S.A. and Canada.

Food: Tender stems and leaves can be eaten raw. Tougher stems and leaves should be boiled for a few minutes. **Medicine:** The leaves can be mashed into a poultice to treat burns and rashes.

CHICORY
Cichorium intybus
Sunflower family
Leaves: Early spring
    or fall
Roots: Early spring

Description: Perennial herb, 1 to 4 feet tall. Stem naked with rigid, angular branches. Leaves 3 to 6 inches long with lobed or toothed edges, radiating from base like those of dandelion; stem leaves often small and clasping. Flowers in disks, 1½ to 2 inches across, deep blue to white, attached directly to stem; petals square-tipped with cleft ends. Flowers close in afternoon or when overcast. Taproot white and fleshy. **Habitat:** Waste areas, fields, and meadows. **Range:** Throughout U.S.A. and Canada.

Food: The white, subterranean parts of young leaves can be eaten raw in salads, while the greens should be boiled for 5 to 10 minutes before eating. Roots can be roasted until dark brown and brittle, then ground into an excellent coffee substitute. Add about 1½ teaspoonfuls per cup of water.

CLEAVERS
Galium aparine
Bedstraw family
Young shoots: Spring
Fruit: Early summer

Description: Weak-stemmed, spreading herb, often supported by surrounding vegetation, 8 to 36 inches long. Stem thin, 4-sided, with recurved hairs that allow it to climb 2 to 5 feet high. Leaves 1 to 3 inches long, lanceolate to linear, usually growing in whorls of 8 from a swollen joint in the stem. Flowers ⅛ inch in diameter, dry, bristly, 2-lobed. **Habitat:** Damp woods and thickets. **Range:** Throughout most of U.S.A. and Canada.

Food: Young shoots can be boiled or added to soups and stews. The fruits make an excellent coffee substitute (without caffeine). Gather them in summer when ripe and roast until brown, then pound into coffee powder. **Medicine:** This plant makes a good general tonic, laxative, and diuretic. Gather it in May or June when in flower, dry in a warm place away from the sun, and make into tea.

CLOVERS
Trifolium spp.
Pea family
Leaves: Spring to summer
Flowers: Spring to summer
Seeds: Spring to summer
Roots: Fall to winter

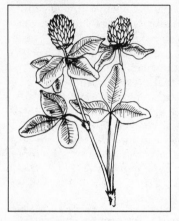

Description: Low-growing herb, 2 to 24 inches long. Leaflets 3, finely-toothed, round, ovate, or heart-shaped, ½ inch to 2 inches long. Flowers in dense heads ½ to 1 inch long; petals pea-like, white, yellow, or pink. **Habitat:** Disturbed soils, dry woods, prairies, and fields. **Range:** Throughout U.S.A. and Canada.

Food: Young leaves can be eaten raw and older ones boiled as a potherb. Flowers can be boiled, steeped as a healthful tea, or fried in fat. Seed heads can be dried and ground into flour. Roots are scraped and boiled like vegetables. **Warning:** Raw clover leaves eaten in large quantities may cause indigestion.

COLTSFOOT
Tussilago farfara
Sunflower family
Stems: Late winter
   to early spring
Leaves: Spring to summer
Flowers: Early spring

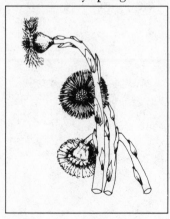

Description: Low-growing, dandelion-like herb, 3 to 18 inches tall. Stems asparagus-like, covered with reddish scales. Leaves 2 to 7 inches long, basal, heart-shaped, dark green, very hairy on undersides. Flowers dandelion-like, in solitary yellow heads 1 inch across. **Habitat:** Streamsides, moist soils, semi-shaded areas, and waste ground. **Range:** Northeastern U.S.A. and eastern Canada.

Food: Young leaves, flowers, and flower stems can be boiled as potherbs and vegetables. Leaves can also be dried and steeped as a tea. Flowers dipped in batter and deep fried make wonderful fritters. The leaves make an excellent salt substitute when dried, parched, and powdered. **Medicine:** Coltsfoot tea is an effective remedy for colds, coughs, asthma, and diarrhea. The smoke from the dried leaves also helps to alleviate lung problems. **Other Uses:** The dried leaves make a good tinder additive for wet-weather fire-starting.

COMFREY
Symphytum spp.
Borage family
Young leaves: Spring
Roots: Fall to spring

Description: Coarse perennial herb, 3 to 5 feet tall. Leaves hairy, ovate to lanceolate, with wavy edges. Flowers 5-lobed, tubular, less than 1 inch long, blue, purplish, yellow, or red, in nodding clusters, subtended by 2 winglike leaves. Nutlets erect, shiny brown to black. Roots thick and spreading, bitterish, mucilaginous. **Habitat:** Damp spots, waste places, and disturbed soils. **Range:** Eastern U.S.A. and Canada.

Food: Very young leaves (high in protein) can be eaten after boiling for 10 minutes. Roots can be roasted until brown and brittle, then ground into a tasty coffee substitute. **Medicine:** The leaves, when crushed and applied as a poultice, are effective in healing wounds. They can also be dried and steeped as a tea to treat respiratory problems.

COTTONWOODS
Populus spp.
Cottonwood family
Inner bark: Spring

Description: Rough-barked deciduous trees growing 40 to 120 feet tall and 1 to 3 feet in diameter. Bark light green when young, turning dark and ridged when mature. Leaves 2 to 8 inches long, finely toothed, usually long-stemmed, heart-shaped or triangular. Buds often gummy. Flowers in long pendulous catkins; female catkin covered with soft, downy "cotton." **Habitat:** Riverbanks, bottomlands, rich woods. **Range:** Throughout U.S.A. and Canada.

Food: The inner bark, or cambium (extremely sweet), can be scraped off and eaten fresh or dried. **Other Uses:** Cottonwood is the best wood for making a fire with a bow drill. The inner bark can also be dried, stripped, and used for tinder.

CRANBERRIES
Vaccinium spp.
Heath family
Fruit: Fall to winter

Description: Low, trailing shrubs or woody perennials. Leaves ¼ to ¾ inch long, evergreen, alternate, oval. Flowers about ½ inch long, pink or white with a pink tinge. Berries red and globose, up to ½ inch in diameter, with many seeds. **Habitat:** Bogs and rocky open soils. **Range:** Northern U.S.A. and Canada.

Food: Berries can be eaten either raw or cooked. They also make an excellent cold drink when mashed and mixed with water.

CURRANTS, GOOSEBERRIES
Ribes spp.
Gooseberry family
Fruit: Summer to fall

Description: Erect or sprawling shrubs with spreading branches, 2 to 5 feet tall. Stems with or without thorns. Leaves ½ to 5 inches long, alternate, palmately lobed, sometimes in clusters on spur branches. Flowers up to 1 inch long, 5-petaled, tubular; greenish-white to yellow, orange, red, and purple; borne on long stems from leaf axils. Fruits ¼ to ½ inch in diameter, red or bluish-black, round or oblong, in smooth-skinned or bristly clusters. **Habitat:** Damp woods and fields. **Range:** Throughout most of U.S.A. and Canada.

Food: Berries can be eaten raw, cooked, or dried. The spiny gooseberries are better if cooked first. **Warning:** Don't confuse these species with poison oak!

DANDELION
Taraxacum officinale
Sunflower family
Leaves: Early spring
Roots: Fall to early spring
Flower buds: Early spring

Description: Common herb, 1 to 18 inches tall. Stems weak and hollow, with milky white sap. Leaves basal, 3 to 15 inches long, with sharp, deep, irregular lobes. Flower heads 1½ inches across, composed of many yellow ray flowers. Taproot with yellow skin. Fruiting mass a silky, downy head composed of seeds with long white bristles. **Habitat:** Waste ground and disturbed soils in full sunlight. **Range:** Throughout most of U.S.A. and Canada.

Food: Young leaves can be eaten raw. Older leaves and buds should be boiled before eating. Roots can be dried, roasted, and ground into a good coffee substitute. The flowers make tasty fritters when dipped and fried in batter. **Medicine:** All edible parts of the dandelion are especially good for blood circulation.

DOCK
Rumex crispus
Buckwheat family
Leaves: Spring to summer
Seeds: Summer to winter

Description: Stout herb, 1 to 4 feet tall. Stem erect and many-branched. Leaves 6 to 10 inches long, oblong to lanceolate, growing mostly from bases in rosettes; thick and coarse, with wavy edges. Flowers very small, reddish or greenish, in slender clusters at top of stems. Fruits borne in whorls on upper part of stem, dark reddish-brown when ripe, 3-sided, each side winged. Taproot red-yellow, up to 12 inches long. **Habitat:** Waste ground and disturbed soils. **Range:** Throughout U.S.A. and Canada.

Food: All species of dock are edible. Young leaves can be eaten raw, but older leaves should be boiled in several changes of water to reduce the bitter taste. Seeds can be dried, threshed, and ground into flour. **Warning:** Do not eat the roots, due to high tannic acid content. **Medicine:** Roots can be mashed into a poultice to treat skin rashes and itches. **Other Uses:** Roots can also be used as a hide-tanning additive.

DWARF GINSENG
Panax trifolius
Parsley family
Tubers: Spring

Description: Small, delicate herb, 4 to 8 inches tall. Leaves compound; leaflets 3 to 5, narrowly oblong, toothed, stalkless, 1 to 1½ inches long. Flowers very small, 5-petaled, dull white to pink, in rounded clusters. Berries in yellowish clusters. **Habitat:** Rich woods, damp clearings. **Range:** Central to northeastern U.S.A. and adjoining Canada.

Food: Tubers can be eaten raw or cooked.

ELDERBERRIES
Sambucus spp.
Honeysuckle family
Flowers: Early summer
Berries: Late summer
   to early fall

Description: Erect, smooth-stemmed shrubs, 3 to 12 feet tall. Bark light gray with thick white pith. Leaves opposite, pinnately compound; leaflets 3 to 11, toothed, oval to lanceolate, 2 to 6 inches long. Flowers very small, white, in flat-topped clusters 2 to 10 inches wide. Berries small, round, juicy; purple, black, red, or white. **Habitat:** Damp, rich soil near roadsides and edges of woodlands. **Range:** Throughout U.S.A. and Canada.

Food: The ripe purple or black berries can be eaten after they are dried or boiled to remove the tartness. Fresh or dried flowers can be simmered as a tea. Fresh flowers can be dipped in batter and fried. **Warning:** Leaves and roots are poisonous. Red and white berries are toxic. Unripe fruits can cause diarrhea or vomiting. **Medicine:** Tea from the flowers induces sweating to help break fevers. Wounds can be washed with a cold tea from the bark or flowers. **Other Uses:** Basket materials, blowpipes, tool handles.

EVENING PRIMROSE
Oenothera biennis
Evening primrose family
Leaves: Late spring
   to mid-summer

Description: Biennial herb, 2 to 5 feet tall. Stems rough, hairy, leafy. Leaves 4 to 8 inches long, slightly toothed, lanceolate, lemon-scented. Flowers 1 to 2 inches wide, with 4 yellow heart-shaped petals and a cross-shaped stigma. Fruit an oblong capsule about 1 inch long. Taproot whitish, carrot-shaped. **Habitat:** Dry waste areas, roadsides, open places. **Range:** Throughout most of U.S.A. and Canada.

Food: New leaves can be peeled and eaten raw or boiled in several changes of water. First-year taproots should also be boiled 2 to 3 times before eating. They are most palatable in late fall or early spring. **Other Uses:** The stem makes a good hand drill for firestarting, and its stringy bark makes good cordage material.

FIREWEED
Epilobium angustifolium
Evening primrose family
Young shoots: Spring
Leaves: Summer

Description: Tall, smooth-stemmed, herbaceous plant, 3 to 7 feet tall. Leaves 3 to 7 inches long, lanceolate, toothless, shiny above, dull below. Flowers about 1 inch wide, 4-petaled, reddish-purple, showy, borne in long terminal clusters on main stem. **Habitat:** Open clearings, logged-over and burned areas. **Range:** Throughout most of U.S.A. and Canada, except in extreme southern U.S.A.

Food: Young shoots can be boiled and eaten like asparagus. Young leaves can be nibbled raw in small quantities or cooked like spinach. Older leaves may require boiling in two changes of water. They can also be dried and steeped as a tea. **Other Uses:** The fibrous inner bark makes excellent cordage and tinder material.

FLY-HONEYSUCKLE
Lonicera villosa
Honeysuckle family
Berries: Summer

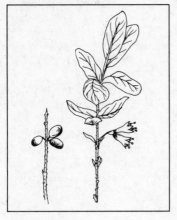

Description: Shrubby plant with stiff, upright branches and exfoliating bark, 1 to 6 feet tall. Leaves opposite, firm, hairy, oval, dark green. Flowers tubular, slender, yellow, in pairs, with 2 slender greenish bracts. Berries glossy blue, with many seeds. **Habitat:** Moist woods and peat bogs. **Range:** Northeastern U.S.A. and adjoining Canada.

Food: Berries are delicious and can be eaten raw or dried for future use. **Other Uses:** Tinder and basket-weaving materials.

GILL-OVER-THE-GROUND
Glechoma hederacea
Mint family
Leaves: Spring
Flowers: Late spring
    to early winter

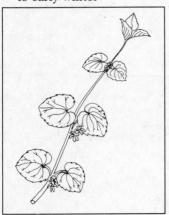

Description: Ivy-like plant with 4-sided, creeping stem, up to 8 inches tall. Leaves ½ to 1½ inches long, kidney-shaped or round, scalloped, opposite, sometimes tinged with purple. Flowers two-lipped, violet, ½ to ¾ inch long, whorled in leaf axils. Fruit 4 nutlets. **Habitat:** Roadsides, lawns, edges of woods. **Range:** Eastern U.S.A. and Canada.

Food: The dried leaves can be steeped in hot water to make a tea that is very high in vitamin C.

GOLDENROD
Solidago odora
Sunflower family
Leaves: Early summer
  to fall
Flowers: Summer
  to early fall
Seeds: Fall

Description: Smooth, licorice-scented annual, 2 to 5 feet tall. Leaves 1 to 4 inches long, lanceolate, smooth, toothless, with parallel veins. Flowers in tiny yellow heads about ¹⁄₁₆ inch long, borne in cylindrical clusters on one side of the plant. Seeds in downy heads. **Habitat:** Dry, open areas well exposed to the sun. **Range:** Throughout central and eastern U.S.A.

Food: Young leaves near flowers can be boiled and eaten as a potherb. Small leaves and flowers can be dried or used fresh to make anise-flavored tea. Seeds can be crushed and added to stews for thickening. **Other Uses:** The fluffy "down" from seeded flower heads makes a good tinder additive.

GRASSES
(see page 83)
Graminiae spp.
Grass family

GREENBRIERS
Smilax spp.
Lily family
Shoots: Spring to summer
Leaves: Spring to summer
Roots: All year
Tendrils: Spring to summer

Description: Vine, 3 to 9 feet long. Stems prickly, woody, and freely branching. Leaves to 5 inches long, leathery, parallel-veined, round, oval, fiddle-shaped, or oblong. Berries bluish-black, in tight little clusters. Roots thick and knobby to long and slender. **Habitat:** Swamps, bottomlands; sandy, fertile soils. **Range:** Throughout central and eastern U.S.A. and Canada.

Food: Young shoots, leaves, and tendrils can be eaten raw or boiled as vegetables. Rootstocks can be dried and ground into flour. The flour mixed with water makes a refreshing cold drink and is also a good thickener for soups and stews. **Other Uses:** Vines are excellent for basket and trap construction.

GROUNDNUT
Apios tuberosa
Apios americana
Pea family
Seeds: Late summer to fall
Tubers: All year

Description: Climbing vine, 5 to 10 feet long. Stems smooth and slender, dry and whitish in winter. Leaves 4 to 8 inches long, pinnately compound; leaflets 3 to 9, lanceolate, about 3 inches long. Flowers ½ inch long, pea-like, brown to purple, strongly scented, borne in long clusters arising from leaf axils. Seed pods straight, slender, clustered, about 3 inches long. Tubers 1 to 2 inches in diameter, in long strings. **Habitat:** Thickets, open woods, low ground, and streamsides. **Range:** Central to eastern U.S.A. and adjoining Canada.

Food: Tubers can be peeled and eaten raw, dried and ground into flour, or prepared and eaten like potatoes. Seeds can be cooked like peas. **Other Uses:** Stems are useful for weaving baskets and other articles.

HEMLOCK TREES
Tsuga spp.
Pine family
Inner bark: Spring
Needles: All year

Description: Tall, straight evergreen trees, 100 to 150 feet tall; trunks 2 to 3 feet in diameter. Top branches drooping, especially in young trees. Bark thick, dark brown to reddish brown, with flat scales. Needles often unequal in length, ¼ to ¾ inch long, yellow-green to blue-green, white below, set in two rows on either side of stem. Cones hanging, oval, ¾ to 1¼ inches long. **Habitat:** Hilly or dry, rocky woods (eastern species); wet, shady woodlands (western species). **Range:** Throughout U.S.A. and Canada.

Food: The inner bark can be dried and ground into flour. The green needles, diced and steeped, make a tea that is very high in vitamin C. **Warning:** Do not confuse the hemlock tree with toxic herbaceous plants of the same name. **Other Uses:** The bark can be boiled to make a wood preservative and red-brown dye. Bark chips also make good kindling, turning quickly into hot coals.

HOG-PEANUT
Amphicarpa bracteata
Pea family
Subterranean seeds:
  Fall to early spring

Description: Perennial twining vine, 3 to 8 feet long. Stems delicate, threadlike, covered with fine brownish hairs. Leaves alternate, compound; leaflets 3, from 1 to 3 inches long. Flowers of two kinds: above-ground ½ inch long, pea-like, lilac to white, borne in clusters from upper leaf axils; subterranean flowers small, without petals, borne on thin runners just beneath the soil. Seeds of two kinds: above-ground in curved, lenticular, bean-like pods about 1 inch long; subterranean pods tough and fleshy, ½ to 1 inch in diameter. **Habitat:** Streamsides, fields, moist woods and thickets. **Range:** Central to eastern U.S.A. and Canada.

Food: Subterranean seeds can be eaten raw, boiled, or roasted. Above-ground seeds are not edible.

JERUSALEM ARTICHOKE
Helianthus tuberosus
Sunflower family
Tubers: Fall to early spring

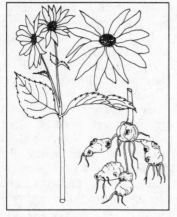

Description: Perennial sunflower, 5 to 10 feet tall. Stems slender, rough, hairy, growing singly in dense patches. Leaves 4 to 10 inches long, ovate to lanceolate, with sharp tapering points, opposite below, alternate above. Flower heads yellow, 2 to 3 inches wide, composed of 10 to 20 ray flowers with notched tips. Roots numerous and creeping, terminated by large knobby tubers, 1 to 5 inches thick. Tubers may be white, yellow, red, or purple. **Habitat:** Fields, waste ground, disturbed soils. **Range:** Throughout most of U.S.A. and Canada.

Food: Tubers can be eaten raw, cooked like potatoes, or dried and ground into flour. **Medicine:** The tubers are easily digestible and contain large amounts of uncrystallized sugar. This makes them valuable for diabetics and those on low-starch diets.

JEWELWEED
(Touch-Me-Not)
Impatiens spp.
Touch-Me-Not family
Young shoots: Early spring
Seeds: Late summer

Description: Soft, fleshy herb, 2 to 5 feet tall. Young stems smooth, unbranched, hollow, semi-translucent; mature stems stronger, swelling at joints, many-branched. Young leaves 1 to 4 inches long, opposite, ovate, pale green, bluntly toothed; mature leaves alternate, semi-fleshy, darker green, up to 3½ inches long. Flowers 1 to 1½ inches long, yellow or orange, sometimes dotted with red or brown. Seeds banana-shaped, 1 to 1¼ inches long, green, borne in explosive capsules. Roots shallow. **Habitat:** Wet, shady area. **Range:** Throughout U.S.A. and Canada.

Food: Young shoots (up to about 6 inches) can be boiled and eaten after removing the leaves. Ripe seeds can be eaten raw. **Warning:** Jewelweed is high in minerals and should be eaten only in small quantities. Ideally, it should be mixed with other vegetables. Older plants can act as a mild purgative. **Medicine:** Poison ivy remedy. Any part of the plant can be crushed and rubbed on the exposed areas. For best results, apply before rash appears. Jewelweed is also good for bee stings and other skin problems.

KINNIKINNIK
(Bearberry)
Arctostaphylos uva-ursi
Heath family
Fruit: Late summer to fall

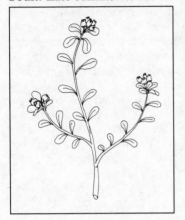

Description: Low, trailing shrub forming dense mats 2 to 6 inches high. Bark reddish and scaly. Leaves ½ to 1 inch long, evergreen, oblong, leathery, rounded at ends and tapering at bases. Flowers pink or white, urn-shaped, in small clusters. Berries ⅜ inch in diameter, round, bright red, mealy and white inside, with large seeds. **Habitat:** Dry slopes, sandy and well-drained soils in exposed areas. **Range:** Northern U.S.A. and adjoining Canada.

Food: The berries are nutritious but dry, mealy, and almost tasteless. They are barely edible raw, slightly better when cooked. **Other Uses:** The dried leaves are a good tobacco substitute.

LABRADOR TEA
Ledum groenlandicum
Heath family
Leaves: All year

Description: Evergreen shrub, 1 to 3 feet tall. Stems densely hairy. Leaves about 2 inches long, leathery, fragrant, densely hairy on lower surfaces, alternate, oblong. Flowers white, 5-petaled, about ½ inch wide, in dense terminal clusters. Seed pods 5-parted. **Habitat:** Swamps, bogs, damp woods. **Range:** Northern U.S.A. and Canada.

Food: Fresh or dried leaves can be steeped in hot water any time of the year to make a tea that is rich in vitamin C. The fresh leaves can also be chewed, but they are quite strong-tasting. **Warning:** *L. glandulosum* and *Kalmia polifolia*, two shrubs with similar growth forms and habitats, are toxic in concentrated doses. They are distinguished from *L. groenlandicum* by the lack of woolly hairs on the undersides of their leaves.

LAMB'S-QUARTERS
(Pigweed)
Chenopodium album
Goosefoot family
Leaves: Summer
Seeds: Fall to early winter

Description: Succulent herb, 1 to 6 feet tall. Stems straight, many-branched, often red-streaked, slightly grooved when mature. Leaves alternate; lower leaves toothed, triangular or diamond-shaped; upper leaves narrow and bluish-green with mealy white scales. Flowers very small, without petals or stalks, in greenish or reddish clusters. Seeds black and very small. **Habitat:** Waste ground and disturbed soils. **Range:** Throughout U.S.A. and Canada.

Food: Young leaves can be eaten raw. Young shoots and older leaves can be boiled as potherbs or vegetables. Seeds can be boiled or ground into flour. **Warning:** Lamb's-quarters resembles Mexican tea, whose aromatic leaves are edible only when dried.

LETTUCES
Lactuca spp.
Sunflower family
Young leaves: Spring
Flower heads: Spring

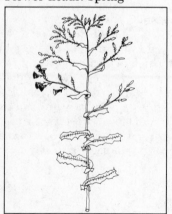

Description: Leafy herbs, 2 to 10 feet tall. Stems and leaves filled with milky sap. Leaves 2 to 12 inches long, deeply cut and toothed. Flower heads ¼ to ½ inch wide, with 6 to 12 ray flowers, in loosely branched clusters, blue, yellow, sometimes whitish. **Habitat:** Clearings, thickets, waste places, disturbed soils. **Range:** Throughout U.S.A. and Canada.

Food: Young leaves (somewhat bitter) can be eaten either raw or as cooked greens. Developing flower heads can be added to soups and stews or fried as fritters.

LIVE-FOREVER
Sedum purpureum
Orpine family
Leaves: Spring
Tubers: Fall to early spring

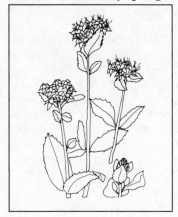

Description: Erect, leafy herb, 12 to 30 inches tall. Stems stout, fleshy. Leaves fleshy, light green, alternate or in whorls of 3. Flowers 5-petaled, pinkish-purple. Roots tuberous, stout, in fingerlike clumps. **Habitat:** Fields, meadows, waste areas, disturbed soils. **Range:** Throughout most of U.S.A. and southern Canada.

Food: Young leaves and stems can be eaten raw. Until the plant flowers they can be cooked and eaten as potherbs. Tubers can be eaten raw or boiled until tender.

MALLOWS
Malva spp.
Mallow family
Young leaves: Spring
Fruit (Cheeses): Summer

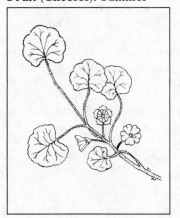

Description: Common annual herb, up to 3 feet tall. Stems spreading, many-branched. Leaves usually roundish, with 5 to 11 scalloped lobes (*M. moschata* with deeply cleft leaves). Flowers 5-petaled, pink or lavender, often with notched petals. Fruits disk-like, in some species appearing as flat clusters of nutlets arranged much like some packaged cheeses. **Habitat:** Fields, waste ground, disturbed soils. **Range:** Throughout most of U.S.A. and Canada.

Food: Young leaves can be eaten raw or added to soups and stews. Cheeselike fruits of species such as *M. neglecta* and *M. parviflora* can be eaten raw or the seeds extracted and ground into flour.

MAPLE TREES
Acer spp.
Maple family
Sap: Early spring
Seedlings: Early spring
Inner bark: Spring
Seeds: Fall

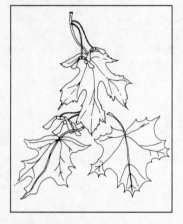

Description: Trees of variable shape and height, from 5 to 60 feet tall. Trunks oppositely branched. Leaves opposite, fan-shaped, with 3 or more pointed lobes. Seeds winged and double. **Habitat:** Damp woodlands and loamy soils. **Range:** Northern U.S.A. and Canada.

Food: The sap can be used as tea water or boiled down into syrup. Young seedlings can be washed and eaten raw. Older seeds can be husked and boiled till tender. Inner bark can be dried and ground into flour. **Warning:** Do not mistake maples for viburnums. **Other Uses:** Stems make good survival bows.

MILKWEED
Asclepias syriaca
Milkweed family
Young shoots: Early spring
Young leaves: Early spring
Flowers: Summer
Seed pods: Late summer

Description: Annual herb, 2 to 6 feet tall. Stem straight, downy, greenish-gray, with milky sap inside. Flowers whitish to dull purple, in domed clusters at bases of upper leaves. Seed pods green, pointed knobby. **Habitat:** Fields, waste ground, disturbed soils. **Range:** Northern U.S.A. and Canada.

Food: Milkweed is only marginally edible. All edible parts must be boiled for a total of about 15 minutes in several changes of water to remove the toxic milky sap. This includes young shoots, leaves, unopened flower buds, and young seed pods. Flowers can be boiled for a minute, dipped in batter, and fried. **Warning:** Do not mistake young milkweed shoots for those of dogbane or butterfly weed, which are poisonous. **Other Uses:** The fibers of the milkweed stem make good tinder and cordage material. The "down" is an excellent insulator and tinder additive. The milky sap makes an effective glue.

MINER'S LETTUCE
Montia perfoliata
Purslane family
Entire plant: Spring to fall

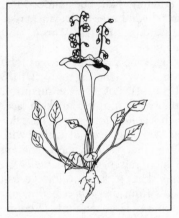

Description: Small, delicate herb, 4 to 12 inches tall. Basal leaves long-stemmed, ovate to lanceolate. Upper leaves encircling or clasping the stem. Flowers ¼ inch wide, white or pinkish, 5-petaled, borne in close clusters. **Habitat:** Shaded, moist woodlands. **Range:** Throughout most of U.S.A. and Canada.

Food: The whole plant can be eaten raw or cooked. The leaves are very rich in vitamin C and iron.

MULLEIN
Verbascum thapsus
Figwort family
Leaves: Summer

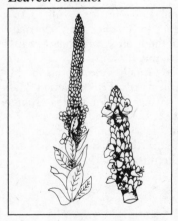

Description: Biennial herb, 1 to 6 feet tall. Stems stout with few upright branches at top. Leaves 3 to 12 inches long, oblong, gray-green, densely hairy. Upper leaves small and stalkless. Flowers yellow, 5-petaled, ¾ to 1 inch wide, in dense, cylindrical, spikelike clusters. **Habitat:** Dry, gravelly waste ground and disturbed soils. **Range:** Throughout most of U.S.A. and Canada.

Food: The leaves can be dried and steeped as a tea. **Warning:** Do not confuse with foxglove, which contains a powerful heart stimulant. **Medicine:** Tea from the leaves is good for coughs and sore throats. Smoke from the dried leaves loosens nasal congestion. **Other Uses:** Mullein stalks make excellent hand drills for firestarting. Heads of stalks can be dipped in tallow or pitch to make torches.

NETTLES
Urtica spp.
Nettle family
Shoots: Spring
Leaves: Summer
Roots: All year

Description: Erect, leafy herbs, 2 to 6 feet tall. Stems unbranched, square, covered with fine stinging hairs. Leaves 2 to 4 inches long, oblong to ovate, coarsely toothed, deeply veined, with stinging hairs on undersides. **Habitat:** Damp, shaded areas, stream banks, rich thickets, swamps. **Range:** Throughout U.S.A. and Canada.

Food: Young shoots and leaves can be eaten after boiling or steaming only 2 to 3 minutes to rid the plant of its toxic qualities. The leaves, either fresh or dried, make a tasty tea. Roots can be boiled to make a base for soups or stews. **Warning:** Do not gather with bare hands. The fine, hollow hairs contain formic acid, which raises stinging welts on contact with the skin. As an antidote, crush and rub on leaves from the jewelweed or another plant containing large amounts of tannic acid. **Medicine:** Tender nettle tops can be brewed as a tea for relief from rheumatism. **Other Uses:** The dried stems can be used as hand drills for firemaking. Fibers from the dried stems make effective tinder and one of the best natural cordage materials.

NEW JERSEY TEA
Ceanothus americanus
Buckthorn family
Leaves: Late spring to early fall

Description: Low, bushy shrub, 3 to 4 feet tall. Leaves 1 to 3 inches long, alternate, ovate, finely toothed, often with heart-shaped bases and 3 prominent veins. Flowers white, 5-petaled, about ¼ inch wide, borne in clusters from upper leaf axils. Fruits 3-lobed. **Habitat:** Dry open woods and hillsides. **Range:** Central to eastern U.S.A. and Canada.

Food: The leaves can be dried and steeped as a tea. **Other Uses:** The red root makes an excellent dye.

OAK TREES
(See "Acorns," page 85)
Quercus spp.

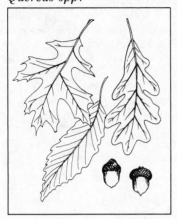

OYSTERPLANT (Salsify, Goatsbeard)
Tragopogon porrifolius
Tragopogon pratensis
Sunflower family
Young leaves: Spring
Roots: Fall to early spring

Description: Stout, perennial herbs, 1 to 5 feet tall. Stems smooth, milky. Leaves linear, light green, clasping, grasslike, with milky sap. Flowers in large dandelion-like heads, purple or yellow, with long slender bracts. Seedballs dandelion-like, often 3 inches in diameter. Taproot tapering downward. **Habitat:** Fields, waste places, disturbed soils. **Range:** Throughout U.S.A. and Canada.

Food: Young basal leaves can be eaten raw or boiled until tender. Roots can be eaten raw or sliced and cooked. They can also be roasted and ground into coffee.

PARTRIDGEBERRY
Mitchella repens
Buckthorn family
Berries: Late summer
  to winter

Description: Trailing herb, 4 to 12 inches long. Stems green, creeping, slightly woody. Leaves ½ to ¾ inch long, opposite, toothless, laced with white. Flowers small, 4-petaled, pink or white, tubular, in pairs. Berries red, about ¼ inch in diameter, borne singly or in pairs at ends of stems. **Habitat:** Knolls and woodlands. **Range:** Eastern U.S.A. and Canada.

Food: Berries can be eaten raw or dried for future use.

PASSION-FLOWER
(Maypop)
Passiflora incarnata
Passionflower family
Fruit: Late summer
  to early fall

Description: Trailing or climbing vine, up to 30 or 40 feet long. Stems with tendrils, tender and weak when young, ribbed and veined when mature, up to 1 inch thick. Leaves palmate, with 3 to 5 deeply cleft lobes; each lobe finely toothed, 1 to 3 inches long. Flowers usually 2 to 3 inches across, with 5 white petals and 5 white sepals below a showy purple corona. Fruit yellowish-orange, 1 to 2 inches long and 1 inch wide, with fleshy covering, filled with red seeds. **Habitat:** Fields, meadows, thickets. roadsides. **Range:** Throughout southern and eastern U.S.A.

Food: Pulp from the ripe fruits can be eaten raw or strained and mixed with water as a refreshing drink. **Medicine:** Tea from the leaves acts as a mild sedative.

PENNYROYAL
Hedeoma pulegioides
Mint family
Leaves: Mid-summer

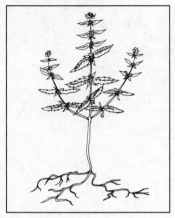

Description: Low-growing herb, usually less than 12 inches tall. Stems square, soft, hairy, sometimes branching. Leaves opposite, small, oval, toothed, with minty aroma. Flowers pale violet to bluish, borne in clusters from leaf axils. **Habitat:** Fields, roadsides, open woods, dry acid soils. **Range:** Central to eastern U.S.A. and Canada.

Food: The leaves make excellent tea when steeped in hot water for 5 to 10 minutes. Don't boil the leaves, however, as the flavor will escape. **Other Uses:** Crushed leaves are a natural insect repellent. Dried leaves can also be stored with woolens as a mothball substitute.

PEPPERGRASSES
Lepidium spp.
Mustard family
Leaves: Spring
Flowers: Early summer
   to late fall
Seed pods: Mid-summer
   to late fall

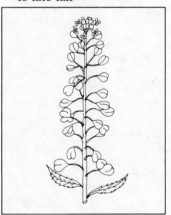

Description: Annual herbs, 6 to 24 inches tall. Leaves about ½ inch long, in basal rosettes, usually deeply toothed and lobed; upper leaves alternate. Flowers very small, 4-petaled, cross-shaped, clustered in terminal spikes. Fruit a dry, rounded, flattened pod, slightly notched at the top, with 2 seeds. **Habitat:** Roadsides and waste places. **Range:** Temperate to warm regions throughout U.S.A. and southern Canada.

Food: The young leaves can be eaten raw or boiled. Seed pods add a peppery flavor to soups and stews.

PEPPERMINT
Mentha piperita
Mint family
Leaves: Summer to fall

Description: Aromatic herb. Stems square, 1 to 3 feet tall, purplish and branching near top. Leaves 1 to 1½ inches long, opposite, on short stems, sharply toothed with pointed tips. Flowers about ¼ inch long, 4-lobed, pink to pale violet, 2-lipped, clustered on terminal spikes. Fruits 4-sided nutlets. **Habitat:** Wet meadows, streamsides, shores, and disturbed soils. **Range:** Throughout U.S.A. and Canada.

Food: Leaves are high in vitamins A and C. They can be steeped as teas or dried and used as a seasoning.

PINE TREES
(See page 84)
Pinus spp.
Pine family

PINEAPPLE-WEED
Matricaria martricarioides
Sunflower family
Flowers: Summer to
early fall

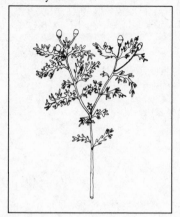

Description: Low-growing, inconspicuous herb, 4 to 8 inches tall. Stems smooth with fine ribbing. Leaves opposite, lacy. Flowers greenish-yellow, with pineapple odor when bruised. **Habitat:** Roadsides, waste places, disturbed soils. **Range:** Throughout northern U.S.A.

Food: Flowers can be steeped in hot water to make a pineapple-flavored tea. **Medicine:** A tea made from the dried leaves acts as a diuretic and antiseptic in the urinary passages.

PLANTAIN
Plantago spp.
Plantain family
Leaves: Early spring
Seeds: Summer

Description: Low-growing herbs, annual or perennial, 6 to 18 inches tall. Stems erect. Leaves in basal rosettes, 4 to 12 inches long, prominently veined, ovate, elliptic, or lanceolate. Flowers minute, greenish-white, in dense spikes on leafless stems. Fruit a small capsule with 2 or more small black seeds. **Habitat:** Waste ground and disturbed soils. **Range:** Throughout U.S.A. and Canada.

Food: Young leaves can be boiled and eaten as a potherb. Seeds can be dried and ground into flour or dried, boiled, and served as a hot cereal. **Medicine:** Crushed leaves are a powerful remedy for minor wounds, stings, bruises, and sprains. Seeds are high in the B vitamins. Take 1 or 2 pods daily as an insect repellent.

POND LILY
Nuphar spp.
Water-lily family
Seeds: Late summer to fall
Rootstocks: Fall to
  early spring

Description: Aquatic plant, with leaves floating on surface of water. Leaves 3 to 15 inches in diameter, round to heart-shaped. Flowers 1½ to 2½ inches wide, solitary, yellow and waxy-looking, with 5 to 6 rounded, petal-like sepals. **Habitat:** Ponds, lakes, marshes, and muskegs. **Range:** Throughout U.S.A. and Canada.

Food: Seeds can be parched, winnowed, and ground into flour or fried like popcorn. Large rootstocks can be cooked and eaten like potatoes. If the flavor is too strong, boil in 2 or 3 changes of water.

PRICKLY PEARS
Opuntia humifusa
Opuntia vulgaris
Cactus family
Pads: Spring to
  early summer
Seeds, Fruits:
  Late summer to fall

Description: Succulent, spiny herbs, up to 2 feet tall. Pads gray-green to deep green, jointed, fleshy, oblong to round, thick and flat. Bristles either single or in groups. Flowers yellow, 2 to 3 inches wide, with 8 to 12 petals. Fruit 1 to 2 inches long, reddish, prickly, pulpy, juicy. **Habitat:** Deserts and dry, rocky, sandy soils. **Range:** Throughout most of U.S.A.

Food: Pads can be peeled and boiled or roasted. Seeds can be ground into flour. Fruit flesh can be eaten raw. **Warning:** Remove spines carefully! **Medicine:** Crushed, mucilaginous pads can be used as a dressing for wounds.

PURSLANE
Portulaca oleracea
Purslane family
Stems: Summer
Leaves: Summer
Seeds: Late summer

Description: Low, sprawling herb, 2 to 6 inches tall. Stems succulent, 3 to 12 inches long, round, often red-tinted. Leaves ½ to 1 inch long, succulent, obovate, flat, alternate. Flowers about ⅜ inch across, stalkless, 5-petaled. **Habitat:** Waste areas and disturbed, sandy soils. **Range:** Throughout U.S.A. and Canada.

Food: Stems and leaves can be eaten raw or cooked in soups and stews. Seeds can be ground into flour.

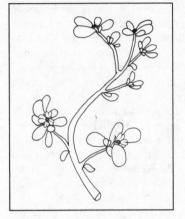

REED
Phragmites communis
Grass family
Shoots: Early spring
Leaves: Early spring
Young stems: Early summer
Seeds: Fall
Rootstocks: Fall to
early spring

Description: Thick-stemmed grass, 5 to 15 feet tall. Stems up to 1 inch in diameter. Leaves gray-green, 1 to 2 inches wide, up to 20 inches long, narrow and pointed, smooth and flat. Flowers very small, without petals, enclosed in scales grouped into purple-brown terminal spikelets. Rootstocks creeping, 6 to 10 feet long. **Habitat:** Swamps, marshes, bogs, shallow water, moist soils. **Range:** Throughout U.S.A. and Canada.

Food: Young shoots and leaves can be boiled and eaten as vegetables. Fleshy green stalks can be dried, ground, and roasted to make a tasty sugar. Seeds can be dried and ground into flour or dried and boiled into cereal. Rootstocks can either be boiled and eaten as a vegetable or dried and ground into flour. **Other Uses:** Mature dried reed stalks make serviceable hand drills and provide good tinder fibers. They can also be used for arrow shafts, thatching, weaving, and insulation.

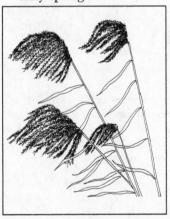

ROSES
Rosa spp.
Rose family
Petals: Summer
Fruit: Late summer
to early winter

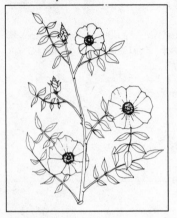

Description: Thorny shrubs, 1 to 15 feet tall. Stems prickly, often growing in clusters. Leaves variable, pinnately compound, with ovate to elliptical finely toothed leaflets. Flowers white, pink, or red with 5 petals. Rose hips orange-red with 5 calyx lobes at end. **Habitat:** Borders of fields and woodlands, thickets, streamsides, springs, moist soils. **Range:** Throughout U.S.A. and Canada.

Food: Flower petals can be eaten right off the bush, added to salads, or steeped as a tea. The pulpy rind of the rose hips can be eaten raw. The entire hip, either fresh or dried, can be steeped to make a tea that is very rich in vitamin C. **Medicine:** Fresh petals can be moistened and used to protect minor cuts. When dry, they form a scab-like bandage. **Other Uses:** Rose stems of varying thicknesses serve well as arrow shafts, basket materials, and other "household" items.

SALAL
Gaultheria shallon
Gaultheria ovatifolia
Heath family
Berries: Fall

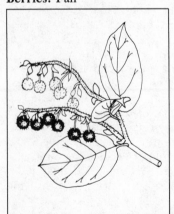

Description: Perennial shrub often forming dense, low thickets 1 to 8 feet high. Stems many-branched, strong, flexible, hairy. Leaves leathery, evergreen, round to heart-shaped, finely toothed, glossy green above, pale beneath. Flowers urn-shaped, pinkish to white, nodding in long slender clusters. Berries purple to black, thick-skinned, hairy, mealy, about 1/3 inch in diameter. (*G. ovatifolia* similar to *G. shallon* except that plants are only 2 to 6 inches high, mainly prostrate, and with red fruit.) **Habitat:** Prefers moist soils in humid areas. **Range:** West coast of U.S.A. and Canada.

Food: Berries can be eaten raw, boiled, or dried and pressed into cakes for storage. **Medicine:** Leaves can be chewed and used as a poultice to treat burns and sores, or brewed as a tea for diarrhea and coughs.

SASSAFRAS
Sassafras albidum
Laurel family
Leaves: Spring to summer
Roots: All year

Description: Shrub or tree, 2 to 50 feet tall. Bark reddish-brown. Stems green, often branched, sometimes hairy. Leaves 2 to 9 inches long, toothless, ovate or lobed. Flowers greenish-yellow, ¼ inch across, 6-parted calyx in long clusters. Fruits ½ inch long, dark blue, fleshy, 1-seeded, ovoid, on thick red stems. **Habitat:** Fields, thickets, edges of woodlands. **Range:** Throughout eastern U.S.A.

Food: Tender young leaves and buds can be eaten raw if nibbled sparingly. Leaves can also be dried and used for thickening soups, or dried and powdered as a seasoning. The root bark makes an excellent tea. Boil it until the water is light red. **Warning:** Contains a chemical that causes cancer in laboratory animals. **Medicine:** The tea can be used as a mouthwash and astringent for minor cuts, poison ivy, and bee stings. **Other Uses:** The wood makes excellent bow-drill materials, spear shafts, and other tools. Smoke from the burning bark is a good shelter fumigant.

SAW PALMETTO
Serenoa repens
Palm family
Fruit: Fall
Terminal bud: All year

Description: Shrublike palm, 3 to 7 feet tall. Stems usually thick and low to ground. Leaf stalks long, with short sharp spines. Leaves 1 to 3 feet wide, stiff, fanlike, segmented into many pointed blades. Flowers white, in fragrant clusters. Fruits black, oblong, up to 1 inch across. **Habitat:** Sandy soils, prairies, pine forests. **Range:** Southeastern U.S.A.

Food: The "hearts" at bases of leaf stalks can be cut out and eaten raw. The bases of terminal buds can be boiled and eaten like vegetables.

SERVICEBERRIES
(Juneberries)
Amelanchier spp.
Rose family
Berries: Summer to fall

Description: Shrubs or small trees, 5 to 40 feet tall. Leaves 2 to 5 inches long, oval, alternate, toothed. Buds reddish. Flowers white, 5-petaled, in drooping clusters; often appear before leaves in spring. Fruits purple-black, juicy, with 5 soft calyx lobes. **Habitat:** Woods and thickets. **Range:** Throughout most of U.S.A. and Canada.

Food: Berries can be eaten raw or dried. **Warning:** Do not mistake this species for the poisonous buckthorns *(Rhamnus spp.)*, whose stems have sharp thorns and whose berries do not have calyx lobes.

SHEEP SORREL
Rumex acetosella
Buckwheat family
Leaves: Spring and summer

Description: Vigorous perennial herb, 6 to 12 inches tall. Leaves ¾ to 2 inches long, arrowhead-shaped. Flowers very small, reddish or greenish, in branching spikelets on upper half of stem. Fruits seedlike, shiny golden brown. Rootstocks slender reddish runners. **Habitat:** Open sites and waste places. **Range:** Throughout U.S.A. and Canada.

Food: Leaves can be eaten sparingly in salads, boiled as potherbs, or steeped as a tea that is rich in vitamin C. **Medicine:** Taken as a tea, the leaves can help to stop internal bleeding and soothe sore throats. Crushed and applied as a poultice, they can help to cure skin diseases and slow external bleeding from minor wounds. **Warning:** May cause stomach cramps if eaten in too large a quantity.

SHEPHERD'S PURSE
Capsella bursa-pastoris
Mustard family
Young leaves:
    Spring to summer
Seeds: Late summer to fall

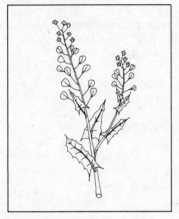

Description: Annual herb, 6 to 18 inches tall. Stems slender, inconspicuous. Leaves with bristly hairs; basal leaves in rosettes, deeply cleft, toothed, dandelion-like, with large terminal lobe; stem leaves clasping, arrowhead-shaped. Flowers small, white, often tinged with purple, in elongate terminal clusters. Fruits flat, heart-shaped, borne on flower stems. **Habitat:** Waste ground, disturbed soils. **Range:** Throughout U.S.A. and Canada.

Food: Young leaves can be eaten raw or cooked. Seeds can be eaten raw or dried and used as a seasoning. **Medicine:** The entire plant eaten raw or cooked helps to relieve diarrhea and to stop both internal and external bleeding.

SOLOMON'S SEALS
Polygonatum biflorum
P. canaliculatum
Lily family
Young shoots: Spring
Rootstocks: Fall to winter

Description: Perennial herbs, 1 to 8 feet tall. Stems arching. Leaves 2 to 6 inches long, alternate, parallel-veined, broadly lanceolate, toothless, unbranched. Flowers ½ to ¾ inch, greenish-yellow, bell-like, dangling in pairs from leaf axils. Berries deep purple. Rootstocks whitish, thick, with characteristic circles, or "seals." **Habitat:** Dry to moist woods and thickets. **Range:** Throughout U.S.A. and Canada.

Food: Young shoots can be boiled without the leafy heads, or whole shoots can be eaten raw in salads. The rootstocks can be added to stews or boiled and eaten like potatoes. **Warning:** Berries are toxic. Do not confuse this species with the May-apple (*Podophyllum peltatum*), whose rootstocks are toxic and do not have the characteristic "seals." Also do not confuse with False Solomon's Seal (*Smilacina racemosa*), whose toxic rootstocks are slender and yellowish.

SPICEBUSH
Lindera benzoin
Laurel family
Leaves: Spring to summer
Berries: Late summer
to early fall
Twigs and bark: All year

Description: Shrub, 5 to 15 feet tall. Stems slender, brittle, spicy-scented. Bark smooth. Leaves 2 to 6 inches long, dark green, oblong, toothless, aromatic, with prominent veins on lower surfaces. Flowers very small, yellowish, clustered, appearing before leaves in spring. Berries reddish, oval, ¼ to ⅜ inch in diameter, aromatic, oily, with one large seed. **Habitat:** Damp woods, streamsides, swamps. **Range:** Eastern U.S.A. and Canada.

Food: Young leaves, twigs, and bark can be steeped in hot water to make a tea that is especially healthful in winter. Berries can be dried and powdered as an excellent general seasoning. **Warning:** Do not eat berries whole. Use only as a seasoning. **Other Uses:** Split twigs make excellent basket material. The natural fragrance of this plant also tends to repel insects.

SPRING BEAUTY
Claytonia caroliniana
Claytonia virginica
Purslane family
Root ball: Spring

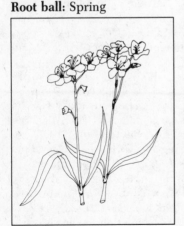

Description: Delicate annual herb, 6 to 12 inches tall. Stems smooth. Leaves 2 to 8 inches long, usually a single pair midway up the stem. Leaves of *C. virginica* narrow, linear; leaves of *C. caroliniana* lanceolate. Flowers ½ to ¾ inch wide, 5-petaled, pale pink to white with reddish-pink veins. Root balls from ½ to 1 inch in diameter, buried 3 to 5 inches underground. **Habitat:** Moist woodlands and semi-shaded areas. **Range:** Throughout most of northern U.S.A. and southern Canada.

Food: Root balls can be dug and prepared like potatoes. They can also be boiled, mashed, and dried to form a starchy flour. **Warning:** To preserve this plant, collect only where it grows in abundance.

SPRUCE TREES
Picea spp.
Pine family
Inner bark: Spring
Young shoots: Spring
Needles: All year

Description: Thick-crowned, steeple-shaped evergreen trees with drooping branches, 50 to 90 feet tall. Bark silvery-gray or brownish, with long deciduous scales. Needles 1 inch long, evergreen, 4-sided, sharp-pointed, stiff, borne in spirals around twigs. Woody bases remain on twigs after needles are removed. Seed cones about 2½ inch long, cylindrical, brown, drooping, woody, with pale brown papery scales. **Habitat:** Well-drained uplands to boggy soils in cool to cold areas. **Range:** Throughout most of U.S.A. and Canada.

Food: Inner bark can be peeled, dried, and ground into flour. Young shoots can be boiled and eaten as vegetables. Green needles can be boiled into a tea that is rich in vitamin C. **Medicine:** Crushed needles can be applied as a poultice for skin rashes. The tea can be used as a mouthwash to treat sores. **Other Uses:** Boughs and branches make good shelter material. Crushed needles can be rubbed on trap parts and skin to camouflage human scent.

SPURGE NETTLE
Cnidoscolus stimulosus
Spurge family
Root: Fall to spring

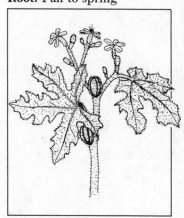

Description: Herbaceous to shrubby plant, 6 to 36 inches tall. Stems stout, covered with stinging hairs. Leaves 2 to 9 inches long, alternate, palmately cleft with 3 to 5 segments, covered with stinging hairs. Flowers about 1 inch long, white, tubular, with 5 flaring lobes. Roots tuberous, often irregularly shaped, white and starchy inside. **Habitat:** Dry sandy woods, fields, and dunes. **Range:** Throughout eastern U.S.A.

Food: Tubers can be boiled or baked like potatoes. **Warning:** Do not touch any part of the above-ground plant with bare hands. The stinging hairs can cause a severe rash.

STORKSBILL (Filaree)
Erodium cicutarium
E. Moschatum
Geranium family
Young leaves: Early spring

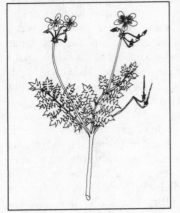

Description: Low-growing herb, 3 to 18 inches tall. Stems and leafstalks stout, fleshy. Leaves often in basal rosettes, fernlike or pinnately compound; leaflets ¾ to 1½ inches long, hairy, toothed, or deeply lobed. Flowers about ¼ inch wide, pink to rose-purple, 5-petaled. Seedpods distinctively beak-shaped, about 1 inch long. **Habitat:** Dry, sandy waste areas and disturbed soils. **Range:** Throughout most of U.S.A. and Canada.

Food: Young leaves can be eaten raw or cooked.

SUMAC
Rhus spp.
Cashew family
Berries: Summer

Description: Small shrub to small tree, 3 to 30 feet tall. Stems upright, mostly branched above. Staghorn Sumac (*Rhus typhina*) has velvety branches. Leaves 2 to 4 inches long, feather-like, compound, with many pairs of finely toothed leaflets. Dwarf Sumac (*Rhus copallina*) has winged leaf stalks and toothless leaves. Flowers small, greenish, in dense terminal clusters up to 6 inches long. Fruits red, small, hard, hairy, clustered to form a conelike structure. **Habitat:** Poor soils, old fields, dry hillsides. **Range:** Throughout U.S.A. and Canada.

Food: Berries can be bruised and soaked in cold water to make an acid-tasting but refreshing drink. They can also be dried and stored for later use. **Warning:** Poison sumac (*Rhus vernix*) causes severe dermatitis on contact. It has white berries and toothless leaves and is found mostly in swamps and bogs. **Medicine:** A strong, hot tea from the fresh or dried red berries makes an effective gargle for sore throats. **Other Uses:** Sumac stems make effective hand drills when thoroughly dried. When green they also make good basket-weaving material. After burning out the center pith, you can use the stems for blowtubes and pipestems.

SUNFLOWER
Helianthus annus
Sunflower family
Seeds: Late summer to fall

Description: Large herbaceous plant, 3 to 12 feet tall. Stems rough and hairy. Leaves ovate to heart-shaped. Flower heads 3 to 6 inches across, with yellow ray flowers and central brown disk flowers. **Habitat:** Fields, prairies, waste places, disturbed soils. **Range:** Central to western U.S.A.

Food: Seeds can be eaten raw or ground into a cereal or flour. Seed shells can be roasted, ground, and used as a coffee substitute.

SWEET CICELY
Osmorhiza claytoni
O. longistylis
Parsley family
Green fruit: Summer
Roots: Spring

Description: Herb, 18 to 36 inches tall. Stems of *O. claytoni* soft, hairy; stems of *O. longistylis* coarse and smooth. Leaves about 12 inches long, fernlike, compound, bluntly toothed or lobed. Flowers very small, 5-petaled, in sparse clusters at ends of stems. Fruits tapered, with licorice odor. Roots thick, with licorice odor when bruised. **Habitat:** Wet, shaded woodlands. **Range:** Throughout most of eastern U.S.A. and adjoining Canada.

Food: Roots and green fruits can be dried, powdered, and used as an anise-like seasoning.

SWEETFERN
Comtonia peregrina
Bayberry family
Leaves: Late spring
  to early fall
Nutlets: Summer to fall

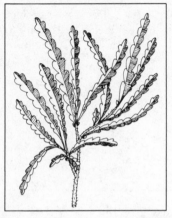

Description: A woody, many-branched shrub. Stems slender, grayish, 1 to 5 feet high, usually with hairy twigs, aromatic when crushed. Leaves fernlike, gray-green, 3 to 6 inches long. Fruits green, burr-like, round, bristly, up to 1 inch long; contain hard, glossy, olive-brown nutlets, ⅛ to ¼ inch long. **Habitat:** Sterile pasture lands, sandy soils, open woodlands. **Range:** Throughout most of eastern U.S.A. and Canada.

Food: Leaves can be steeped as a tea. Nutlets can be eaten raw. **Medicine:** Crushed leaves can be applied externally as a poison ivy remedy and insect repellent. Tea from leaves and twigs is an effective treatment for diarrhea. **Other Uses:** Dried leaves make an excellent tinder additive. Flexible stems are good for weaving survival baskets. Leaves and twigs can be burned as a shelter fumigant.

SWEETGALE
Myrica gale
Wax-Myrtle family
Leaves: Late spring to fall
Seeds: Early summer to
  winter

Description: Low-growing shrub, 1 to 8 feet tall. Branches strongly ascending in dense thickets. Leaves wedge-shaped, aromatic, slightly toothed on upper half, grayish-green with yellow resin dots beneath. Fruits aromatic, yellowish-green drupes, about ½ inch long, in conelike clusters. **Habitat:** Wet, sunny areas along lakeshores and bogs. **Range:** Throughout northern U.S.A. and Canada.

Food: Leaves can be steeped as a tea. Both leaves and seeds can be dried and ground into a sagelike seasoning. **Medicine:** The tea is a good cold remedy. **Other Uses:** Leaves are useful for camouflaging human and food scents.

TAMARACK
(American Larch)
Larix laricina
Pine family
Shoots: Spring
Inner bark: Spring

Description: Slender, pointed tree, 40 to 80 feet tall. Bark thin, gray to reddish brown. Needles deciduous, pale green, turning yellow in fall, in dense tufts on short, warty spurs. Cones oval, reddish brown. **Habitat:** Swamps, bogs, and open woodlands. **Range:** Northern U.S.A. and Canada.

Food: Young shoots can be boiled as vegetables. The inner bark can be dried and ground into flour. **Other Uses:** Tamarack makes effective bow-drill implements.

THISTLES
Cirsium spp.
Sunflower family
Leaves: Spring to
    early summer
Stalks: Summer
    (before bloom)
Roots: Spring to fall

Description: Biennial herbs, 1 to 6 feet tall. Stems straight, branched or unbranched, with or without spines. Leaves 5 to 10 inches long, alternate, spiny, lanceolate, with wavy edges. Flower heads 1 to 1½ inches wide, single or many per plant, with white to purple disk flowers. Taproots fleshy or stringy, on horizontal rootstocks. **Habitat:** Meadows, pastures, waste soils. **Range:** Throughout U.S.A. and Canada.

Food: Young leaves and stems can be eaten raw or boiled after the spines are removed. Older stems and roots can be peeled and boiled as vegetables. **Other Uses:** The stems, when well dried and de-thorned, can be used as hand drills. The downy part of the seed head makes good insulating material and a good tinder additive.

TOOTHWORT
Dentaria spp.
Mustard family
Rootstock: Spring

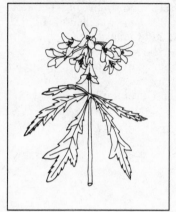

Description: Low-growing herbs, 8 to 12 inches tall. Stems weak, often sprawling. Leaves compound; either opposite, alternate, or in whorls of 3; leaflets 3, ovate to linear, deeply toothed or lobed. Flowers 4-petaled, white to pinkish, about ½ inch across, in terminal clusters. **Habitat:** Moist woods, streambanks, fields. **Range:** Throughout most of U.S.A. and Canada.

Food: Rootstocks can be dried and used as a peppery seasoning.

VIOLETS
Viola spp.
Violet family
Leaves: Spring
Flowers: Spring to
    early summer

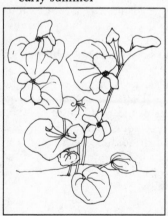

Description: Dainty, low-growing herbs, 3 to 10 inches tall. Stems thin. Leaves 1 to 4 inches long, ovate, with heart-shaped bases. Flowers blue, violet, yellow, or white, 5-petaled; lowest petal thickly veined, others usually bearded. **Habitat:** Wet meadows, damp woodlands, semi-shaded areas. **Range:** Throughout U.S.A. and Canada.

Food: Most species edible, though some yellow species may act as a mild purgative. Young tender leaves and flowers can be eaten raw, added to soups or stews, or dried and steeped as a tea. **Medicine:** Leaves and flowers are both very rich in vitamin C.

WALNUTS
Juglans nigra
Juglans cinerea
Walnut family
Sap: Early spring
Nuts: Fall

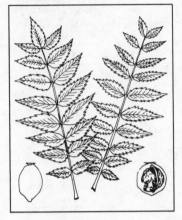

Description: Irregularly branching tree, 40 to 100 feet tall. Trunk 2 to 6 feet in diameter. Bark rough, furrowed, pale gray to dark. Leaves 12 to 24 inches long, pinnately compound; leaflets 7 to 17, toothed, spicy-scented when crushed. Fruits spherical or elongated, with thick green husk covering rough, brown or black nutshell. **Habitat:** Loamy, sandy soils, streamsides. **Range:** Central to eastern U.S.A. and Canada.

Food: Sap can be extracted from the trunk and boiled into syrup. Nut meats can be eaten raw or roasted, or dried and ground into flour. **Other Uses:** Nut meats can be boiled and the oil skimmed off for a variety of food and utility purposes. The dried inner bark makes good tinder and cordage.

WATERCRESS
Nasturtium officinale
Mustard family
Young leaves: All year
Stems: All year

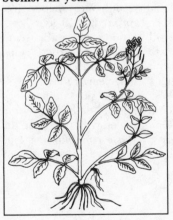

Description: Creeping perennial herb, 4 to 10 inches tall. Stems fleshy, smooth, sometimes form dense mats in water or mud. Leaves pinnately compound, with 3 to 9 oval leaflets, the terminal leaflet the largest. Flowers very small, white, borne in elongate clusters. Seed pods ½ to 1 inch long, slightly upcurving. **Habitat:** Streams, springs. **Range:** Throughout U.S.A. and Canada.

Food: Raw leaves and stems are excellent in salads. **Warning:** When gathering, make certain the water in which the plant grows is not polluted. **Medicine:** Very high in vitamins A and C, watercress is an effective remedy for scurvy.

WILD ASPARAGUS
Asparagus officinalis
Lily family
Young shoots: Early spring

Description: Fernlike plant, 2 to 6 feet tall. Young shoots stout, fleshy, up to ¾ inch thick. branching into smaller, green, thread-like stems. Leaves scale-like, brownish. Flowers ¼ inch long, bell-shaped, greenish-yellow, dangling on weak stems. Berries red. **Habitat:** Moist, rich soils, fields, roadsides. **Range:** Throughout most of U.S.A. and Canada.

Food: Young shoots can be cooked and eaten exactly as cultivated asparagus.

WILD CARROT
(Queen Anne's Lace)
Daucus carota
Parsley family
Roots: Fall to
   early spring

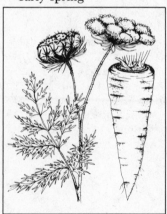

Description: Biennial, aromatic herb, 1 to 3 feet tall. Stems erect, with tiny hairs. Leaves 2 to 8 inches long, cleft many times. Note 3-forked bracts just below main flower clusters. Flowers small, white, in flat-topped, lacelike clusters 3 to 5 inches across; single small, deep purple flower in center of cluster. Seeds in dry clusters, old ones shaped like small birds' nests. Taproot 2 to 3 feet long, white, with carrotlike odor. **Habitat:** Meadows, fields, waste places, disturbed soils. **Range:** Throughout U.S.A. and Canada.

Food: Prepare first-year roots as you would carrots. **Warning:** Do not confuse with toxic species such as poison hemlock (*Conium maculatum*—stems grooved with purple spots) and fool's parsley (*Aethusa cynapium*—stems smooth, beardlike bracts beneath flower clusters.)

WILD GINGER
Asarum canadense
Birthwort family
Rootstocks: Early spring
to fall

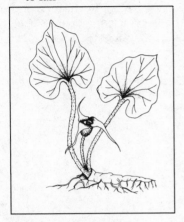

Description: Hairy-stemmed herb, 6 to 12 inches tall. Leaves 3 to 6 inches long, heart-shaped, opposite, dark green above, light green below. Flower a single red-brown, bell-shaped blossom with 3 lobes, 1½ inches across. Roots long, horizontal, with ginger odor. **Habitat:** Rich, rocky woods. **Range:** North central to northeastern U.S.A. and adjoining Canada.

Food: Rootstocks can be boiled and eaten or dried and used as a seasoning.

WILD GRAPES
Vitis spp.
Vine family
Leaves: Early summer
Fruits: Late summer to fall

Description: High-climbing vines with forked tendrils. Stems twining, with peeling bark, thornless, the branchlets usually with brownish pith. Leaves large, coarsely toothed, heart-shaped, often lobed. Flowers greenish, fragrant. Berries ¼ to ½ inch in diameter, fleshy, with 1 to 4 pear-shaped seeds, purple, black, red, greenish, or white. Buds with single pair of scales. **Habitat:** Moist, fertile ground, thickets, edges of woods, streambanks. **Range:** Throughout U.S.A. and Canada.

Food: Leaves can be eaten as a cooked green after boiling 10 to 15 minutes. Fruits can be eaten fresh or mixed with water as a cold drink. In springtime the live vines can be cut and drained to yield a refreshing watery sap. **Warning:** Grape roots are poisonous. Do not mistake wild grapes for poisonous species such as Canada moonseed (*Menispermum canadense*—lacks tendrils and has only 1 crescent-shaped seed) or common nightshade (*Solanum nigrum*—leaves usually with 2 small lobes at bases). **Other Uses:** Excellent basket-weaving material.

WILD ONIONS
Allium spp.
Lily family
Leaves: Spring
Bulblets: Summer
Bulbs: All year

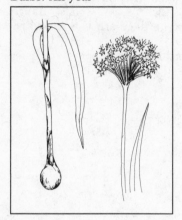

Description: Erect-growing herbs, 6 to 24 inches tall. Leaves 4 to 18 inches long, slender, quill-like, tubular or nearly flat. Flowers in umbels at ends of stems, with 3 petals and 3 petal-like sepals. Bulbs oblong, up to ½ inch in diameter, often in clusters, with onion odor. **Habitat:** Fields, open slopes, rocky soils. **Range:** Throughout U.S.A. and southern Canada.

Food: Bulbs and leaves can be eaten raw or boiled. Bulbs can also be used as a seasoning. **Medicine:** Juice from the bulbs serves as an antiseptic.

WILD PARSNIP
Pastinaca sativa
Parsley family
Roots: Fall to early spring

Description: Biennial herb, 2 to 5 feet tall. Stems stout, deeply grooved, hollow, branched. Leaves pinnately compound, with 5 to 15 ovate, sharply toothed leaflets. Flowers with 5 petals, gold to orange, in clusters up to 6 inches across. Taproot white, up to 20 inches long. **Habitat:** Deep, moist soils, waste ground, disturbed areas. **Range:** Throughout U.S.A. and Canada.

Food: First-year roots can either be eaten raw or boiled. **Warning:** Contact with leaves can cause a severe rash if the skin is wet or sweaty. Do not confuse with poisonous species (hemlocks or fool's parsley) with carrotlike leaves or purple-spotted stems.

WILD POTATO VINE
Ipomoea pandurata
Morning glory family
Roots: All year

Description: Trailing or climbing vine. Stems smooth. Leaves 1½ to 4 inches long, heart-shaped or arrowhead-shaped. Flowers 2 to 4 inches long, bell-shaped, solitary or in clusters of 2 to 3, white with pinkish centers. Root large (up to 4 feet long and as heavy as 30 pounds), deeply buried. **Habitat:** Dry, light, sandy soils in partial shade. **Range:** Central to eastern U.S.A.

Food: Smaller roots (up to 6 pounds) can be baked or boiled like potatoes. Larger roots may require boiling in several changes of water. **Warning:** Do not eat the roots without cooking, as they may have a strong laxative effect.

WILD RAISINS
Viburnum lentago
Honeysuckle family
Fruits: Fall

Description: Shrubs or small trees. Stems upright, branched. Leaves opposite, finely toothed, ovate or elliptic. Flowers small, white, in clusters 3 to 5 inches across. Fruits small, fleshy, oblong, blue or blue-black, each with a single large seed. **Habitat:** Streamsides, edges of moist woods and thickets. **Range:** Northeastern U.S.A. and adjoining Canada.

Food: Fruits can be eaten raw or boiled to make a sauce. **Other Uses:** Straight, stout stems can be used for hand drills, arrow shafts, and bow staves.

WILD STRAWBERRIES
Fragaria spp.
Rose family
Leaves: Summer
Fruits: Summer

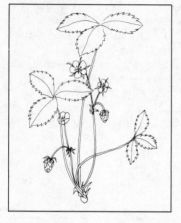

Description: Low-growing perennial herbs, 3 to 6 inches tall. Leaves long-stemmed, with 3 coarsely toothed leaflets, each 1 to 1½ inches long. Flowers ¾ inch wide, white, with 5 rounded petals, several per stem. Berries soft red, resembling small cultivated strawberries. **Habitat:** Open woodlands, clearings, moist woods. **Range:** Throughout U.S.A. and Canada.

Food: Leaves can be dried and steeped in hot water to make a clear, sweet tea that is rich in vitamin C. Berries are delicious either raw or dried.

WILLOWS
Salix spp.
Willow family
Inner bark: Spring and
    summer

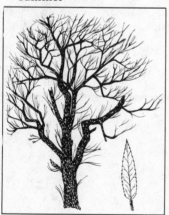

Description: Low, creeping shrubs to tall, spreading trees. Leaves mostly long, narrow. Buds with single scale. Bark mostly yellow-ridged. Flowers small, aggregated in catkins. **Habitat:** Low, marshy areas, moist woods, thickets, streamsides. **Range:** Throughout U.S.A. and Canada.

Food: The inner bark can be brewed as a tea or dried, mashed, and powdered into flour. **Medicine:** Bark tea is good for reducing fevers and treating rheumatism. **Other Uses:** Stems of various lengths and thicknesses are useful for making arrow shafts, trap parts, and baskets. The bark is also a source of tannic acid, used as a cleanser and insect repellent.

WINTER CRESS
Barbarea vulgaris
Mustard family
Leaves: Late winter
to early spring
Flowers: Spring

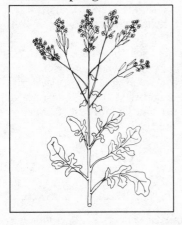

Description: Perennial herb, 1 to 2 feet tall. Lower leaves 2 to 5 inches long, dark green and glossy, pinnately lobed, with a rounded terminal lobe. Upper leaves clasping, alternate, coarsely toothed. Flowers very small, bright yellow, 4-petaled. Fruits narrow, erect seedpods ¾ to 1½ inches long, with short beaks. **Habitat:** Wet fields, meadows, streamsides. **Range:** Central to northeastern U.S.A. and adjoining Canada.

Food: In late winter, young leaves can be eaten raw. Later in the season they can be eaten after boiling in 2 to 3 changes of water. The clustered flower buds can be thoroughly boiled and eaten as a cooked vegetable. **Medicine:** Crushed older leaves make a good poultice for bee stings and other skin ailments.

WINTERGREEN
(Checkerberry)
Gaultheria procumbens
Heath family
Leaves: All year
Fruits: Fall to
early spring

Description: Low evergreen shrub, 2 to 6 inches high. Rhizomes subterranean, horizontal, with vertical branches. Leaves 1 to 2 inches long, oval, aromatic, with small bristly teeth; light green when young, dark glossy green and stiff when mature, mostly clustered near top of branch. Flowers about ¼ inch long, white, bell-shaped, nodding in leaf axils. Berries round, red, ⅛ to ¼ inch in diameter, hidden beneath leaves. **Habitat:** Well-drained, acid soils, most often in pine woods or under evergreens. **Range:** Throughout most of U.S.A. and Canada.

Food: Young leaves can be eaten raw or steeped as a tea. Berries can be eaten fresh or dried. **Medicine:** The leaf tea can be gargled to relieve sore throats. It can also be taken internally to relieve minor aches, pains, and fevers. Applied externally as a poultice, the crushed leaves reduce swelling, inflammations, and rheumatic pains. **Other Uses:** Leaves can be crushed and lightly wiped on trap parts or the body to reduce human scent.

WOOD SORRELS
Oxalis spp.
Oxalis family
Leaves: Spring to summer

Description: Delicate woodland herbs, 3 to 11 inches tall. Leaves alternate or basal, palmately compound, with 3 segments resembling 3-leaf clovers. Flowers ¾ inch wide, showy; white, pinkish, violet, or yellow; one to several per stem. **Habitat:** Moist, cool woodlands, mountainous areas. **Range:** Many edible species throughout northern U.S.A. and Canada.

Food: Leaves (rich in vitamin C) are excellent eaten raw in small quantities, or steeped as a tea. **Warning:** Do not eat sorrel leaves in large quantities over a long period. Excessive amounts may inhibit the absorption of calcium into the body.

YARROW
Achillea millefolium
Sunflower family
Leaves: Early summer to fall

Description: Erect herb, 1 to 3 feet tall. Leaves 4 to 6 inches long, usually hairy, grayish-green, lanceolate, aromatic. Flower heads ¼ inch wide, white, with 4 to 6 ray flowers; numerous heads clustered to form compound, flat-topped clusters. **Habitat:** Fields, roadsides, meadows, waste soils. **Range:** Throughout U.S.A. and Canada.

Food: Dried leaves can be steeped as a tea. **Warning:** Do not confuse yarrow with species such as fool's parsley (*Aethusa cynapium*) and poison hemlock (*conium maculatum*). The leaves of the poisonous species are more carrotlike—broad, lacy, and cleft many times. **Medicine:** Crushed leaves can be applied to wounds to stop bleeding and heal cuts. Fresh leaves can be chewed to relieve toothaches. For year-round use, gather while in bloom, dry, and store.

YUCCAS
Yucca spp.
Lily family
Stalks: Early spring
Flowers: Late spring to
summer
Fruits and seeds: Late
summer to fall

Description: Perennial herbs, 2 to 10 feet tall. Stems straight, woody, sometimes branched. Leaves up to 30 inches long, evergreen, stiff, swordlike, whorled at bases. Flowers 1½ inches wide, cream-colored to waxy white, with 3 petals and 3 sepals, bell-shaped, in large terminal clusters. Fruits oblong capsules, dry or fleshy, 6-sided. **Habitat:** Sandy woods, dunes, old fields. **Range:** Throughout southern U.S.A.

Food: Stems can be sliced, peeled, and boiled as a vegetable. Flower petals can be eaten raw. Fruits are good raw, roasted, or baked (remove rind before eating). Seeds can be ground and boiled into cereal. **Other Uses:** The dried stems make excellent hand drills. Leaves can be dried and twisted into cordage. Yucca roots make a good soap when mashed in water or diced and boiled.

6. ANIMALS

Listen to a chorus of frogs by a pondside. Follow a flock of birds through the sky. Watch a fish dart for cover in a clear pool. No matter where you go, the message is clear: Everything wants to live. From the smallest beetle to the largest whale, all creatures express a vitality and an eagerness to experience the world in their own unique way. Even plants show these basic urges in their upward striving toward the sun.

But while a plant can live on little more than soil and water, no animal can live without taking other life. In a survival situation, eating plants is rarely enough. The body's demands for balanced nourishment cannot always be met by berries, nuts, roots, and greens. There are times when plant food is so scarce that, in spite of your wishes to the contrary, you may be forced to take the life of another animal.

Hunting Ethics

There is a responsibility in the taking of any life. To pull up a plant by its roots for no good reason is the same as wantonly killing an animal. But it is only natural to feel a greater burden in taking the life of an animal. Animals eat, breathe, and bear young as we do; and many of them have feelings very similar to our own. As our closest relatives in the great chain of being, they are constant reminders of our dependence on other life.

This was the attitude that Stalking Wolf tried to pass on to Rick and me when we were growing up in the Pine Barrens, but we did not learn it through words alone. I remember a day when Rick and I caught more fish than we could possibly use. We fished without respect, pulling one animal after another from the stream and the flow of life. We did a butcher job of the cleaning and scaling, wasting many of the fish's usable parts. In the end, we cooked and ate only a few of them and left the rest. It was a sad mistake.

Stalking Wolf was very angry when he discovered what we'd done. "Did you pray for your fish brothers and sisters?" he asked. "Is this how you treat a person who gives up his life for you?" We had nothing to say.

We finally ate all the fish and felt very badly for what we'd done, but our lessons were far from over. The next day, Stalking Wolf took us to a desolate place in the Pine Barrens—a place with very little water and very few animals. In fact, the only available edibles were pine and oak trees and a few scattered greens. We went hungry for many days, and we deeply appreciated every morsel we could find.

As our hunger grew, we thought back on the fish we had treated with such disrespect. We remembered their vitality, the way they had flashed

145

in the sun when they jumped, the way they had fought to hold on to life, and the gift of nourishment they had offered us. In the end we paid dearly for our thoughtlessness, and before we left that desolate place, we had made peace with the fish and with ourselves.

Part of our peacemaking was the realization that life is essentially no different in a man than it is in a paramecium, a fly, a salamander, or a deer. All share the same spark of life and spirit. All are part of the same superconsciousness, living in one place under the sun, connected by a frail umbilical cord to the nourishing Earth Mother. Everything moves within our movements, and we move within the movements of everything else. Understanding these things with our innermost beings, we also understood that to remove an animal from the flow of life, without respect and without utilizing everything, is a sacrilege.

Many people today are quite lackadaisical in their approach to hunting. Perhaps this is a result of a technology that has created long-range weapons and lifestyles more separate from the forests and fields. Whatever the reasons, many modern hunters stumble on their game by chance, shoot from a great distance, and take only the best parts home to the freezer with little feeling of connection to the animal's life. By contrast, the native Americans felt intimately connected to the animals they hunted. Knowing starvation all too well, they hunted from the heart, using skills that took years to perfect. They felt a true thanks for every morsel and fiber of an animal's being.

In some ways, the Indians' hunt was a sacred ritual. They customarily spent days in careful preparation. They fasted to rid their bodies of impurities and to feel the sting of hunger. They prayed to the Great Spirit, giving thanks for the gifts they were about to receive. They performed sweat lodge ceremonies to lessen their scent and to calm their minds and bodies. When such hunters finally took to the woods, they went with little more than bows and arrows—and sometimes nothing more than knives. There, with tracking skills honed to a fine edge, they sought fresh signs and chose animals that would be worthy of their efforts.

A hunter often followed a track for days. At nightfall, he either slept beside the trail or tracked in darkness, feeling for hoofprints in the ground with his fingers. Whenever he examined a print, he learned more about the animal until he fit into the fabric of its life like a shadow. Long before he saw the quarry, he knew it well and felt bound up in its destiny by a power much greater than himself. This often worked both ways; for the animal was not always unaware that it was being followed—and for what reason.

Finally, when the hunter glimpsed the animal, he began the stalk— the slow, soundless approach to within striking distance (usually from ten to thirty feet). With the stealth and patience of a cat, the hunter moved unseen, blending and flowing like a whisper across the landscape. The stalk might take as long as six or eight hours. By the time the bow was poised, hunter and hunted moved almost as one. And when the arrow was loosed, a mutual exchange took place. The hunter released the animal's spirit to the Creator, and the animal left the gift of its body in return. The hunter then prayed to the animal's spirit, offering thanks for the gift of life.

The Indian's thanksgiving only began with the animal's death. For in death the lives of hunter and hunted were joined, and the hunter's responsibility continued until he had utilized every part of the animal. Over time, various members of the tribe prepared and served the meat as part of their daily meals, or dried and preserved it for hunting and gathering parties. They tanned the hide with the animal's brains and made it into clothing. They boiled the hooves into glue and oil. They made strands of sinew into fish line, thread, snares, and bowstrings. They fashioned bones into awls, hooks, needles, and scrapers. Even the entrails were used—the stomach as a cooking container or fishing float, the intestines as storage pouches or sausage skins, the glands for medicinal purposes. Nothing went to waste. To discard anything would be both disrespectful and very foolish; for life itself depended on making full use of all the Creator's gifts.

I remember the gift of my first deer. It was a small buck. I dropped from a tree and thrust my knife into its throat, but it would not die. It held onto life with unbelievable tenacity. It kicked, bucked, and strained to get me off its back. Finally I was forced to choke the life out of it with my bare hands.

That was a powerful experience for me. I became a part of the deer's final struggle. I saw the horrified look in its eyes and felt its spirit slip through my fingers. That deer's death brought me closer to the essence of life than I had ever been before, and it taught me a grave lesson. It is so easy to stand behind the barrel of a gun and kill an animal at a distance. But to experience an animal's death firsthand, to feel the awesome struggle as it clings to its last spark of energy, teaches what a great sacrifice it is for a being to give up its life for another.

These stories bring up several important points. One, the taking of an animal's life should be viewed with the utmost seriousness. It can be justified only by a real need, and only if you plan to use every part of the animal. Secondly, you should take every precaution to avoid inflicting needless pain and suffering. Among other things, this means good craftsmanship. Once you see an animal writhing and squealing in a poorly made trap, it is unlikely that you will ever do a shoddy job on that trap again.

Finally, it does take practice to learn to trap, fish, and hunt effectively. These arts involve the mastery of many complex and interlocking skills. To be an effective hunter, you must not only know how to make weapons and be able to use them with accuracy, but you must also understand your quarry's habits and master the rudiments of tracking and stalking. To trap with any success, you must not only know how to make traps, but how to set, camouflage, and bait them with the least possible disturbance. You may be able to read about these skills in an evening, but it will take time to learn them well and iron out the kinks. As with other survival skills, I recommend practice before it becomes necessary.

What Animals Are Edible?

The wilderness contains a tremendous variety of animals that will provide sustenance in time of need. Aside from the difficulties of capturing these animals, your biggest problem may be overcoming your aversion to eating them. For many people, wild animals are objects of curiosity, affection, and wonder; and the mere idea of killing them—let alone eating them—is repugnant. Second, chipmunk stew and rattlesnake steak are not standard fare and may take some getting used to. In most cases, nagging hunger will be enough to make you see these animals in a different light. If not, remind yourself that most animals are not only highly edible, but very tasty and nutritious.

As a general rule, you can eat anything that is finned, scaled, feathered, or furred—that is, any fish, reptile, bird, or mammal—as long as the animal is not diseased or contaminated, and as long as it is properly prepared. Most of the insects and amphibians are also edible.

Before you go out to capture a flock of sparrows, though, consider several things. In a survival situation, the kinds and numbers of animals will be determined by the area, not by your hopes or preferences. You must first check the area thoroughly to see what is available so that you will not expend useless energy pursuing an animal that doesn't exist. For example, I once tracked a hunter who had become lost following an elk trail more than three months old.

Second, many animals are so small that it is not worth the trouble to catch them unless there are great numbers in a given area. Generally speaking, keep your eyes open and gratefully accept any edible within easy reach. But don't go out of your way for anything smaller than a bullfrog unless you can gather it in sufficient quantity.

Finally, if you are in a situation where you can choose your prey, it's usually wise not to go after an animal that is acting strangely—for example, badly limping or walking in circles. Such behavior may be a sign of disease. On the other hand, some animals, such as bears and squirrels, can get literally drunk on berries in the late fall and may be seen staggering or teetering even though otherwise in perfect health.

Insects and Grubs

These little beasts generally fall into the "not-worth-the-trouble" category, unless you run into an anthill or termite mound and can gather them in bulk. However, nearly all insects are edible (if cooked first to rid them of parasites) and contain rich amounts of proteins and vitamins that will considerably strengthen soups and stews, even in small quantities.

Grasshoppers, crickets, katydids, and cicadas can often be gathered in small quantities when they cling in a torpid state to grass stems or shrubs in the cool of the early morning. At times, some species infest grassland or plains areas so thickly that they can even be swatted to the ground with saplings and collected in a basket. When the Indians found a field of grasshoppers, they sometimes set the field on fire, killing and cooking the insects at the same time. However, this is not a method I recommend in an age when preservation of natural habitats is of such critical concern.

Ants are usually edible, but it is almost fruitless to try to gather them by hand unless they are of the large black carpenter variety found in old stumps. For the smaller species of red and black ants that nest in large mounds on the ground, dig into the anthill with a shallow basket (see "Weaving Clothes and Baskets," page 254) until the basket is filled with a mixture of ants and nest material. This should stir up the ants so much that they will soon be scrambling about on top of the heap. Then you can simply roast them over a fire or add coals to the basket to cook them. As they cook, everything will shrivel up except the abdomen—which is a source of sugary, black powder that is very enticing to bears and other insect eaters, including survivalists.

Insect eggs and larvae should not be neglected if you can find a nest of bees or termites and safely gather a meal without getting stung. You may first have to temporarily smoke the bees out with a judiciously placed firebrand, but afterwards you may find many succulent larvae—or even a few pounds of energy-rich honey. You will have more luck with such insects if you approach them with calmness and a sense of sharing rather than with the idea of raiding their home. It is possible to pick a comb of honey from an active nest of bees without getting stung once if you let the bees know by your manner that you are grateful and will take no more than you need.

Larvae and nymphs of other insects such as stoneflies and mayflies can often be found in springtime under rocks in swift-flowing water, or at the water's edge. Don't neglect the adults of these species, either, if you can easily catch them. Grubs and caterpillars are also edible, with the exception of the furry varieties, which are often poisonous.

Unmentionable Edibles

There are a number of edible animals you may come across that will not make your mouth water, but which you should also consider fair game. Among these are maggots, earthworms, and slugs—all of which can be fried or boiled and eaten with stews. For the faint-hearted, it might be worth mentioning that such foods are considered delicacies in some parts of the world; and, as the robin will testify, they are all too abundant a food source to ignore in some areas. Worms, of course, can be gathered with a flat-tipped digging stick simply by turning up moist, rich soil as you would with a shovel before a fishing trip. Slugs often appear in large numbers in damp meadows and forests in spring and summer—particularly just before or after a good rain. Just plunk these into a boiling stew and forget they're even there.

Fish

Most freshwater fish are edible, as long as they are not diseased or contaminated by poisons. Depending on their location and habits, they can be caught with hooks, spears, traps, or even with your bare hands. (For a complete discussion of fishing techniques, see "Fishing," page 203.) All fish should, of course, be cleaned and cooked or dried before eating (see "Preserving Food," page 237).

Frogs and Other Amphibians

Most frogs are a little small to be considered prime survival game; but the large bullfrogs, identified at some distance by their deep, resonating honk, are often worth stalking with a three-pronged spear (see "Trident," page 205). And sometimes a pond will be overrun with small frogs caught up in their early spring mating frenzy. Toads are also a frequent find among the damp forests and can often be caught with the hands alone as they seldom have a water sanctuary in which to hide. The eggs and tadpoles of many amphibians are also a good source of protein.

Be certain before you eat a frog, toad, newt, or salamander, however, that you can positively identify the species, as some are quite poisonous. For instance, if you cannot tell the difference between a pickerel frog and a leopard frog, you may be in for the worst diarrhea of your life. The pickerel frog has toxic glands embedded in its thighs, which are otherwise the most edible part of the animal. Many amphibians also emit poisons from glands in their skin, which should always be removed before cooking and eating.

Snakes and Lizards

Yes, the reptiles are edible, too. In fact, our scaled friends are a better survival bet than the amphibians because they're all safe if properly prepared—even rattlesnakes. Don't go out of your way to hunt reptiles, since they are loners by nature and usually either very elusive or very quick. However, if you should come upon a snake or lizard sunning itself on a rock, tucked away in the shade of a tree, or caught in one of your pit traps, you can often get close enough to stun it with a rock or a stick.

These animals should also be skinned, cleaned, and cooked until well done. If you kill a rattlesnake, be very careful to avoid the fangs during the kill and to cut off and bury the head before skinning. The poison is just as powerful whether the animal is dead or alive. The Indians often used such poisons to tip their arrows and spears, but I don't recommend this in a survival situation because there is too much danger of accidentally poisoning yourself through cuts or scratches.

Birds

Most of our feathered friends are so small and so quick—with the added advantage of wings for a final getaway—that there is no point in actively pursuing them. In fact, once you have plucked the feathers from a small songbird and realize what a tiny spark of life is beneath that warm coat, it seems a pitiful waste for the single bite of meat it will afford. But some birds, because of their size and habits, are another matter. Included in this category are the ducks, geese, and gallinaceous birds such as grouse and ptarmigan, all of which are quite large and spend a considerable amount of time either on the ground or in the water. Once you are proficient with various hunting skills, these can be effectively taken with a variety of weapons, including sticks, bolas, slingshots, and the bow and arrow. They can also be trapped or snared on land and water using various techniques (see "Other Traps," page 200).

As with most animals, it is especially important to observe the birds' habits before choosing a particular method. Geese, for example, like to graze in flocks and are especially vulnerable to a shallow trench trap that gives them a feeling of security but that makes it impossible for them to take off. Grouse and ptarmigan will often allow a person to approach to within a few feet and fly only short distances, which usually affords a hunter one or more good shots with a throwing stick. Any such large bird will make a delicious and hearty meal—and perhaps several such meals. These animals should all be plucked (save the feathers!) and cleaned before cooking. With the exception of the fish-eating ducks, they usually taste better if they're not skinned.

Eggs and Young. Take a tip from the fox and the raccoon and look for fresh bird eggs in the spring and early summer. Eggs are a quick, safe source of protein at any stage of development and can be easily gathered once you locate the nest. Do not take all the eggs, however. If you leave one or two untouched (marking them for identification) and do not cause too much disturbance, a bird will often keep laying until she has a full clutch. This way, you may be able to gather an egg each day for several days. If you're not starving, leave the last few eggs to hatch.

If you are starving, don't rule out the possibility of taking babies or adults out of the nest. If you feel queasy about this, remind yourself that over half the eggs and young of most birds fall to predation each year. A hungry owl or weasel would not hesitate for a second to take advantage of an easy meal, and neither should you. Nests can often be located by patiently observing a single bird during the nesting season. Most birds' territories are quite small, and most of them make frequent trips while building nests and feeding babies.

Mammals

Almost all of the furred animals are edible. A partial list includes shrews, voles, moles, mice, rats, squirrels, chipmunks, opossums, gophers, aplodonts, weasels, minks, skunks, muskrats, beavers, badgers, wolverines, foxes, dogs, coyotes, wolves, raccoons, armadillos, bobcats, cougars (good luck catching one!), porcupines, rabbits, bears, deer, goats, and sheep—not to mention the many marine mammals such as otters, seals, and whales. Most of your hunting and trapping efforts should be directed toward this category—especially those animals about the size of a rabbit. Not only are the mammals relatively abundant and easily captured, but they are usually large enough to provide at least one sustaining meal. Some, such as the deer, provide meat and other useful parts that can sustain a survivalist for weeks (see "Utilizing the Animal," page 229).

In determining the proper method of capture, there is no substitute for a thorough knowledge of the animal and its habits. If you are unfamiliar with the lifestyle of a delectable-looking squirrel, for example, it would probably pay dividends to spend some time watching that squirrel to see where it lives, what it eats, where it travels, how it protects itself, when it feels curious, relaxed, frightened, or angry. In short, try to discover its weaknesses so that you can coax or fool it into getting caught.

Two obvious areas of vulnerability are food and water, since all animals must eat and drink. This might indicate the use of a well-placed trap or an ambush with a bow and arrow. Other weak points are curiosity and territoriality. Using these, you may be able to coax the animal to within range of a spear or throwing stick. But remember that every species has its own distinct lifestyle, and that every individual is a little different. There is no substitute for spending study time in the library and then watching an animal firsthand.

It is not tedious work getting to know animals in this way. Nor is it time wasted on any outing to watch a bird or beast go about its daily rounds. In fact, one of the joys of practicing survival skills is that in the process you become a sort of practical ecologist—one who understands and appreciates the complex interactions of animals, whether or not you ever need them for food. (For general information on the habits of various animals, read the sections under "Finding and Approaching Animals," below—especially "Tracking," page 155. For more specific information on animal identification and habits, I recommend the Peterson Field Guides published by Houghton-Mifflin.)

Finding and Approaching Animals

As anyone who tries it will quickly discover, it is not enough to arm yourself with a primitive spear and go blindly thrashing through the brush in search of game. Before you can successfully hunt or trap, you must first have some notion of what animals live in your area, where to find them in the greatest numbers, and how to get close to them without scaring them off. This will involve some practice in the arts of observation, tracking, and stalking.

Observation

There is a certain amount of logic to finding animals. All animals need food, water, and cover. As you survey the landscape, then, seek out the areas that offer these three things in the greatest variety and abundance. Look for transition areas—the meeting of forest and field, the banks of rivers and lakes, old clear-cut areas with a healthy mix of grasses, shrubs, and young trees. Such areas support many small animals such as voles, mice, and rabbits. These are called "indicator animals" because their presence usually indicates the proximity of a host of other animals—foxes, weasels, owls, hawks, snakes, and coyotes. Such areas are also the best feeding grounds for larger herbivores such as deer and elk.

Thick, mature forests, on the other hand, usually have a great scarcity of animals because they lack the necessary underbrush and low, succulent vegetation. A deep forest is very quiet when compared to a meadow at its fringe. You may hear a few songbirds high in the trees and see a squirrel or two, but most animals will only be passing through on their way to more promising feed areas.

This does not mean that you cannot hunt or trap successfully in such areas, but you will have to look more carefully for promising spots. Every forest has its clearings and creekbeds with their occasional congregations of animals. In desert and scrub environments, you may find a promising rock formation near a seep or spring. In high alpine areas, a collection of large boulders near a small lake may shelter an abundance of marmots and pikas.

Wherever the potential hunting or trapping area, be on the lookout for an abundance of animal signs (see "Tracking," page 155). Scat and gnawed vegetation are particularly good indicators. However, once you have found a likely area, don't disturb the flow of life by going into it right away. Survey it carefully from a distance. Ask yourself what kinds of animals it might support. Take note of broken branches, disturbed brushwork, and matted grasses. Listen for animal sounds and try to catalog the residents of the area. Even the presence of a particular insect or rodent may give you a good idea of what other animals are living nearby. Two skills will come in especially handy in this initial inventory—splatter vision and focused hearing.

Splatter vision is the practice of unfocusing your eyes so that they take in a panoramic view instead of a single object. It allows you to detect any movement that occurs within your total field of vision. Just to show you what it will do, look straight ahead and spread your arms out wide so you can't see your hands. Then, wiggling your fingers, slowly bring your hands forward until you notice the first finger movements out of the corners of your eyes. That is your peripheral range of vision. Now stretch your arm straight over your head and look for the moving fingers as you lower your hand in front of you. That is your vertical range of vision.

With splatter vision, most people are able to detect any movement that occurs within a radius of nearly 180 degrees—a span enormously greater than when the eyes are focused on a single object. Using this method in an open field, you can easily detect swaying grasses, fluttering leaves, and passing planes in a single glance. But you will also notice the movements of birds and insects. And with practice you'll even be able to pick out the flick of a deer's tail or the blink of a rabbit's eye.

Splatter vision should become a habit while walking, stalking, hunting, setting traps, or even while sitting in camp. Eventually you should be able to snap in and out of it whenever you want, frequently shifting your gaze from the minute to the majestic and taking in far greater information about your environment than ever before.

Focused hearing is an even simpler skill that allows you to locate and amplify sounds. In a way, it is like splatter vision in reverse. Normally, humans hear sounds coming from all directions. To zero in on a particular sound, simply cup your hands behind your ears and push them forward slightly with thumbs and index fingers. No doubt you've seen the ears of a dog perk up and change direction as it focuses on a new sound. You can do the same thing by turning your head with your hands cupped to your ears. Experimenting with this technique will help you amplify almost any repetitive sound. A slight tapping in a tree may become the sturdy rap of a woodpecker. A high-pitched hum in the distance may turn into a chorus of frogs. A soft rustling may reveal the movements of rodents through the grass. All these things will tell you volumes about what lives in the area.

Tracking

At its best, tracking is a fine art that takes many years to learn well. For purposes of survival, you need not be an expert by any means, but you should know enough of the fundamentals to be able to locate and identify the greatest concentrations of animal life in your area.

It is unusual for an animal to leave a perfect print—especially in areas of thick ground cover. But often enough you will run across excellent prints in mud, sand, or soft soil that will allow you to positively identify an animal—or at least narrow its identity down to a family or group of animals with similar habits. This will make your trapping and hunting infinitely easier and more effective.

Following, then, are track classifications and habits for various families of animals. As you will see, a family or order can usually be determined by the relative numbers of toes on front and hind feet. Once you know the family, you can usually determine the specific animal by the size and shape of the print. Unless otherwise indicated, all the tracks described below are for walking gaits, which is the normal gait for most animals ninety percent of the time.

THE CAT FAMILY leaves very rounded tracks showing four toes on the front feet and four on the hind feet, with no clawmarks. This, of course, does not mean that cats have no claws—only that the claws are retracted and do not show up in the print unless the animal is climbing, pursuing game, or suddenly escaping danger. Also, cats are the only family of animals that directly register when they walk. This means that as the animal picks up its front foot, the rear foot on the same side of the body falls directly into the front print, making what appears to be a single track.

The most common North American cats include the house cat (or feral cat, as there are many wild ones), bobcat, lynx, and cougar. With their sharp claws and fangs for raking and ripping, cats are excellent hunters. About ninety-five percent of their diet consists of other animals—usually small mammals such as mice, moles, and squirrels. Even giant cats such as the cougar, which often take animals as large as a deer, first go for

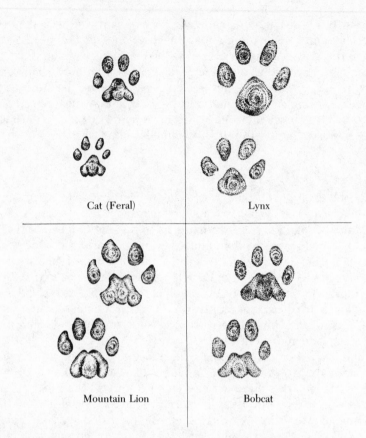

Cat (Feral)   Lynx

Mountain Lion   Bobcat

an easy kill such as a raccoon or porcupine. So if you find a cat track of any kind, it is an excellent indication of smaller animals nearby.

Cats have large territories, which they mark periodically and randomly with pungent "scent piles"—droppings of urine or scat that can often be smelled for days or weeks at quite a distance. Generally, cats are loners, very elusive, and excellent climbers. They like to hunt at night, holing up during the day in hollow trees, under secluded bushes, and inside protected rock formations. They often range a great distance, returning to one of several dens perhaps two or three times a week as they make their rounds. (As an illustration of some of these traits, in August of 1981, a male cougar was found in Seattle's 530-acre Discovery Park. Before his capture, the cougar successfully eluded Game Department trackers and hounds for a week, feeding on raccoons and small rodents within the area. He was finally treed and captured after midnight on a steep bluff, where his primary scent posts were still detectable two months later.)

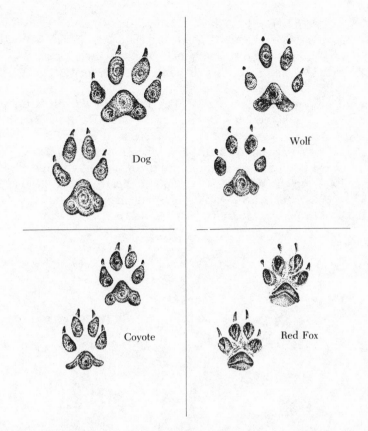

Dog

Wolf

Coyote

Red Fox

THE DOG FAMILY makes tracks showing four toes on the front feet and four on the rear, all with claws visible. The fox is the only member of the dog family that directly registers when it walks. All other dogs (and most other mammals) show indirect register, meaning that as the front foot is picked up, the back foot falls slightly behind and to the right or left.

The dog family includes all dogs, foxes, coyotes, and wolves. Like cats, dogs are excellent predators with sharp canines and clawed, well-padded running feet. Most of them also eat some vegetable matter. And some, such as the coyote, are real scavengers. Dogs hunt singly, in pairs, or in packs over territories ranging from a few square miles for the fox to several hundred square miles for the wolf. All dogs mark their territories—usually in prominent places—with scat or urine. They return frequently and unfailingly to such posts, and may visit up to several dens on consecutive days.

THE WEASEL FAMILY shows five toes up front and five in the rear, usually with sharp claws. The normal gait varies from bounding to shuffling, depending on the species (see "Track Patterns," page 163). This family includes weasels, martens, fishers, mink, ferrets, skunks, otters, badgers, and wolverines.

One of the most characteristic things about the weasels is their very pungent scent glands, which leave an acrid skunk-like smell not only on their scent posts, but wherever they go. So use your nose when investigating unknown tracks or animal signs. The weasels are also generally short-legged and long-bodied, well adapted to burrowing and digging. Most are exceptionally ferocious predators—equally at home on the ground or in trees. They consume large numbers of small mammals, birds, fish, and frogs, along with occasional fruits, nuts, and greens.

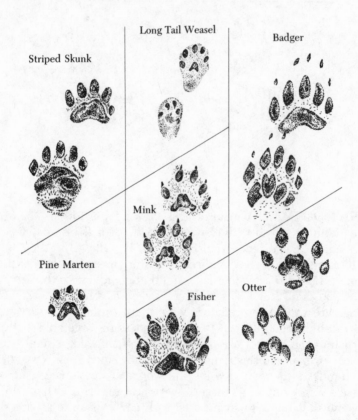

Raccoons, opossums, and bears are not in the weasel family, but they have the same five-and-five track classification (with nonretractile claws). All of these animals have very flat, human-like feet (although of greatly differing sizes), and the opossum has distinctively opposing thumbs for climbing.

The raccoon prefers to travel around water and has a very loose territory covering up to about fifteen acres. It takes refuge in trees and dens in any number of hollow logs, stumps, or protective nooks and crannies. It eats almost anything, which is one of the reasons for its great success around human populations.

The opossum is a very slow animal. Like the raccoon, it holes up in hollow logs or stumps and eats just about anything, dead or alive. Its range is usually between fifteen and forty acres.

The bear is a solitary scavenger for the most part, eating anything from berries and insects to small rodents, fish, and tin cans. Depending on the species, it may range from fifteen to fifty miles in a very loose territory. Bears usually den in the ground, hibernating during the winter months. In spring the females may have one to three cubs, which they will defend ferociously if threatened. Needless to say, the bear is an animal to be respected and avoided—and under no circumstances should it be hunted with basic survival weapons.

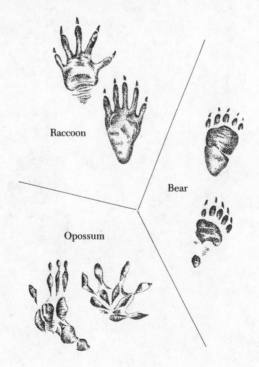

Raccoon

Bear

Opossum

THE RODENT ORDER includes most of the gnawing mammals. Rodents show four toes up front and five in the rear, with three exceptions: The beaver and muskrat show five-and-five some of the time, and the aplodont (or mountain beaver) shows five-and-five all the time. The normal gait of the rodents varies from bounding to shuffling to galloping, depending on the species (see "Track Patterns," page 163).

Rodents include a wide variety of animals: voles, mice, rats, squirrels, chipmunks, gophers, porcupines, muskrats, and beavers, to name some of the most common. Rabbits, hares, and pikas, while they do not belong to the same order, nevertheless exhibit many of the same characteristics, including the sharp incisors for gnawing. Rodents are generally nocturnal and herbivorous, living on a strict diet of grasses, bark, fruits, seeds, and nuts. They are often found in great numbers within a small area. They are a survivalist's delight because they are abundant, easy to trap, and offer some of the best-tasting meat of any of the mammals.

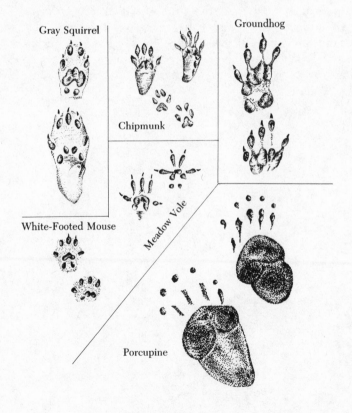

Gray Squirrel

Chipmunk

Groundhog

White-Footed Mouse

Meadow Vole

Porcupine

Voles, mice, lemmings, and rats are small to medium-sized rodents—primarily ground dwellers that feed on grasses, seeds, insects, and nuts. They make their homes in nests beneath roots or among thick grasses or brush. Often present in great numbers within a small area, they may constitute the principal food of other predators such as hawks, owls, and most carnivorous mammals.

The squirrel family (including chipmunks, ground squirrels, prairie dogs, woodchucks, and marmots) are mostly daytime animals. With the exception of the tree squirrels and flying squirrels, this family likes to burrow into the ground or hole up in hollow logs, boulder piles, and such.

The pocket gophers are all burrowing animals, rarely emerging into the light. Instead, they prefer to pull vegetation down into their burrows by the roots. The pocket mice, kangaroo mice, and kangaroo rats are small desert and plains animals that get most of their water from their food. Living mainly on seeds, they burrow into the ground beneath bushes and shrubs.

The beaver is readily recognizable by its stick-and-mud dams. These are so sturdily built that it is pointless to try to tear them apart in order to get to the animal. However, the beaver can often be captured with a snare set carefully in one of its runways, or stalked with a weapon when it comes ashore at night to fell trees or to chew on bark and twigs.

The porcupine, with its prickly quills, is primarily a nocturnal, tree-dwelling rodent that likes to feed on bark, twigs, and buds. Its gnawings can often be seen as thick scars on tree trunks. Frequently the animal can be seen clinging to a tree trunk or shambling along the forest floor.

The pikas, hares, and rabbits fall into an order called Lagomorpha. They are not rodents, in spite of their size and chisel-like gnawing teeth. Their tracks show four toes up front and four in the back.

Pikas are small, gray, squirrel-sized mammals without tails that are active mainly during the day among the talus slopes of high alpine areas. They feed on grasses (which they often pile into miniature haystacks) and are very elusive—often identified only by a fleeting shadow or a high-pitched squeak among the rocks.

Hares and rabbits include many widely dispersed species. They have very large hind feet for leaping. Primarily nocturnal, they feed on low-growing plants and grasses and usually sit in a protected lair of some kind. Various species are found among trees, bushes, and brush in open fields, forests, prairies, and deserts.

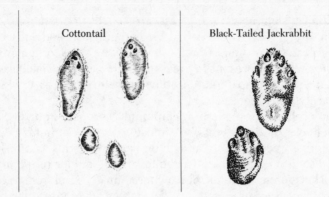

Cottontail   Black-Tailed Jackrabbit

THE HOOFED MAMMALS are easily recognized by their heart-shaped prints. They include the pronghorns, goats, sheep, deer, caribou, musk ox, moose, reindeer, and elk. Some of these, such as the moose, are quite solitary; but most tend to travel in herds for greater protection. Some species also have distinct summer and winter territories and often migrate great distances with the changing seasons. Most hoofed animals are very habitual. They are especially active mornings and evenings. They

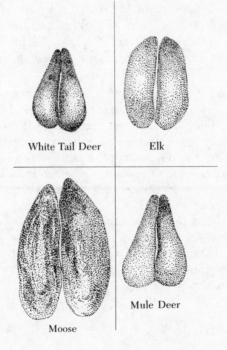

White Tail Deer   Elk

Moose   Mule Deer

also tend to follow well-established trails, browsing on a variety of vegetation from grass and succulent shrubs to bark and lichens.

Pronghorns are animals of the prairies and plains that eat mainly grass, weeds, and sagebrush. Wild goats and sheep inhabit rugged mountain slopes and cliffs, while the musk ox and the caribou are animals of the tundra that feed on almost any vegetation available—mostly lichens. Deer, elk, and moose (all three of which grow and shed antlers each year) tend to prefer a mix of forest and field with an abundance of cover and succulent feed.

The deer is one of the most preyed upon animals in the U.S.—and also one of the most useful in a survival situation. Because of the abundance of winter feed provided by modern farmlands, there are probably more deer in this country than there were hundreds of years ago. Deer generally have small territories and stay within a single square mile for long periods of time. They are creatures of habit, usually bedding down in the same location every night, browsing at the same three or four feeding areas, and drinking from the same water source day after day.

Track Patterns

Animals are no more eager to wear themselves out than humans. Ninety percent of the time, they walk or shuffle from one place to another. (Hearing this, one of my survival students blurted out, "Well, almost every time *I've* seen an animal, it's been running the other way!") This means that ninety percent of the tracks you find will be representative of the animal at its slowest gait. However, there are four different "slowest" gaits you should be able to recognize and link up with specific animal families. Once you are familiar with them, you will then be able to see that these same four patterns are used by different animals moving at different speeds.

Diagonal Walkers include all cats, dogs, and hoofed animals. These animals move limbs on opposite sides of the body at the same time. For example, a walking cat or dog lifts and places its right front and left hind feet at the same time, alternating sides of the body as it goes. At progressively higher speeds, these animals move into trotting, loping, bounding, and finally galloping.

Bounders include all members of the weasel family except for the wide-bodied skunks, badgers, and wolverines. These animals hop in a series of sewing-machine-like jumps in which the front feet come down first and the back feet pull up right behind them. No matter what the speed, bounders rarely change this basic pattern.

Gallopers include most rodents and rabbits. These animals hunch their bodies even more than bounders, bringing their hind feet down in front and to either side of the front feet. This usually creates an easily

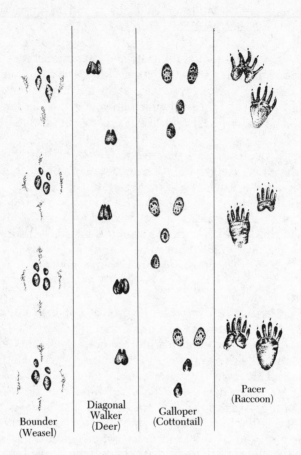

Bounder
(Weasel)

Diagonal
Walker
(Deer)

Galloper
(Cottontail)

Pacer
(Raccoon)

recognized U-shaped track pattern. If the two front feet regularly hit side by side, it is probably a tree-dwelling rodent such as a squirrel. A diagonal hit indicates a ground-dwelling animal such as a rabbit. (Tree-dwelling and ground-dwelling bird tracks can be distinguished in the same way.) The speed of a galloper can be determined primarily by the increasing distance between sets of tracks.

 Pacers include wide-bodied animals such as raccoons, opossums, bears, beavers, porcupines, wolverines, badgers, and skunks. For these animals, it is usually easier to move both feet on one side of the body at the same time in a shuffling or lumbering fashion. As speed increases, the wide-bodied members of the weasel family (wolverines, badgers, and skunks) go from pacing to bounding. Other pacers move first into a diagonal trot, then into a bounding lope, and finally into a full gallop.

Animal Highways and Signs

Individual tracks are usually the least obvious signs of an animal's passage. More apparent, as you move through the landscape, are well-traveled trails, runs, and bedding and feeding areas. These may be difficult to recognize at first; but with practice you will be able to survey an area and identify them like major thoroughfares on a highway map. And where you find these markers, you'll also find more subtle signs.

Trails are well-worn animal pathways (comparable to our highways) that connect feeding, watering, and bedding areas. Usually following the easiest route of travel over a given terrain, trails may be used by many species of animals and do not change very often. Animals are usually very wary of danger on trails, so these are not the best trapping and hunting areas.

Runs are less obvious pathways (much like our sidestreets) that connect trails to feeding, bedding, and watering areas. They resemble trails but are less heavily traveled—often only by one or two different species—and are very subject to change. Some, such as rabbit runs, are very obvious. Others, such as those of the mice and voles, are hidden. But in

almost every case, the width and depth of the run is a good indicator of the species that uses it. Runs are often good hunting and trapping areas.

Pushdowns are places where an animal has suddenly pursued or fled from another animal. They are indicated by vegetation smashed in one direction. An animal that has recently escaped an enemy in a particular area is not likely to be back for some time.

Beds are frequently used sleeping spots. They are about the size of the animal's body and appear as well-worn depressions in thickets, grasses, hollow logs, and under rocks. Beds are sometimes lined with fur or other debris and are not very subject to change. Some species, such as the fox and the bobcat, may have several different bedding areas and change them four to six times a year. Others, such as the deer, might use the same bedding area for a lifetime if food and water were always available. Animals in their bedding areas are usually very aware of danger, making such spots unlikely places to hunt or trap.

Lays are infrequently used rest spots near feeding or watering areas. They are indicated by depressed vegetation that often takes on the outline of the animal but that does not have a well matted look. (I have often

come across elk lays, for example, that have shown the whole animal's body splayed out on the ground, from antlers to hooves.) A lay is usually an indication that the animal feels secure enough to lie down and rest, which makes the immediate vicinity a prime hunting and trapping area.

Rubs and nicks are bare spots on branches and trunks where animals have rubbed or scraped themselves in passing. A well-worn alder trunk may indicate the purposeful rubbing or scraping of an elk during the rutting season. Less obvious but even more frequent are the scars left by the hides and hooves of passing animals on well-worn trails. A fallen log, for example, may contain hoof nicks from many a passing deer, while a tree trunk or branch beside a trail may have the bark worn off. Sometimes, in exchange for the bark, such vegetation extracts a few hairs that an alert survivalist can use to identify the animal.

Scratchings are similar indicators of an animal's presence. A bear or bobcat may rake its claws on a tree or leave telltale claw marks as it climbs. A skunk, fox, or coyote may grub for insects or rodents at the base of a fallen log and leave the pattern of its digging—perhaps also along with a few telltale hairs.

Gnawings are also excellent animal signatures. One of the most obvious is that of the beaver, which cuts down whole trees with its chisel-like teeth. Every piece of gnawed vegetation leaves the signature of the feasting animal. Rodents and rabbits slice grasses and twigs with sharp incisors at forty-five-degree angles. Lacking top teeth, hoofed animals clamp down and yank at the vegetation, leaving a flat, serrated cut. Members of the dog and cat families usually leave plants and grasses with a crushed, masticated appearance after chewing on them.

The height of a gnawing usually indicates the size of the animal that has been feeding. If you've ever seen vole or mice runways, for example, you've probably noticed that the grasses are mowed down to within a fraction of an inch of the ground in places. Rabbits can chew on vegetation up to a foot or two off the ground, while deer and elk can reach much higher. Snow on the ground also extends an animal's reach in the winter, leaving marks much higher than you would expect to find them at other seasons.

Animal droppings (scat) are extremely useful signs. They are not only species indicators, but positive proof of an animal's diet. Once you begin to recognize specific kinds of scat and learn to tell the difference between day-old and year-old droppings, this information will be invaluable for trapping and hunting. A fox scat, for example, may contain the bones of several small mammals and several different kinds of wild edibles in a given area.

Other Signs. The tracks left by animals are endless. Keep your eyes open for broken or abraded twigs, crushed or unnaturally tangled vegetation, stones that have been flipped or rolled out of their beds, and unusual compressions in the ground. Anything unnatural or out of place may indicate the passage of an animal, and the recognition of these signs can be your meal ticket.

The Fox Walk

Since most of us are used to walking on flat ground, we have developed an unnatural, shuffling gait that is not conducive to observing or approaching wild animals. On pavement, we usually walk on the insides of our feet—heels first, heads down, and bodies leaning forward in great, lurching strides. Such a gait is frightening to most animals because it's so out of step with the flow of nature. In the woods, a far better gait is the fox walk—a short, smooth stride in which you roll quietly from the outside to the inside of your feet, with the body and head held erect. Such a gait uses the large thigh and buttock muscles rather than the calves, and it puts the emphasis on lifting rather than sliding the feet.

One of the most obvious advantages in walking this way is that you

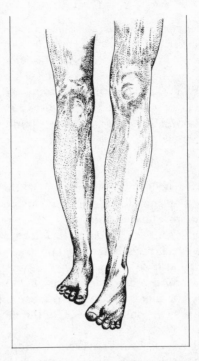

don't trip so frequently on roots and rocks. A less obvious advantage is that, by keeping the body erect, you have better balance and weight control. This allows you to move, change directions, or stop smoothly at any time. Your feet also come down more softly. And with your eyes fixed on the horizon rather than the ground, you can be more alert to changes in the environment.

You may find the fox walk uncomfortable and awkward at first. You may even have to fight a strong tendency to lower your gaze when you become anxious about unseen obstacles in your path. But in time, your feet will coordinate with your eyes, automatically avoiding obstacles that are picked up in your peripheral vision. In fact, the more time you spend in the woods, the more you will walk this way as a natural response to the demands of the environment.

The Weasel Walk
Once you are within sight of a potential hunting or trapping area, you should be even more careful to avoid detection or disturbance. You should become more cautious and alert, taking on the aspect of a hunter. The best example of this in the animal world is the weasel. Its body is low to the ground. It is always looking, always thinking, moving smoothly and quietly in search of prey.

To successfully perform the weasel walk, first try to feel like a hunter. Then, calling on ancient instincts, drop into an easy crouch, your hands close to your sides. Slow down until you are moving at less than half the pace of a normal walk. Move the feet as before, but be more cautious of what you're stepping on. Take care to keep from rustling brush and snapping twigs. Scan the area more intently and listen even more carefully for animal sounds. Your object, as you approach a hunting area, is to see the animal before it sees you.

Stalking

Once you have spotted an animal or reached a promising area, move so slowly and carefully that animals in the area cannot detect any sound or movement at all. Try to blend so perfectly with your surroundings that you seem to be nothing more threatening than a tree. Some animals (such as the deer) are so nearsighted that they may look repeatedly at an approaching human and mistake it for a stump if there is no telltale movement. Others, such as squirrels, often approach to within a few feet of a motionless person out of sheer curiosity. To most animals, no movement means no danger. That's why stalking is one of the most important survival skills you can learn.

Stalking is a logical extension of the fox and weasel walks. Crouch down even more, with the arms in close and the hands folded in front. Keep your eyes fixed constantly on the animal, and take each step with the deliberation of a heron stalking a frog. Lift the feet high to avoid obstacles. Your balance should be so controlled that if the animal suddenly looks up, you can freeze in any position for as long as necessary.

You should also bring the feet down with special care. Touch first on the outside ball of the foot and lightly roll to the inside and back before lowering the toes or applying weight to the step. Next, relax the toes and try to feel what's under your foot. Then apply more weight so you can really feel the ground. Finally, apply full weight and glide the body smoothly forward until the back foot lifts off naturally. Do not push off with the back foot.

The main reason for such precision is that you can't afford to commit your weight until you know what is under your foot. Bringing it down all at once, you might easily snap a twig or crush some vegetation that would alert the animal. A slow, rolling motion, however, applies pressure gradually. It allows your foot to feel the ground and to compress vegetation slowly and soundlessly. That way, if you encounter an obstacle at any point, you can place your foot somewhere else.

Regardless of where you step (forward, backward, sideways, over logs or brush), always touch down so that you won't have to pivot once the foot

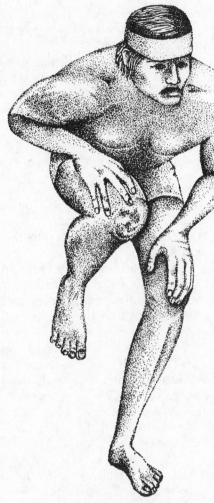

Stalking crouch,
bracing hands on knees
for extra support.

STEPS IN STALKING

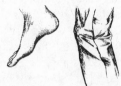

Lift foot high and maintain balance.

Come down on outside ball of foot.

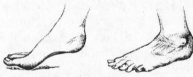

Roll to inside ball of foot.

Lower heel and toes, then apply weight.

is in place. Always roll from the outside to the inside of the foot. Try to maintain the attitude of the weasel, flowing imperceptibly across the landscape.

If you should cause a disturbance that alerts the animal during your approach, simply freeze until the animal relaxes and returns to its normal activities. Then continue the stalk. If you need to scratch your nose or use your hands in any way, do so with infinite slowness; for hand or arm motion will immediately give you away as a human. At very close range, even the blink of an eye or the glint of a pair of glasses might reveal your presence.

Normally the stalk is done in a crouch. If this posture becomes tiring, you can ease your back somewhat by resting your hands on your knees. You can even help to lift your knees by pulling on your pant legs. You may also find occasion for stalking on hands and knees—or even on your belly. In such cases, simply remember to lift one limb at a time in a slow, flowing motion—moving around vegetation instead of through it.

When crawling, lift the knees high instead of sliding. Keep the toes pointed so they don't catch on anything. Come down on the hands just as you would normally come down on your feet, rolling from outside to inside and back before committing the weight. In the belly stalk, inch the whole body along on hands and toes, keeping the arms in close to the sides.

At its best, stalking is a fine art. Stalking Wolf taught it to Rick and me very slowly and reverently, and we practiced for hours on end. We did stalking gymnastics to make our muscles rock-hard. We stood motionless on one leg for an hour or more at a time. We practiced weaving with the trees and grasses and blending ourselves with the mottled coloring of mud and herbs. We prayed for the proper attitude, yearning to understand the full wisdom of the stalk.

We practiced on flies and birds and other small animals until we could get close enough to touch them. It was years before I touched my first deer. But I will never forget the thrill of feeling its hair under my hand and watching its muscles flinch as it reacted to my presence. It is a great delight to touch a wild animal, because to touch it you must truly know it.

Camouflage and Cover

As you have probably gathered, the key to approaching animals is to blend so well with the flow of nature that your presence goes undetected. Minimal sound and movement are only part of the process. When stalking, setting traps, or sitting in ambush, you must also take advantage of camouflage and cover to mask your movements.

If possible, wear mottled clothing such as plaid that mixes well with your surroundings and breaks up your outline. You may also find it useful to darken your skin with dirt or charcoal, and to cover up your scent by rubbing on pungent plants found in the area. Do not follow well-beaten trails and paths into a hunting area. Instead, approach along a little-used route with plenty of vegetation. Stay out of direct sunlight. Use shadows, trees, and bushes to hide your body. Crouch low to blend with the vegetation, and move with the sounds of wind or rain.

There are two types of cover: primary and secondary. Primary cover is anything so thick that you can't see through it. This might be a tree stump, a tangle of brush, or even a field of tall grass. Secondary cover is composed of thinner material such as leafy branches that do not completely obscure your view. When stalking, keep most of your body hidden behind primary cover, even if you have to crawl or inch along on your belly. Utilize secondary cover either to watch animals or to plot your direction.

Ambush

Once you have determined an animal's habitual trails and runs, you can often sit in ambush with a weapon until it comes by. Pick some cover just beside the thoroughfare and stalk to it from the least used direction. Do this well in advance of the animal's expected arrival. Enter the cover very carefully, making sure that it breaks up your outline, and get as comfortable as possible. This need not be primary cover, for you will want to have an unobstructed view of the trail or run in front of you. You will also want to have enough room to use your weapon when the time is right. There is nothing more disheartening than taking an easy shot with a thrusting spear and having it tangle up in a bunch of briars.

Once you are comfortably in place, wait patiently until an animal approaches. This can be very trying if you're not used to it, and you may experience heavy spells of restlessness. If you feel the need to scratch or shift position, go ahead; but always do so in a stalking manner. In general, try to calm the body and mind while waiting. Attune yourself to the flow of nature. If you remain still enough, even in secondary cover, an approaching animal will pass right by unaware. And if you are equally patient and skilled with your weapon (see "Hunting Tools," page 211), you will be rewarded for your efforts.

Attracting Animals

It is possible to attract animals to your hiding place in a number of ways, but this takes a thorough knowledge of the specific animal and its habits.

Lures. You can often attract an elk or moose in the rutting season by scraping an antler against a tree within its territory. Such a lure can be made even more irresistible by first baiting a strategic spot with urine from another animal of the same species (another example of how to utilize everything from an animal). In fact, artificial scent posts of urine and scat will arouse the curiosity or indignation of almost any territorial animal. Near a known scent post, simply mound up a pile of dirt that is well impregnated with these substances and wait in ambush for the animal to make its accustomed rounds. Another lure that works well, especially for curious predators such as bobcats and foxes, is to hang up a feather or part of a bird wing so that its movement attracts attention.

Calls. When you become familiar with the sounds of various animals, you may be able to entice a predator within range by imitating the distress call of a bird or rodent. The high-pitched squeal of a mouse can be effectively imitated by sucking your lips against your top teeth. You can also create many birdlike calls by sucking the back of your hand in different ways. Two fingers scratching against a leafy surface is sometimes enough to fool a fox into thinking there's a mouse nearby. And an occasional slap of the ground can get you anything from a coyote to a rabbit.

Attunement

Whether you are waiting in ambush or setting a trap, your state of mind will have a lot to do with your success. Time and again in my survival classes I've had individuals who seemed to notice every animal and insect in their path, and whose calm presence brought on curious visitations from jays and weasels alike. Conversely, other people walk through the woods seeing very little, repelling animals instead of attracting them. The difference is attunement. The successful hunter is the one who is able to empty his mind of all other concerns. He blends so well with the environment that he becomes one with it in body, mind, and spirit. This was the meaning behind the Indian prayers and sweat lodge ceremonies.

Before a hunt or trapping excursion, then, take time to prepare yourself by calming your mind and adopting the flowing "weasel" attitude. When sitting in ambush beside a rabbit run, don't give in to fears, boredom, irritations, or restlessness. Try to live in the moment. Concentrate on your surroundings—the beauty of a plant, the texture of a leaf, the sound of the wind or rain, the erratic travels of an ant or beetle. These things will not only help to keep you occupied, but will also prevent you from inadvertently warning the animals of your presence.

Trapping

One of the best ways to catch animals is by setting traps. The beauty of trapping is that you don't have to wait around for an animal to show up. It also causes little disturbance to the environment and little alarm to animal residents.

Trapping is an age-old art used by natives the world over. As opposed to hunting, which is based primarily on concealment and sudden attack, trapping is a more passive form of food getting based on deception. In a word, your aim is to fool an animal into getting caught. For this reason, it is very important to know the animal's habits—where and how it travels, what it eats, what arouses its fright or curiosity, and how to take advantage of its weaknesses. You can only learn these things through study and observation.

Most of the traps described in this section are nonselective; that is, they catch dogs and cats just as effectively as they do squirrels and rabbits. Most of them, if properly made and set, are also quick and lethal. Since it is difficult to release the neighbor's dead cat, various governments (the U.S. and Canada included) have outlawed these traps for all but survival emergencies. Use them only if your life is on the line. Remember, too, the pain and suffering you can cause your animal brothers through shoddy craftsmanship. Practice making and setting traps before it becomes necessary. You can do this without danger to the animal simply by leaving out the lethal component or by rendering it harmless. (See "Deadfalls" and "Snares.")

Location

Before you even start building a trap, first decide on a specific animal and location. Find a transition area with a good supply of water, food, and cover. (Water need not always be in the immediate area. In fact, in some desert areas, animals get water from vegetation.) Survey this area from a distance, noting obvious animal trails, runs, and other signs. Determine what animals the area supports and what they have been feeding on. If necessary, scout the area in a stalking manner to determine the best trap locations. A promising spot will have an abundance of scat and gnawed vegetation. If you go into the area, take note of any natural materials you can use. But spend as little time there as possible until you are ready to set your traps.

Do not set traps on well-used trails. Animals know their territories like you know your own house. If someone put a freshly baked apple pie inside a big noose on your living room floor, chances are you wouldn't touch it. If you found a partially eaten pie inside a kitchen cabinet or refrigerator, though, you might be tempted to take a bite. Likewise, if you set up a baited trap in the middle of a trail, an animal will become suspicious and avoid it no matter how delectable the bait. In a less prominent spot, the animal will likely think he discovered it himself. The best trap locations, then, are marked by less traveled trails or runs among resting and feeding areas. Baited traps are most effective in semi-open spots, while unbaited traps are usually set directly on runs where vegetation or force of habit channels the animal in the proper direction.

Construction and Camouflage

Most traps require one or more pieces of wood to serve as supports or triggers. These can be either green or dead, but they should be very straight and strong, and easily carved or abraded. The bark on such pieces should be left on unless it has been naturally weathered away. A trap made of freshly whittled wood will stick out in a meadow like a sore thumb.

All notches on the trap should be cut as cleanly and precisely as possible. Carved or abraded portions should be darkened with dirt or charcoal. Your hands, knees, shoes, and all trap parts should also be smoked lightly (ten minutes or so beside a medium fire) or rubbed with ashes or charcoal to camouflage any human scent. The smell of smoke and charred wood is so common in the woods that most animals do not give it a second thought.

You can also cover up your scent by rubbing the trap parts with common nonpoisonous plants found in the area. (A student of mine once rubbed a trap with poison ivy, which did nothing to attract animals or to improve his health.) Once the trap is made, try it out a few times in camp to make sure it works well. Then stalk quietly into the trapping area to set it up.

Baiting

It is not always easy to decide what bait will lure an animal into a trap. Indeed, baiting is a science that involves some understanding of animal psychology. Fortunately, though, wild animals are not so different from humans when it comes to food habits. They need a mixture of salts, oils, proteins, and carbohydrates to maintain good health, and they prefer some foods more than others. If you can offer them something they crave, you will be well on the way to successful trapping. There is hardly an animal alive that will turn down peanut butter. But since the wilderness does not provide a ready supply of such foods, you will have to study the landscape for baiting clues.

Following is a likely scenario: You go into an area and find that X type of bush has been thoroughly nibbled by rabbits. There are lots of X bushes around and they are easy for rabbits to get to. But you also notice that wherever Y tree's buds are close to the ground, they have all been nibbled, and there are no more within easy reach. Logically, then, you will reach up higher and gather some of Y tree's buds to bait your trap.

Another example: In most areas of the country, two of the groundhog's favorite foods are clover and alfalfa. But the groundhogs on my farm can hardly stand clover and alfalfa because that's what they have to eat twenty-four hours a day. There I would bait them with something like sassafras buds—a food that is not generally preferred but that I know they would welcome for variety's sake. The general rule is, don't bait with corn in the middle of a cornfield.

For carnivores such as weasels, bobcats, and foxes, the preferred food is soft viscera. Liver, kidney, heart, lungs, and other internal organs make the best bait. However, most carnivores prefer their food fresh, so you may have to re-bait these traps frequently. Scavengers such as raccoons, skunks, and opossums, on the other hand, will eat decayed meat or viscera.

Avoid touching the bait with any part of your body. If you're using meat, skewer it right onto the bait stick and carry the stick from the other end. When you're transporting bait from one place to another, don't touch the part you're going to use. Most animals will not go near bait that has been tainted with human scent.

The Importance of Mastery

The following sections include descriptions of many different kinds of animal traps. My intent is to give you an arsenal of traps that can be used under varying conditions and locations to catch a wide variety of animals. But don't confuse versatility with mastery. Mastery comes only through practicing one trap at a time until you can carve it and set it with your eyes closed. I mean that literally, for there may be times when you will have to set traps at night.

Another point to remember is that many of the traps below are variations on a common theme. Once you thoroughly learn a single trap in each category, the variations will be easy. With this in mind, I strongly suggest that you first learn and master the following traps: figure-four deadfall (page 178); Paiute trap (page 184); rolling snare (page 190); and T-bar snare (page 195).

Deadfalls

The deadfall is a heavy object such as a rock or log that is propped up with an upright stick attached to a trigger mechanism. Almost all such traps are baited and set in semi-open areas. When triggered, they fall and ideally crush the animal beneath them. Some deadfalls are constructed to come down on an animal's head or neck; others to cover the entire body. As a general rule, though, the rock or log should be about twice the weight of the animal's body and wide enough to catch it even if it's moving.

This points out the importance of knowing the animal. If the deadfall is too heavy, you will gut and tenderize the animal all at once. If it is too light, the animal may escape or suffer unnecessarily. To harden the blow and prevent escape through burrowing, it is also advisable to put a slab of bark or other solid material beneath a deadfall—especially on soft ground.

Finally, you can't always count on finding the right-sized rock or log in the trapping area itself. For large animals you will have to hope for the best; but for small ones it is wise to import your deadfalls if you don't already have too much to carry.

In practice, of course, you will want to use a deadfall that is too light to cause any harm at all. The best one I know of is a cardboard box. My students and I have used it successfully on a variety of animals. One night in a backwoods cabin, I remember, we were particularly plagued by mice. So each of us set up a deadfall with a cardboard box and baited it with anything from cheese to peanut butter. Within minutes we heard the first box drop—and shortly thereafter a second and a third. No sooner did a box fall than a student rushed up to release the mouse and reset the trap. Most of the night that cabin was alive with the sounds of falling sticks and boxes—and by morning all of my students were experts with deadfalls.

Deadfalls Without Cordage

Initially you may want to set up deadfalls without the aid of cordage. These traps are not usually as quick as deadfalls with cordage or as versatile as lightning-fast snares; but if carefully constructed, they can catch animals of almost any size.

The Figure Four is the most common of the deadfalls. It is composed of three sticks in the shape of a "4" supporting a flat rock or log weight. When learning this one, it is probably best to place all three sticks on the ground in proper relation to each other and first mark where the notches will go.

The upright should be dovetailed at one end and squared off to a right-angled edge about halfway down. The diagonal stick should be beveled at the top and dovetailed at the bottom so it supports the deadfall and fits snugly into the notch at the end of the bait stick. Also notch the bait

Figure-four Traps

Top View

stick in the center so it fits cleanly against the squared-off edge of the upright. Then skewer the bait with the pointed bait stick, set up the apparatus, and carefully place the very edge of the deadfall onto the diagonal. Do not place the apparatus farther in, or the deadfall may fall onto the upright. If the upright is positioned beneath the deadfall, either push the deadfall back a bit or make a longer diagonal stick.

Ideally, when an animal goes for the bait, it pulls the bait stick away from the upright, causing the whole structure to collapse. For a large animal with a substantial pull, the upright can be pushed well into the bait stick notch. For a small animal, pull the bait stick out until it is barely held by the upright and will trip with the slightest tug. To prevent the animal approaching from the wrong direction and pulling the bait stick against the upright (which may twist the trap around without tripping it), place a barrier of sticks or brush on one side of the trap. Make sure the barrier sticks do not lean against or interfere with the movement of the deadfall.

Finally, make sure the ground beneath the trap is hard and devoid of sticks or brush that could prevent the weight from giving it a good whack. In soft ground, bury a small log or flat rock beneath the deadfall to insure a good hitting surface. Always be careful to avoid disturbing the area any more than necessary while approaching the site or setting the trap. If you do cause a disturbance, be sure to camouflage it before you leave.

The standard figure four is most effective in catching animals from the size of a rabbit up to the size of a fox. Animals smaller than a rabbit often have a hard time tripping the trigger or are too quick for the falling weight. If you use this trap for very small animals, then, take extra care to make a hair trigger so the weight will fall with no hesitation.

Penned Bait Area. This is a variation on the figure-four system that can be used to catch animals as large as a deer or a bear. It is composed of a semicircular fence with either a single or double figure-four system at the entryway supporting a heavy log. The bait is placed inside the pen, and the trigger stick—well branched at the end—is tripped when the animal pushes its head through to get the bait. The log then comes plummeting down and breaks the animal's neck. For especially large animals, the double-triggered trap with a log suspended horizontally is more effective. This usually requires the efforts of two or more people.

Whether you use the single or double trigger, the trap is made in basically the same way. First, place a log on the ground and drive four long wrist-thick stakes on either side near the ends. These will hold the lower log in place and stabilize the suspended log on top of the figure-four diagonals. Next, set up the figure-four apparatus and—using a lever, if necessary—heft the suspended log carefully into place. Put the bait on a

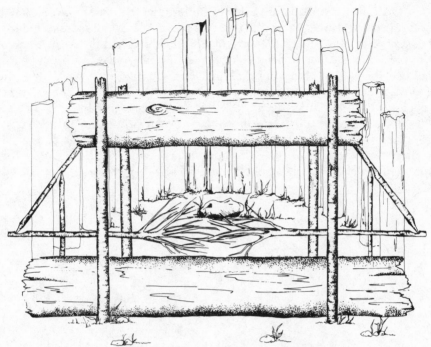

Penned Bait Area—Double Figure Four

stake just beyond the long, branched trigger stick and fence in the entire area behind the trap. Finally, if you're using a double trigger system, check both triggers to be sure they will trip at the same time. The upper log should fall smoothly and hit perfectly flush with the lower one so the animal cannot escape. For an even more lethal effect, you can taper the lower edge of the top log so that it drops like a guillotine.

The Bait Stick Deadfall is even simpler than the figure four, although not quite as reliable. All you need is an upright, a bait stick, and a deadfall. Carve the top end of the upright to a fine point and flatten one end of the bait stick so that it fits between the deadfall and the upright while holding the bait at the proper height. The key (and this may take some experimenting) is to establish such a delicate balance that the slightest touch on the bait stick will flip out the upright and topple the deadfall.

A variation on this trap can be made by inverting the entire trigger mechanism and setting it near the ground on a rounded stick or rock. If you do this, though, be sure the upright and ground stick are placed so that neither of them will impede the deadfall when the trap is triggered.

Bait Stick Deadfall

The Branch Deadfall is an unbaited trap meant primarily for use on animal trails and runs. Its only disadvantage is that it is quite difficult to set up. Cut the upright stick cleanly in half and whittle or abrade the end of one piece to a sharp point. When you set the trap, place this point on a small, rounded pebble. Between the two halves of the upright place the flattened end of a small branch—one with enough twigs to brush against a passing animal. Balance is critical with this trap. But once you get the alignment right and set up a twig fence to funnel the animal toward it, you'll find it's as quick and lethal as any deadfall.

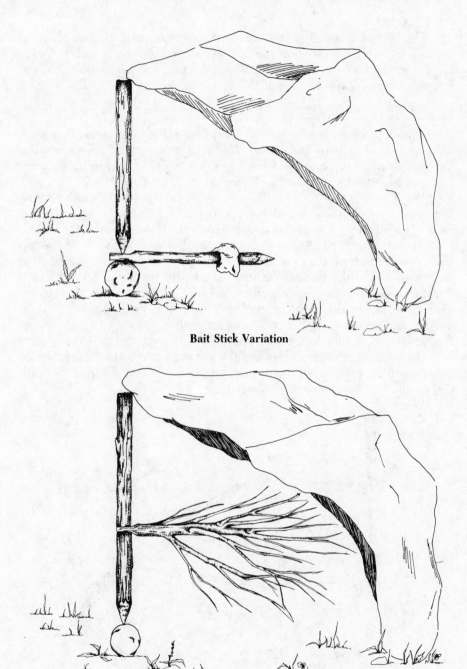

Bait Stick Variation

Branch Deadfall

The branch deadfall is also excellent for catching birds. Just set it up inside a pit in such a way that the bird must perch on the branch before it can get to the bait on the ground. When the bird touches the branch, the trigger is tripped and the deadfall drops into the pit.

Deadfalls With Cordage

If you have access to cordage or have time to manufacture some (see page 241), you can use it to make your deadfall triggers even more versatile. Usually, deadfall cordage need not be very strong. In fact, in most cases, you'll need little more than the thickness of a few threads.

The Paiute Trap is much like the figure four but with a more sensitive trigger mechanism that makes it especially useful for very small animals. The upright is made exactly as with the figure four—flat on the bottom and dovetailed at the top. Again, the diagonal is beveled at the top and notched underneath to receive the upright. But instead of dovetailing the lower end of the diagonal as you would with the figure four, tie on a fine piece of cordage. Tie the other end of the cordage to a short twig. When you are ready to set up the trap, wrap this twig once around the upright and secure it on the point of a long, thin bait stick lodged against the underside of the deadfall. In the end, this trap is also shaped like a "4." Once again, make sure the upright will not impede the falling rock or log. And if the ground is soft, place a piece of bark or a flat rock beneath the deadfall to insure a solid impact.

Paiute Deadfall

The Paiute trigger mechanism is extremely quick. It can be tripped equally well from either direction, so you don't need to wall in one side of the trap. To make the trigger even more sensitive, carve the end of the short stick to a dull point before securing it with the bait stick. This makes the Paiute one of the quickest of all deadfalls. Although it is most effective for small animals, it can be used to catch game as large as a raccoon or a fox.

The Hook Deadfall is especially effective for weasels and other small, quick animals that are adept at stealing bait from traps. It is identical to the Paiute deadfall except for the trigger mechanism, which uses two hooked sticks such as twigs with tiny branches. First, dig a small depression beneath the deadfall—just large enough to momentarily shield the animal's view of the falling rock or log. Push a long twig into the bottom of this depression with the hooked end facing downward. Tie the other twig to the baited cordage and hook it to the first so that the slightest disturbance will trigger the trap.

Hook Deadfall

The **Broken Stick Deadfall** is almost identical to the branch deadfall described above—again, except for the trigger. Once more, cut the upright in half (or simply snap it in two) and balance it between a pebble and the underside of the deadfall. Attach a piece of cordage on the pointed end of the upright just above the pebble. Run this cordage into a small depression beneath the deadfall and staple it in place with a small Y-stick—allowing enough space for the cordage to move freely beneath the "Y." When the animal pulls on the bait at the end of the string, it dislodges the lower half of the upright and brings the deadfall crashing down before it knows what has happened.

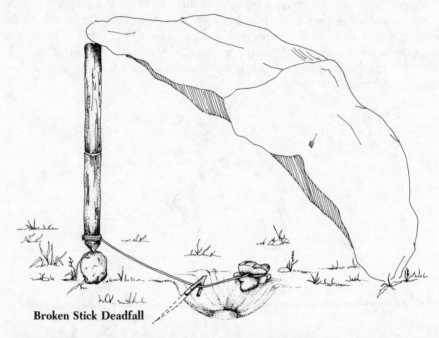

Broken Stick Deadfall

Greased String Deadfalls are variations on the broken stick deadfall that use a piece of cordage greased with animal fat (or some other irresistible, salty substance) for bait. The string is tied around the deadfall and then attached to the critical part of the upright. In the first type, it is tied to the upper part of a broken stick just above the joint; in the second, to the downward-curving hook on a leaning stick.

The **Ramp Pitfall** is a complicated but very sensitive Paiute-style trap that employs a board-and-fulcrum trigger held by a tiny hook. The idea is to lure the animal up the ramp past the fulcrum until its weight depresses the board and drops the deadfall. The upright and diagonal are made in standard Paiute style, with a length of thin cordage trailing from the end

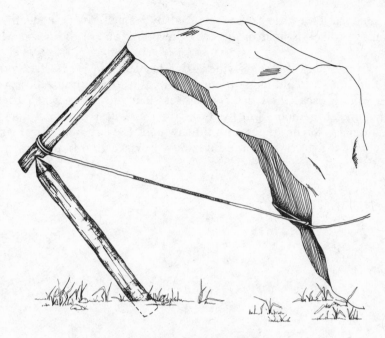

Greased String Deadfall

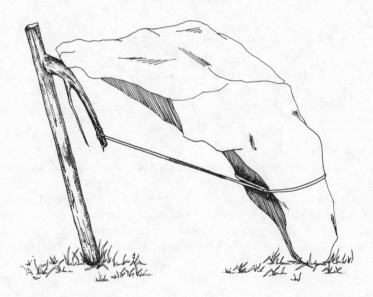

of the diagonal to a little hook supported by a small Y-stick beneath the deadfall. The hook is held in place by the upper end of the board when the trap is set.

Make the ramp at least as wide as the deadfall. Elevate it slightly on a round fulcrum stick and lodge the low end against the upright to prevent it from rolling back when the hook is set. Bait the board well past the fulcrum and set the hook. Finally, fence the trap with sticks on either side so the animal is forced to enter on the low end. If everything is just right, the slightest weight beyond the fulcrum will trigger the trap.

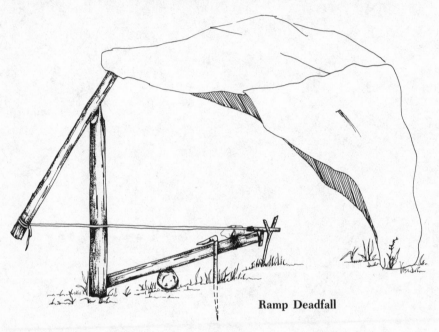

Ramp Deadfall

Spring Snares

Spring snares are loops of cordage set on or near animal runs with a sapling or springy branch held down by a trigger mechanism. When tripped, the sapling suddenly springs up, tightening the loop around the animal's neck and strangling it. Most snares have very fast triggers and arouse little or no sense of danger in an animal before it is too late.

A few things to keep in mind: The cordage on any snare should be as thin and inconspicuous as possible, but strong enough to withstand the spring of the sapling and the weight of the animal (see "Cordage," page 241). A few strands of reverse-wrapped sinew are usually ideal—except for practice, in which case you should always use an easily breakable material such as fine thread. Set all snares for specific animals, or for animals of about the same size. Make the loop large enough so the animal can easily get its head through, but not its shoulders or legs. Choose a spring stick that has enough strength and resiliency to lift the animal completely off the ground. When snared, the animal should be dangling free by its neck, unable to reach any nearby branches or trap parts.

If you cannot find a well-located, springy sapling or branch, you can set up a lever-and-fulcrum system using a Y-stick and a pole weighted at one end. To prevent the pole from jumping out of the Y-support when it springs up, tie a small stick or a length of cordage to both arms of the "Y." Also, groove the pole at the fulcrum so it will not slide in and allow the animal to get to the Y-stick.

Finally, it is a good idea to mark all spring sticks with a piece of cloth or other material that will be visible from a distance. This way, you will be able to determine which traps have been sprung without having to disturb the area.

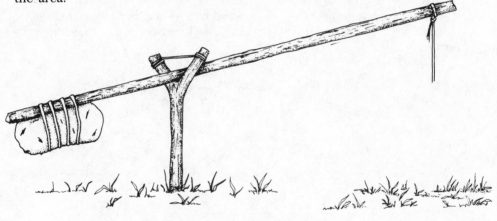

Lever and Fulcrum

Unbaited Snares

If you have a supply of strong cordage, you can place any number of un-baited spring snares on various animal thoroughfares in very little time. Most of these traps are very simple, needing only cordage, a sapling, and a trigger. Since they do not use bait, however, they must be placed on known trails or runs. There, most of them will catch an animal with equal dispatch from either direction—especially if you place a few vertical sticks on either side of the run to funnel the animal into the noose.

The Rolling Snare is a versatile trap that can be used to catch animals of almost any size. The trigger is made with two hooked sticks—one long and one short. Just beside the run, pound the long stick securely into the ground with the hook curving downward. Tie a knotted loop in one end of the cordage (see "Knots," page 244) and slip the other end through to form an easily adjustable noose. Next, tie the end of the cordage to the spring stick. A short distance farther, tie on the other hooked stick. Bend the sapling over and secure it under tension by joining the two hooks, bark to bark. (This is important, as carved surfaces can actually grow together if the sap is running—or freeze together in cold weather.) Test the trigger mechanism by lightly tapping on the lower hook. (Watch the eyes!) The spring stick should snap back instantly. If not, carve or abrade the two trigger surfaces to a finer point of contact.

After you have reset the spring stick, place the noose just high enough over the run so the animal will push its head through when it comes by. If necessary, use sticks to help hold the noose in place, and set sticks or brush on either side of the run to prevent the animal from going around. To assure good timing, avoid slack between the noose and the trigger.

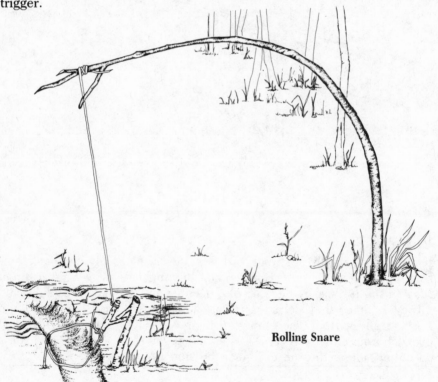

Rolling Snare

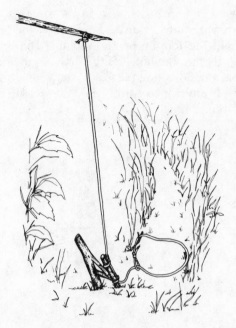

Rolling Snare

The Hook Snare is a variation on the rolling snare that uses a single hooked stake for a trigger. In this case, the sapling is bent nearly to the ground and set directly against the flat part of the hook itself. This trap does not allow for much variation in the bend of the spring stick, but it is very simple—and excellent for use with a lever and fulcrum.

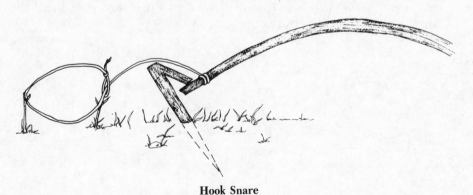

Hook Snare

The Notched Peg Snare is similar to the standard rolling snare, but its trigger is made with notches instead of hooks. One peg is pounded into the ground to hold the tension on the sapling. The other, carved into a small "L," fits neatly into the notch of the first. A potential disadvantage of this trigger is that the adjoining pieces of wood sometimes bind or freeze together, making it difficult to spring. For this reason, it should be used primarily with larger animals.

Notched Peg Snare

The Peg-Rock Snare is very simple and very touchy—suitable for the smallest and quickest of animals. Drive a peg into the ground and place a smooth, egg-shaped rock beside it. Bend the sapling down so it's just resting against the rounded edge of the rock. When the animal pushes its head through the loop, the sapling springs off the edge of the rock. Take care, though; this trap is so touchy that it sometimes trips even in a light wind.

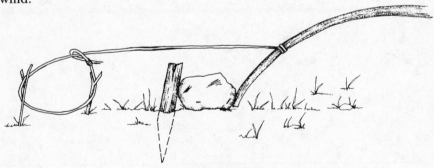

Peg-Rock Snare

The Peg Snare is a medium-speed snare used primarily for animals ranging in size from a ground squirrel to an eastern cottontail. In this case, the spring stick is held against nothing more than the smooth edge of a single peg driven into the ground. If the trigger is too touchy, adjust it by flattening the edge of the peg with a knife or rock.

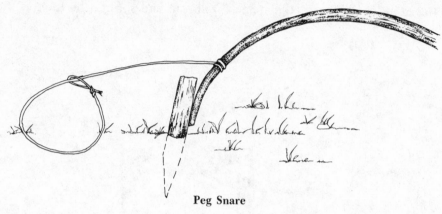

Peg Snare

The Plug Snare is a variation on the peg snare that uses a plug flattened at one end and inserted into a notched peg. With this snare, the cord from the spring stick should be tied right next to the flattened end of the plug. On an unbaited snare system, the plug should be very short; however, a longer one can be baited and used with the snare systems described in the following section. As with the notched peg snare, there is a potential here for binding or freezing; hence, it should be used mainly for animals that will give it a good tug.

Plug Snare

The Pencil Snare is potentially the fastest unbaited snare trigger of all. It is made with two notched pegs holding a smooth, cylindrical trigger stick. The notches face inward, like two sets of fingers delicately grasping a pencil. The cordage is tied to the trigger stick, and the noose is placed on a run—either to the side or between the two pegs. With the slightest tug in either direction, the "pencil" rolls out and springs the trap.

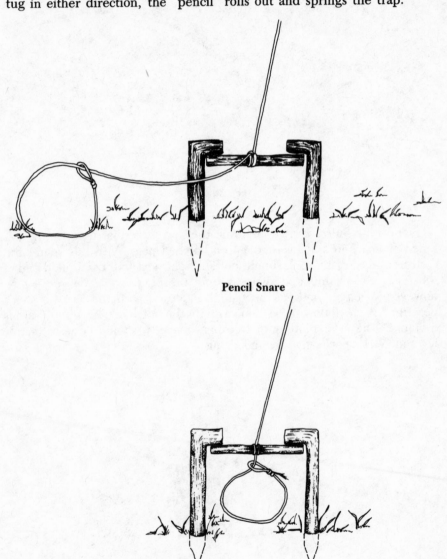

Pencil Snare

The Burrow Snare is used to catch animals as they emerge from their homes in trees, logs, or ground. Again, the noose should be only slightly larger than the animal's head and placed just in front of the burrow so that the animal must push through it to get out. For most ground burrows, you will be able to use one or more of the systems just described. In more difficult spots, such as vertical tree trunks, you may have to improvise. There you can often use a springy branch (or even a suspended rock) and hook the cord carefully into the bark.

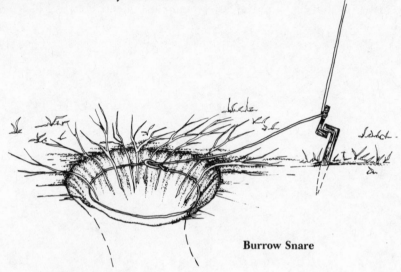

Burrow Snare

Baited Spring Snares

If you have both bait and cordage, it is advisable to set some baited snares. Like baited deadfalls, these traps should be set within feeding and resting areas but not directly on trails or runs. With almost every type, the baited trigger is enclosed in a circle of sticks to force the animal to enter from a specific direction.

The T-Bar Snare is much like the pencil snare. Pound two notched pegs firmly into the ground. Instead of facing the notches toward each other, though, place them side-by-side to hold a T-bar trigger. Place the bait at the end of the T-bar and flatten the top of the "T" just enough so it will be held parallel to the ground when the spring stick is set. If it is carved correctly, the slightest upward pull on the end of the bar should cause it to flip out of the notches.

Tie the cordage from the spring stick to the joint of the T-bar and place the noose carefully on the outward-beveled edges of tiny stakes encircling the bait. This "fence" forces the animal to stick its head down through the noose to get to the bait. When it tries to pull the bait up, it springs the trap and instantly rockets into the air.

In most cases, the fence stakes for the T-bar trap are about six inches high. For smaller animals, you can make a variation that allows for a frontal entry by placing the loop in front and carving the T-bar so it points toward the ground. (With this trap, of course, there is no need to bevel the edges of the fence stakes.) The T-bar snare and its variations take some time to set up, but they are the fastest and most effective traps I have ever used.

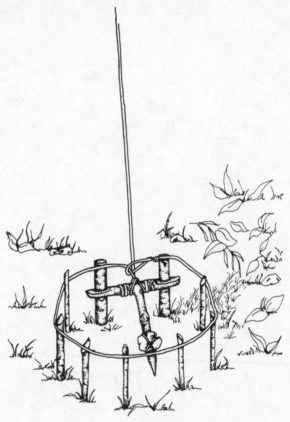

T-Bar Snare

The Lever Snare is a variation on the T-bar that uses one peg and a triangular support system with a lever. The peg has two notches—a rectangular notch in the middle and a beveled notch toward the top. The bait stick is beveled on the near end and notched in the middle. The lever (beveled at one end and dovetailed at the other) completes the triangle,

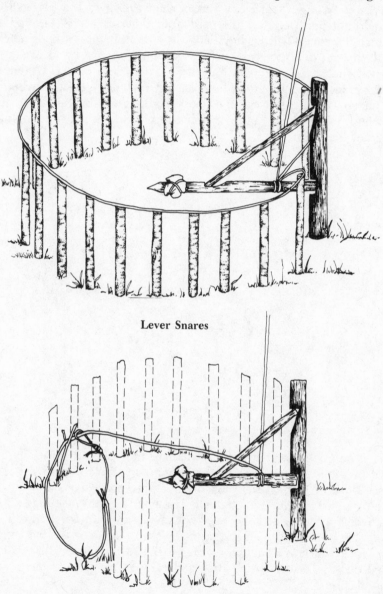

Lever Snares

fitting snugly into the notches in peg and bait stick. Make the notch in the bait stick so shallow that the slightest downward push dislodges the lever and springs the trap. Tie both the spring stick cord and the noose cord to the bait stick. As with the T-bar, this trap employs a circular fence of stakes and can be set for either top or front entry.

The Wedge Snare is a variation on the lever snare—again using a single notched peg. Tie the cord from the spring stick around a small, squared wedge. This wedge should fit so loosely into the peg notch that it will flip out unless it is secured. Secure the wedge by inserting the flattened end of the bait stick into the bottom of the notch. Wedge the bait stick in just enough so that it will fall out and spring the trap when the bait is taken. With this trap, the noose cord should be tied directly to the spring stick. You can set it for either top or front entry, depending on the size of the animal.

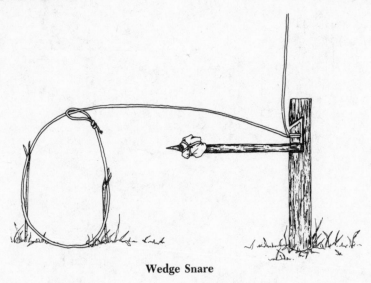

Wedge Snare

The Peg-Rock Bait Snare is similar to the peg-rock snare described in the previous section. Again, the spring stick rests precariously against a rock—which in turn rests against a simple peg driven into the ground. The trigger on this trap, though, is a pointed bait stick lodged carefully between the rock and the peg. Balance is critical and often difficult. All components must be set so that when the animal jars the bait stick loose, the rock will move enough to trigger the spring stick. The noose cord is tied directly to the spring stick and placed on top or to one side of the circular fence.

Peg-Rock Bait Snare

The Greased String Snare is a simple variation of the above traps that uses a single peg inside a circular fence. Two pieces of cordage come off the spring stick. One goes to the noose on top or in front of the fence and the other is tied to the peg inside. This second piece of cordage is greased with animal fat. It is placed so that the animal will just get its head through the loop before biting down on it and tripping the spring stick.

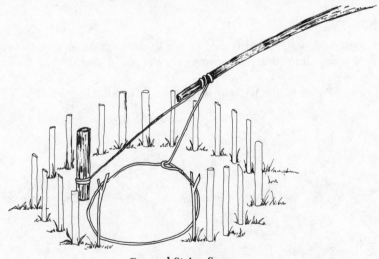

Greased String Snare

   The Ramp Snare is similar to the ramp deadfall. It is composed of a board set on a stick fulcrum, like a teeter-totter. Lodge this board lightly against a small peg at the low end and secure it with the tip of the spring stick at the high end. Place the noose in the middle of the board and the bait near the high end. Set the fulcrum so that the board will fall just after the animal pushes its head through the noose. To force the animal to enter at the low end of the ramp, fence in the upper half with sticks. Use the first two sticks to hold up the noose.

   The ramp snare is a very touchy trap. It is especially effective for small, quick animals such as mink and weasels that often travel on logs and branches in the woods.

Ramp Snare

Other Traps

Although you will probably use deadfalls and spring snares to catch the bulk of your game, there are many other kinds of useful traps. Several are described below.

   The Water Snare is a non-spring snare used to catch animals such as

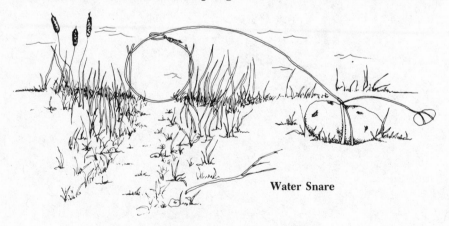

Water Snare

beaver, muskrats, and waterfowl. The noose is set up on a run leading to water and tied around a rock at the water's edge. The end of the cordage is then secured around a nearby stake. When the animal gets its head caught in the noose, its first impulse is to head for water. When it jumps off the bank, it pulls the rock in and drowns. To keep the animal from escaping or suffering unnecessarily, be sure that the water is deep enough to drown it and the rock heavy enough to hold it under.

The Goose Trench is nothing more than a ditch about a foot wide, a foot deep, and twenty feet long with a gentle ramp leading in at one end. Dig it at night where you have found an abundance of goose droppings and tracks; then sprinkle grain inside and near the entrance to lead the birds to it. Get rid of the excess dirt and camouflage the trench so that it looks like a natural part of the landscape. Then hide nearby and wait for the geese to march down in. Once in the trench, the geese have a sense of security because they can periodically raise their heads to look over the sides. But in fact they are helpless because they cannot jump out and they cannot spread their wings to take off. This allows you to simply walk up to the trap and pick out as many birds as you need.

The Duck Blind. A trench will not work for ducks because they are capable of explosive, near-vertical takeoffs. When paddling on the water, though, they can often be fooled by an innocent-looking patch of vegetation. Tie a thick matting of reeds around your head so you can just barely see out. When you spot a flock of feeding ducks, stalk into the water and slowly float toward them. Bob with the wind and waves. If you move carefully enough, you will be able to float to within an arm's length of a feeding duck, where you can reach out and pull it under by the feet. If you yank quickly enough, chances are you can then get another bird, since ducks are seldom alarmed by the sudden submergence of one of their fellows.

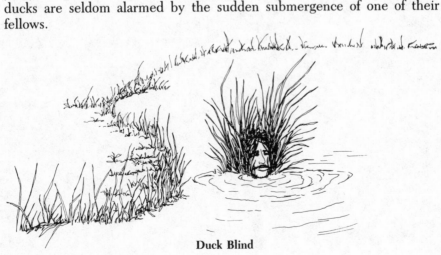

Duck Blind

The Mouse Bottle Pit. This trap is geared for small meadow rodents such as mice and squirrels. In the middle of a field, dig a bottle-shaped pit about arm deep. The pit should have a narrow neck and widen toward the bottom to prevent the animals from climbing out. Use several small stones to support a flat rock just above the pit. Choose a rock that is large enough to completely cover the hole, and set it up so it looks like a logical hiding place.

When all is set, walk to the outer edge of the field and gradually spiral back in toward the center. As you walk, your movements will scare small animals toward the trap, where they will mistakenly take refuge beneath the rock and fall in. Since the mouse bottle pit catches snakes and scorpions as easily as mice, never reach your arm into the trap. Instead, first pound the bottom with the flattened end of a log, or break the sides down so you can examine the contents without danger.

Mouse Bottle Pit

Fishing

If you are close to a major water source, fish and related animals may be an easy source of survival food. They can be taken with spears, traps, lures, baited hooks, baskets, bows and arrows, and—believe it or not—even with your bare hands. The method you use will depend primarily on your abilities, but also on the type of fish you're seeking and where you're trying to catch it.

Again, there is no substitute for observing fish and getting to know their habits. If you are near a lake or stream, stalk up to the water's edge and spend some time there trying to find out what is available. (You may soon realize that the water contains a whole host of edibles, from nymphs and polliwogs to frogs, mussels, and crayfish—in addition to various finned species.)

In general, fish like to feed in the early morning just before the sun comes up and again just after sunset. The onset of a storm may also cause a sudden feeding frenzy. At such times you may notice the surface of a lake frequently broken with concentric ripples made by fish rising for insects. During the heat of the day, fish usually try to hole up somewhere cool and protected. In lakes they take to deeper water. In creeks and rivers they seek out hidden rock outcroppings or logs in quiet pools. Study the water and imagine where a fish might feel comfortable, safe, and secure.

Before you choose a particular method of fishing, also try to find out what the fish are feeding on. If you use bait, it should be enticing but not very different from the fish's accustomed foods. Ideally, it should duplicate or mimic what the fish is feeding on at that time. This may be flies, worms, small amphibians, or even the eggs and entrails of other fish. After you catch your first fish, examine the contents of its stomach for other clues to its diet.

Bare Hands

The most primitive, although not the easiest, way of getting fish is by picking them up with your bare hands. This method requires no equipment at all, but it takes a great deal of patience and should be used only in shallow water in a place that is known to contain fairly good-sized fish. It can be very effective for catching salmon in their spawning grounds or for taking large trout from protected pools in streams.

Stalk into the water as silently as a heron. When you have reached the fish's lair, stand absolutely still and slowly reach your hands down into the water. Try to become part of the flow of the creek, your fingers no more intimidating than sticks or fronds of grass. If possible, approach the fish from behind, gradually bringing your hands under its belly. If it moves away, be patient and it will likely return. Then, at just the right moment, rake your fingers up into its gills and flip it out of the water.

Baskets

The use of baskets is a variation on the bare hand technique that is especially good for smaller fish and minnows. Again, the water should be shallow and the fish visible. Make a shallow basket with a weave that is loose enough to move quickly through the water but tight enough to contain the fish (see "Weaving Clothes and Baskets," page 254). Follow the same careful stalking procedure you would use for catching fish by hand. When the basket is beneath the fish, quickly lift it up and flip the fish onto the bank.

Spears

In shallow water where fish are readily visible, a spear may be the most effective. The size of the spearhead should be determined by the size of the fish. A double-pronged, six-inch tip is usually adequate for trout, perch, whitefish, and the like; whereas a much larger and more durable spear may be necessary for salmon-sized fish.

Most spears are easily made. Even so, carve them with care. If you are patient and careful in every aspect, you will probably be rewarded with as much as you need. Also, when you practice with spears, use submerged logs or sticks as targets. This not only conserves the fish, but protects you as well, since most states forbid fishing with spears and arrows except for survival purposes. There are many different spear types, but the following are all you will need for short-term survival purposes.

The Straight Spear is the simplest of all. It is nothing more than a straight green sapling—or better yet, a fire-killed sapling—that is pointed or barbed on the end. Choose a sapling that is about a foot longer than your highest reach. Carve or abrade it to a sharp, barbed point at one end, and fireharden the point before using it (see "Firehardening Wooden Tools," page 252). This spear is very quick to make, but the single prong will not hold a squirming fish as well as a double or triple prong. Therefore, it should be used with special care (see "Using Fish Spears" on the following page).

The Straight "V" Spear is a little more complicated, but quite a bit more effective at holding a fish. Again, it is made from a long green sapling—this time firehardened, split, and carved at one end into two sharp prongs with inward-pointing barbs. Before carving, force the two halves apart with a wedge lashed between them. The lashing can be done with sinew, rawhide, or cordage made from strong natural plant fibers such as dogbane, velvet leaf, evening primrose, and fireweed. If you secure the wedge with sinew or rawhide, wet it thoroughly and wrap it as tightly as possible, since both these materials tend to loosen in water.

The Straight "Y" Spear is another double-barbed spear made from a long forked sapling. The fork should be as symmetrical as possible, and wide and long enough to accommodate the fish you have in mind. Carve barbs into the prongs (both barbs pointing inward), then fireharden the fork (see "Firehardening Wooden Tools," page 252). Finish the spear by bending the prongs closer together and securing them with a length of cordage a short distance above the fork.

The Trident is a triple-pronged spear made just like a straight "Y" spear except for the additional third prong. It is a little more difficult to make, but it greatly increases your chances of spearing and holding a fish. To make a Y-stick into a trident, split the fork carefully down the middle, groove it slightly, and insert a single or double-barbed piece of bone or firehardened wood. Then wrap the shaft tightly along the split. Finally, bend in the two outer barbs and secure them with cordage. If you have the equipment, another way of installing the third barb is to drill a hole at the fork with a bow drill and glue it in place with a mixture of pitch and ashes (see "Glues and Oils," page 263). With this technique, it is not necessary to wrap the shaft unless it splits, but wrapping will help prevent splitting.

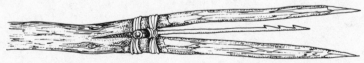

Using Fish Spears. Fish spears must be handled skillfully to be effective. As with any prey, try to spot the fish before it spots you. Stalk quietly and carefully without making any quick movements. If you are in the water, be especially careful to avoid detection.

Hitting a fish from above the surface of the water is chancy because the fish is not where it appears to be. Refracted light distorts both its size and position. Once within range, establish the proper alignment by slowly lowering the tip of the spear into the water. Then, holding the spear near the end of the shaft with your throwing hand and supporting it farther down with the other, push it close enough so you can make a quick jab at the fish. Double- and triple-pronged spears will usually lock the fish onto the spearhead so you can pull it right out of the water. If you are using a single-pronged spear without a sharp barb, try to pin the fish to the bottom. Then, holding the spear with one arm, carefully reach down and slide the creature up the shaft a few inches before lifting it out of the water. Or flip it out onto the bank with a quick thrust of the spear.

Fish Arrows. Fish can also be speared with arrows shot from survival bows (see "Bows and Arrows," page 216). These are made in the same way as hunting arrows, but they are twice as long and barbed at the tip like a harpoon—or even fitted with double- or triple-pronged points like spears. A length of cordage is also tied between the arrow and the lower end of the bow so the arrow can be retrieved. As with spears, the bow and arrow is more accurate with fish if you can get the tip of the arrow in the water before releasing it. If this is not possible, aim a little below the fish to compensate for refraction.

Hook and Line

Initially, you may find that fishing with hook and line is the most effective for a given water source. This technique is familiar to most people, takes relatively little time or skill, and is sometimes the only way to get fish out of deeper water. Its only disadvantage is that it often requires a sizeable length of cordage and proper bait.

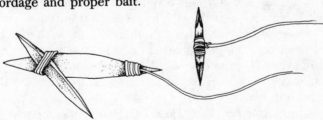

Hooks can be fashioned from wood or bone. One of the simplest is the skewer gorge hook, which is nothing more than a needle of material sharpened at either end, notched in the middle to receive the cordage, and baited so that it lies almost parallel with the line. This makes it easy for the fish to swallow. Once you pull on the line, though, the skewer opens up and catches on some part of the fish's anatomy and you have yourself a meal. A variation on this is the scissor hook—two needle-like pieces of bone or wood lashed together with cordage. These lie almost parallel when baited, but open up like a pair of scissors when the fish bites down.

You may be able to find thorns that will make serviceable fishhooks. You can also carve or abrade the branch of a small stick into a sharp barb. Better yet, lash two or three of these thorns or barbs together. If you have already caught a small rodent or bird, various bones can be sharpened into excellent barbed hooks and secured to a length of cordage at the end of a stout sapling.

The cordage should be as inconspicuous as possible, long enough to reach the fish's lair, and strong enough to land the fish without breaking. Milkweed, dogbane, and stinging nettle make excellent fishline. Sinew, although it is incredibly strong, tends to stretch and loosen when it gets wet. If you use sinew, be sure all knots are tight and secure. Wrapping a sufficient length of cordage from natural vegetation may be time consuming. But if you take pains to insure a good line, you will avoid disappointment later on (see "Cordage," page 241).

To tie on an eyeless hook, one of the best methods is to cover the shank with hot pitch and wrap the cordage along its entire length, securing it finally with a second layer of pitch (see "Glue," page 263). If you don't have pitch, taper the shank toward the barb and tie it on with a few half hitches (see "Knots," page 244).

Lures

Fish lures can be carved from wood and "decorated" to imitate small fish, frogs, and insects. One of the simplest is an oval button of cedar with tiny feather tufts glued to the ends. Another is a somewhat thicker button, shaped flat on the top and rounded on the bottom, with "legs" made of pine needle tufts to imitate a frog. There are many possible variations, so use your imagination to make something that imitates the most popular insects and animals.

Such lures can be made either with or without hooks. To attach a hook, drill a hole at the back and tie on a barb with cordage or sinew. Attach the fishing line through a drilled hole at the front end and work the lure on the surface of the water with a long sapling. Hookless lures can be dangled from a pole with one hand while you hold a spear ready in the other. Just as the fish is about to take the lure, stop all movement. When the fish stops, jab and pull out your meal.

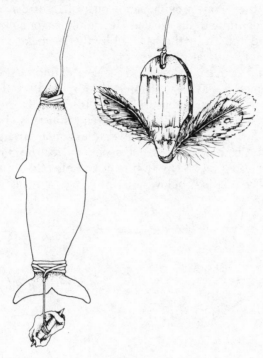

Snares

You can also catch fish using various types of spring snares. These work on the same principles as those described in "Trapping," page 175. For best results in calm water, use a hair trigger such as the one used for the rolling snare (page 190). Set the spring stick by the water's edge with a piece of cordage leading first to the trigger stick, then to a float. From the float, tie another piece of cord with a baited hook trailing beneath the water. When the fish takes the bait, the spring stick snaps back, sets the hook, and pulls the animal out of the water. Ideally, it is held high enough above the bank so it won't be bothered by other animals. To prevent the spring stick from ripping the hook out of the fish's mouth, weight it with a rock near the tip.

Traps

Once you have provided for your immediate food needs, you may want to set up a fish trap. These are often quite time-consuming to make, but in the long run they may provide large quantities of fish and other water creatures for continued sustenance. Remember, though, that such traps are frowned upon both by the fish and by the lawmakers in various states. So use them for survival purposes only.

The Fish Funnel is a fencing of stakes pounded side-by-side into a creekbed in such a way that it forces water dwellers through a narrow passageway into an open enclosure. There the animals are speared, caught with the hands, or netted with baskets. The funnel is always set up with the wide end facing upstream; however, the actual arrangement of stakes depends on the creekbed. It is not necessary for the funnel to span the entire width of the creek. The trap is just as effective in the shallows of a larger waterway—or just below a set of riffles or pools where you know fish are hiding.

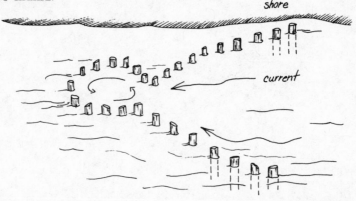

Once you have set up the trap, herd fish and other water animals into it by throwing rocks far above the opening of the funnel. As the fish swim into it, they will be channeled right by and you can try your hand at spearing. Better yet, wade downstream from above the trap, systematically turning over rocks and causing a commotion that makes all the animals flee for cover. By the time you reach the trap receptacle, you should find an abundance of finned, clawed, and shelled edibles temporarily detained there. You can then block the entry with a log or rock and use a spear or basket to gather them up.

The One-Way Gate. If you're not skilled with a spear, you can make a gate to keep your fish in the trap by lashing several vertical bars to a crosspiece. Tie these sticks close enough to prevent the fish from getting through. Then lash the crosspiece lightly to the two stakes in the narrowest part of the funnel so that the bars nearly reach the bottom of the creek. The gate should open inward very easily. To prevent it from opening outward, lash another horizontal stick near the bottom so that the ends of the stick will catch on the two vertical stakes. Finally, weight the bottom of the gate with a rock that is just heavy enough to keep the current from pushing it open. When a fish swimming downstream butts its snout against the gate, it should open and close as easily as reed grass and contain the animal for as long as you like. (This is one way of storing fresh fish without a refrigerator!)

Basket Trap. You can just as quickly make a loosely woven trap from saplings by following the directions given for construction of survival baskets (page 256). Use long, strong saplings. Make the weave loose enough for the current to flow through, but tight enough to contain whatever fish and animals you're seeking. Interweave the saplings until you've created a large pot; then attach a gate like the one described above. Finally, bait the trap with animal entrails or decaying meat, camouflage it with sticks or water grasses, and place it in a promising spot. Whether you place the trap in a gentle current of shallow water or lower it into a deep, crayfish-infested pool, be sure to weight it or stake it down so it will be there when you come back. Within a few hours, if you're lucky, it may be so full of fish and animals you can hardly lift it.

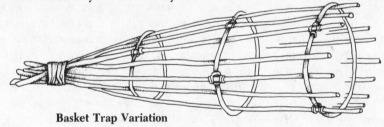

Basket Trap Variation

Hunting Tools

By now you are well on the way to comfortable survival in the wilderness. You have built a warm shelter, gotten a fire going, gathered an abundance of wild edibles, and perhaps even secured a few small animals with traps and snares. The streams are providing fish, and you are beginning to feel more confident about your survival abilities. For the first time, you may have some leisure to begin thinking about longer term survival aids and comforts. Among these are carefully crafted hunting tools.

Our earliest ancestors used stones, bones, and sticks as hunting tools millions of years ago. Over time, they invented more complicated weapons such as spears, slingshots, bolas, and bows and arrows. Today, high-powered rifles have largely replaced such primitive weapons. But handmade survival tools are still in use wherever people live close to the earth—and they are by no means crude or ineffective. In many cases, their construction and use have been honed to a fine art. Primitive though they are, we should look on such hunting tools with respect; for the people who were most skilled at using them were those who survived to build our present civilization.

Among the native Americans, every hunting tool was manufactured to perfection. Even the collection of materials for these tools was considered a sacred art. Much fasting and praying was done before a hunter went to find a bow stave or a set of arrow shafts. Staves, shafts, knives, handles, feathers, and other materials were all considered gifts from the Great Spirit—as well as gifts from the trees, rocks, plants, and animals that gave themselves for the Indians' use.

Making your own hunting tools is not at all like buying them in the store. A fine, handcrafted tool is like an intimate friend. You know its strengths and weaknesses, what it can do and can't do. It is an embodiment not only of the natural materials used to make it, but also of the effort and skill that went into its construction.

All of the hunting tools described below are extensions of the human arm; yet all are relatively short-range weapons. To be successful with them, you must not only be adept at observation, tracking, and stalking, but you must be able to throw or shoot accurately. You will have more luck if you remember several important points. (1) Before embarking on any hunting expedition, warm up and take at least ten practice shots with the tool you intend to use. (In most cases, success or failure depends on a single shot.) (2) Stalk to within range of the target, holding the weapon close to the body. (3) Bring the weapon back slowly on the final step so that when you are poised for the shot, your opposing foot is pointing directly at the target. Make the shot as quickly as possible to take full advantage of your position.

Stones

A stone held comfortably in the hand can secure many animals when thrown at close range. You can certainly stalk close enough to bag a grouse, ptarmigan, or slow-moving porcupine, and many other animals can be taken this way if the throw is fast and accurate. Your throwing ability is far more important than the size of the stone. Gather several small ones and hold them in your non-throwing hand as you stalk toward the animal.

Keep your eye on the target. Whenever practical, aim for the animal's head, since a sharp blow on the skull will probably stun it long enough for you to retrieve it. On the final step, slowly bring your throwing arm back, plant your foot, and release the stone with a final snap of the wrist. Lean forward and follow through with your arm as though pitching a baseball. Then quickly transfer another stone to your throwing hand. For small game, throw a whole handful of stones at the same time.

Throwing Sticks

To the ancient Neanderthals, sticks were the most useful of survival tools. They served as clubs, hammers, shovels, prying bars, and, not least of all, throwing weapons. A rapidly spinning stick could knock firemaking materials out of trees and had a far greater killing radius than a stone. Times have changed, but the usefulness of the throwing stick remains the same.

Pick a strong, light stick that fits easily into your hand. Ideally, it should be free of branches, about two to three feet long, with a smooth

Overhand Throw

handle. In some cases you may have to use whatever you can find, without taking time to shave off the bark or carve the stick to fit your hand. For the long term, though, choose one that is easy to throw and that serves many of the other purposes mentioned above.

The stick is usually thrown either overhand or sidearm. The overhand throw is used to reach animals such as squirrels on tree trunks or rabbits hiding in tall grasses. Hold the stick at the small end, just as you would a tennis racket. As you take the final step, bring it straight back over your shoulder so it hangs loosely against your back. As you throw, keep your shoulders square and bring the stick straight past the ear. At the end of the throw, snap it so that it whirls rapidly through the air like an unleashed propellor, perpendicular to the ground.

The sidearm is a little more difficult but much more effective in open areas. Most animals will be sitting or standing on the ground, and a horizontally spinning stick has a chance of hitting them even on the rebound. Hold the stick as before, bringing it back slowly until it is well extended behind you. Then curl the wrist and forearm out to the side. Finally, plant the opposite foot and snap the stick toward the target as though cracking a whip. Do not follow through or you may throw off to the side.

Sidearm Throw

At times, you may have to throw somewhere between overhand and sidearm. Practice stalking and throwing until you are comfortable with almost any angle. Throw at trees, stumps, rocks, cans, high targets and low—anything that will not be damaged by the twirling stick. Even in practice, remember to flow smoothly and quietly up to the moment you release the stick.

Given time and tools, there are many things you can do to make a throwing stick more serviceable. At the very least, you can shave off the bark and carve the handle so it leaves your hand more easily. You can also taper the edges so that it slices more quickly through the air. You can even carve it into the shape of a modified boomerang. If you taper the edges, though, keep the stick heavy enough so it doesn't take off like an airplane wing. Such weapons in the hands of skilled hunters have been known to kill at ranges up to several hundred feet!

For heavier animals, you might use a stick with a root ball or knot on the end. Carve off the roots and smooth both the stick and the handle. When you throw this stick, the added weight of the ball will give it more power. Finally, you can even split the stick and lash on a round or oblong rock at one end with a rawhide thong or piece of sinew to simulate a tomahawk.

Rodent Skewers

Most rodents escape danger by ducking quickly into their burrows. However, many of them don't go very far down. And sometimes, when they feel comfortably surrounded by the old familiar soil, they venture back toward the entryway out of sheer curiosity. You can sometimes take advantage of these habits with a rodent skewer—a long-handled, Y-pronged stick with firehardened barbs at the ends. Push and prod the skewer into the burrow until you feel the animal. Then thrust and turn the stick at the same time, locking flesh and hair into the barbs. Maintaining the twist on the skewer, pull the animal to the surface and quickly put it out of its misery with a club. Needless to say, this is a very crude way of catching an animal. Because of the pain it inflicts, I don't recommend it unless you are near starving.

Bows and Arrows

The bow and arrow is the most versatile of all primitive weapons—easily adapted to catching fish, frogs, reptiles, and mammals of almost any size. For most native Americans its construction and use were nothing less than an art form. Experienced hunters spent years curing and shaping bows, which they presented with elaborate ritual to younger members of the tribe. Various tribes spent centuries adapting the size, shape, and function of these weapons to their specific needs. As a result, the variations are astounding.

The simple weapons discussed here are crude when compared to such fine tools. However, they are by no means ineffective. In about an hour you can construct a short-term survival bow that will be perfectly adequate for small animals. Then, using the materials thus gained, you can build a longer-term bow that should last for the duration of your stay in the wilderness.

Double Bows

Most fine bows are made of strong, resilient, long-grained wood that has been cured and oiled to prevent cracking. In a survival situation, you may have neither the time nor the wood to fashion such a tool. But you can get along with green wood of lesser quality if you make a long bow and reinforce it with an extra stave.

The main bow can be made from any green or fire-killed sapling that has a good spring to it. (Fire-killed wood is hard to find, but it's better because it is already seasoned.) Fir, cedar, yew, maple, and alder are usually adequate. Cut a stave that is free of knots and branches, with a slight natural bend to it. It should be from one to one-and-a-half inches thick in the middle and about chin high. Test the stave for strength and symmetry by tying a piece of cordage to the ends and gently pulling on it, or by bracing the center of the bow with one foot while pulling on the ends. If the stave shows signs of weakness or cracking, choose another one.

Next, cut a second stave about a foot shorter and test it in the same way. Shave the back of the staves flat in the middle and fit them back-to-back so they bend in opposite directions. Bind the staves together in this position by wrapping cordage tightly along the entire length of the grip.

Finally, notch all four tips and join the two bows at either end with cordage. Then string the main bow with a durable bowstring. All three lengths of cordage should be very taut so that when you pull back the main bowstring you will take full advantage of the natural strength and bend of the staves. Ideal cordage for bowstrings is wrapped sinew or twisted, dried rawhide. Twisted, dried intestine from some animals is also

very strong. However, any strong natural fiber will do temporarily if it is wrapped thick enough to withstand repeated pulls and "twangs" (see "Cordage," page 241). To prevent weakening the stave, it is best to keep the main bow unstrung except when in use. To do this, tie a permanent knot at one end and a small loop at the other that can be slipped over the bowtip when the stave is bent. Another way of doing this is to bend the bow slightly and secure the free end of the string with a few wraps and a half hitch or two (see "Knots," page 244).

The spring or "cast" of this makeshift double bow is not as great as with fine woods or well-cured staves. The backup stave increases its power to the point where it might be able to stop a deer. But don't expect it to last a long time. Within a week at most it will probably crack and you will have to make another one. You can add strength and life to such bows by shaving the bark, curing and oiling the wood, and fitting the backup stave with a bowstring. If you're going to take such pains, though, you might as well start from scratch and make a longer-term survival bow.

Single Stave Bows

For a more durable bow that is easier to handle, start with a strong, resilient sapling such as greasewood, yew, osage orange, ironwood, hickory, or ash. Unlike the wood for a short-term bow, this wood should be as straight as possible—again with no knots, branches, or weak points. Start with a stave about one-and-a-half inches thick and chest- to chin-high. Peel the bark off and allow the stave to cure for at least twenty-four hours before shaping it.

Next, determine the natural bend of the wood. If the stave is perfectly straight, prop one end against your foot while holding onto the other with one hand. Grasp the middle of the stave with your free hand and

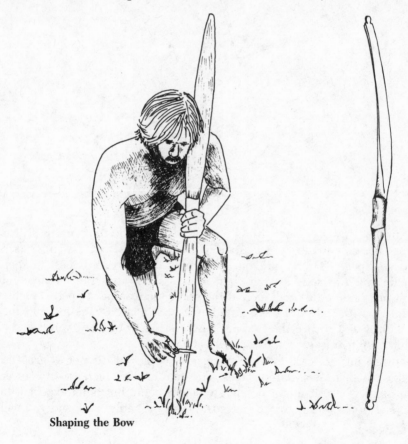

Shaping the Bow

push it in a circular fashion until you discover the direction it bends most easily. Mark this bend well; for you must shape and string the bow so that it curves in the opposite direction.

Shape the bow in one of two ways—either into a double rattail or an elongated double cone, as shown in the illustration. The cone shape is more powerful, but a little more difficult to achieve. Whichever you choose, both halves of the bow must be tapered smoothly and evenly all the way around. Work on one half at a time, starting in the middle and tapering toward the ends. Do not carve the wood or you may cut in too far and weaken it. Instead, hold the blade at right angles to the wood and shave it as though planing or using a drawknife. When you finish with one half, taper the other in identical fashion. Except for slight bending to gauge the evenness of the pull, avoid testing the bow until it is completely finished.

When you are done shaping the bow, lay it down in a warm spot and allow it to season for another two days. The longer you let it season, the better. Next, warm the bow near the fire and grease it thoroughly with oil or rendered animal fat (see "Oils," page 263). Repeat this process, alternately heating and greasing until the bow is nearly saturated with oil. Every few days afterwards, rub on another layer of oil. This will make the wood more pliable and keep it from cracking.

Finally, make a durable bowstring of sinew, twisted rawhide, or twisted intestine and tie it to the bowtips as explained above. If the tips are too smooth to hold a knot, you can notch or roughen them slightly with a blade. But this is risky, since the tips have already been tapered and will have to take quite a bit of stress. A much better method is to wrap them with strands of wet sinew. As the sinew dries, it hardens, both reinforcing the tips and providing a rough surface for the bowstring.

Arrows

The arrows made by native Americans were amazing in their variety and craftsmanship. They were nocked with feathers to fly specific distances and fitted with heads that adapted them to securing game of all conceivable kinds. Individual hunters even marked their arrows with colorful dyes so they could identify them when a kill was made. Survival arrows may be fashioned more quickly, but it is good to remember that their straight flight and effectiveness depend on careful craftsmanship.

Making the Shaft. Survival arrow shafts can be made from any strong, light, resilient, straight-grained wood that is free of knots and branches. Best are the shoots or suckers found growing at the bases of willow trees. Others are ocean spray ("arrowwood"), yew, greasewood, and cedar. Even cattail and foxtail reeds work well if you strengthen the notches with wrapping and fit the ends with wooden foreshafts.

Since arrows are easily lost or broken, it is best to make them in sets of five or six. Cut a number of saplings or strips of long-grained wood a quarter-inch to three-eighths-inch in diameter and about as long as your arm. (If you're going after fish or frogs, make the shafts twice that length.) Then, shave off the bark and smooth the bumps by scraping—*not carving* —with the blade held at right angles to the wood. Set the debarked shafts near the fire to cure for at least several hours, preferably overnight.

Finally, straighten the shafts by heating and bending them over coals. Begin in the middle of the shaft and work toward each end a little at a time. Heat and straighten each crook, holding the shaft in place until it cools. Use steam heat for particularly stubborn bends. Keep checking the straightness of the shaft by sighting down its length from time to time. A few minor crooks will not hamper the arrow's flight, but when you are done, both ends of the shaft should be lined up and it should be nearly as straight as a dowel. When the shafts are straight, sand them smooth by scraping at a right angle with a blade or rock.

If an arrow is too heavy in front, it will tend to rock up and down as it flies, while a back-heavy arrow will tend to fly askew. The ideal point of balance on a finished arrow is slightly to the front of center. Before the head is attached, then, balance the shaft on your finger and determine which end should receive the head. Ideally, tie the head on temporarily to check the balance. If it is just a little off, you may be able to correct it by shaving one end of the shaft a little more. If it's too far off, though, consider using a different head or cutting the arrow a little shorter.

Fletching. With most arrows and spears, you should lash on three stabilizing feathers at equal distances around the end of the shaft. Fish or frog arrows require only two, while long-range spears may have as many as four.

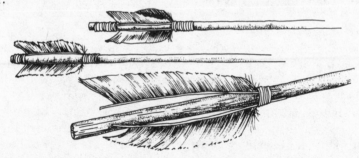

Although feathers are the best fletching materials, they aren't required to make an arrow fly straight. In fact, you can get by with several short lengths of coarse grass or pine needle tufts. About two to two-and-a-half inches up the shaft, wrap on the thick end of the material and secure it with half hitches (see "Knots," page 244). Then bend the tuft into a gentle arc (about three-eighths of an inch high—just enough to catch the air) and tie it down to the end of the shaft. Cut off the excess material.

The leaves of the yew tree are another possibility. Like feathers, they grow in the same plane on opposite sides of the branch. Split the branch down the middle, tie on your "feathers," and trim them to suit your needs as explained below.

If you have found or killed a bird, by all means use wing or tail feathers for fletching. Tail feathers are best because they are flat and give the arrow maximum range. Feathers taken from wings are slightly curved and catch the air in a way that makes the arrow spin. This slows it a little, but keeps it on a very stable course—which is fine for arrows with round heads. If you use flight feathers, take them from the same wing, since feathers from opposite wings curve in opposite directions and will slow the arrow too much. For flared points such as those made from bone or stone, it is best to use tail feathers.

When you have chosen a feather, split the quill down the middle so that it lies flat on the shaft, then cut and trim the vane to size. The length and trim will depend on the arrow. In most cases, feathers two to three inches long and a half-inch wide are fine. Cut them at similar angles in front and back as on regular arrows, leaving about a half inch of bare quill on the front and an inch on the tail. Then trim the top according to your needs. Wider feathers produce slower flight, shorter range, and fewer lost arrows. Use them for very close shots while stalking or waiting in ambush. Narrow feathers increase speed and range but lessen stability. If you're in an area with lots of thick brush, trim the feathers close to the shaft.

Bind the feathers to the shaft with thread-thin cordage—preferably sinew that is wet with saliva. Start by looping a clove hitch over the shaft (see "Knots," page 244) and sliding the forward end of all the quills underneath the thread. Tighten the hitch and wrap to the ends of the quills so nothing sticks out. Finish the wrap with a half hitch—or, if you're using sinew, simply cut the thread and roll it to the end. As the sinew dries, it will harden and serve as its own glue. Seal it off with boiled pitch.

Follow the same procedure for the back of the feathers, occasionally pulling on the quill ends to make sure the feathers stay flat. Wrap tightly to within an eighth inch of the end of the shaft before you secure the thread. This will reinforce the shaft and prevent it from splitting after the notch is made. Finally, cut off any excess quill and notch the arrow by filing a narrow groove at the back end of the shaft. Do not carve the notch, as this may split the shaft.

Arrowheads. In a pinch, you can simply carve or abrade the arrow shaft to a point and fireharden it with flames or coals (see "Firehardening," page 252). In fact, this method works quite well for game up to about raccoon size. However, if time permits, you can make more durable heads from hard wood, bone, or stone (see "Bone Tools" and "Stone Tools," pages 247-52). The size and shape of these heads will depend on the game you're after. Generally, arrowheads for birds and small game are narrow, while larger game requires heads with sharp, flared edges for extra cutting power. For fish, make heads with sharp barbs, or even double-pronged spearheads.

For best results, the arrowhead should have a notched stub, or set of tabs, at the back end. This makes it much easier to attach to the shaft. Prepare the shaft by filing a deep notch at the tip. Make it wide and deep enough to accommodate the stub without splitting the shaft. Perhaps with a little glue, fit the head into the notch. Then, starting above the stub, secure the thread with a clove hitch and wrap toward the tabs. (If you start wrapping lower, it tends to close the notch and squeeze the arrowhead out.) When you reach the tabs, crisscross back and forth two or three times and continue the wrap about half an inch down the shaft. This will keep it from splitting on impact. When you are done, the arrowhead should be almost like part of the shaft—immovable, with no irregular lumps in the wrapping. File the tip of the shaft so it fits flush with the head, and make sure the stub is narrower than the head's flaring edges.

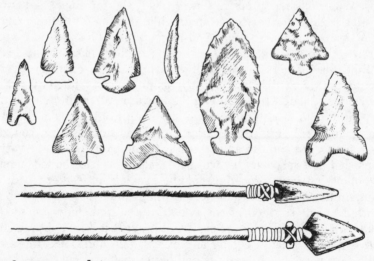

Using the Bow and Arrow

A short, single-stave bow is easier to carry than an unwieldy double bow, but their use is basically the same. Stalk to within striking distance, holding the strung bow and a single arrow in one hand alongside the body. Carry additional arrows under your belt or in a makeshift quiver slung at your side for easy access.

To prepare for the shot, grip the bow in the middle with one hand and rest the arrow shaft above it while fitting the notch onto the bowstring. Curl the first three fingers of your pulling hand around the bowstring—the first one above the shaft and the other two below. Then slowly pull the bowstring back the entire length of the arrow. Sight down the shaft toward the animal, aiming at the most vulnerable spot—in most cases, the rib cage just over the heart. Then, at the right moment, release the arrow by allowing the bowstring to slip away from your fingers. Do not jerk the string suddenly or you will throw off the shot. As you become a better archer, you will be able to take quicker shots, but always keep them smooth, flowing, and in tune with the movements around you.

Spears

Most spears are made just like arrows, only longer. The very long thrusting varieties are discussed under "Fishing," page 203. These featherless spears can be just as easily used with firehardened wood, bone, or stone heads for other small game at very short range.

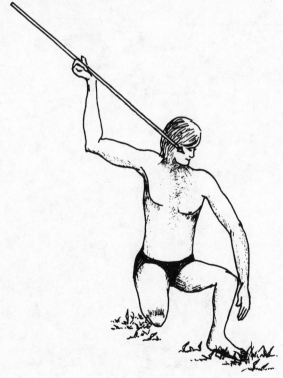

Throwing spears are generally shorter than thrusting spears—about as long as you are tall—and should be fletched with feathers. The longer the spear and the longer the range, the longer the feathers. In fact, you can even lash several whole wing feathers to the very end of the spear to help stabilize it in flight. A slight spin is also good.

A spear thrown by the power of the arm alone should generally be used for ambush at a range no greater than half your maximum throwing distance. That is the only way it will have enough accuracy and momentum to be effective. As you stalk, carry the spear close to your body. Prepare to throw by grasping the spear at the point of balance and slowly bringing it up to shoulder height, parallel to the ground. Cock the throwing arm beside your ear and stretch the other arm toward the target. As with arrows, aim for the heart. Fire by thrusting the hand straight past the ear.

Dart Thrower or Atlatl

You can increase the power of your arm—even without a bow—by using an Indian device called an atlatl, or dart thrower. In fact, the atlatl was the forerunner of the bow and arrow. Its stone heads have been found embedded in prehistoric mastodon bones.

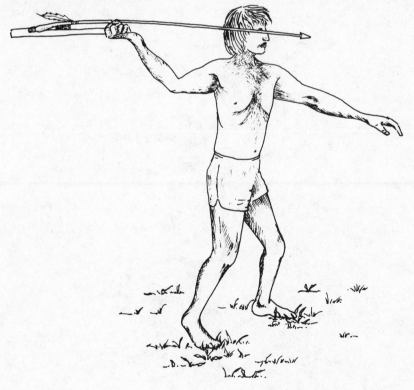

This tool, which can be used for "darts" ranging in size from four to seven feet, gives you more than twice the leverage and range of a normal throw. It can be carved from a limb about as long as your arm and half as thick. The handle at one end can either be smoothed to fit in your throwing hand or fitted with a crosspiece so you can grasp it more firmly. If you prefer, you can even attach loops of rawhide or sinew for a two-fingered throw. The back end has a protruding point that fits into a corresponding notch in the back of the dart.

There are many different variations of the atlatl, including grooved throwers, throwers fitted for front release, and those with counterweights. Experiment to discover what works best for you.

Using the atlatl is a delicate art. If your thrower is not grooved, place the back end of the dart on the point and rest the shaft on your fingers after grasping the handle. While bringing your arm back to throw, you must keep the dart balanced and gauge the distance at the same time. As you throw, the dart will buck into the air a little before it settles into a smooth, arcing path. For these reasons, it may feel awkward at first. But with practice you'll see why primitive peoples preferred it to the naked arm.

Throwing Board

For especially heavy spears and large game at close range, you can magnify the thrust of your throw many times by using an Eskimo throwing board. This is a variation on the atlatl that was often used to hunt marine mammals from kayaks. It is a grooved board, somewhat wider but only half as long as the atlatl. It is similarly fitted in the back with a point to receive the spear. On the front end, carve a short handle with a thumb hole or loop of thong just to the side. Use the weapon just like an atlatl— but at the end of the throw, thrust down sharply with the fingers and wrist as you would with a throwing stick.

Slingshot

With a slingshot, you can throw stones many times faster and farther than with the hand alone. This tool consists of two thongs tied to either side of a patch of rawhide about the size of your palm (see "Rawhide," page 257). The thongs should be about two feet long. One of these ends in a loop that

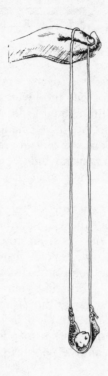

slips over the thumb of your throwing hand, while the other (slightly longer) is knotted several times and held in the palm or between the first two fingers.

To use the slingshot, secure the loop and knot in your throwing hand, letting the rawhide patch hang toward the ground. When you're ready for the throw, place a smooth, round stone in the patch, cock your arm, and thrust your hand past your ear just as you would with a spear. As your arm moves forward, the stone will rotate in a semicircle at the end of the thongs. Then, just as your arm becomes fully extended, you let go of the knotted thong. The stone will go sailing toward the target—ideally, the animal's head.

Another way of throwing a slingshot is to spin it around your head once or twice before releasing the thong. This gives the stone added momentum, but the extra movement may also warn the animal of your presence. When you become proficient with the slingshot, it can be used effectively on animals up to the size of a fox. However, keep in mind that it takes many years to perfect. When practicing, stay well away from other people, since the first few shots might go anywhere!

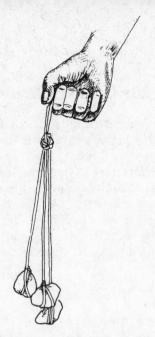

Bolas

Bolas were used extensively by such tribes as the Chocksaw and Seminole, primarily for catching waterfowl. But you can also use them for small mammals. They consist of three or more weights attached to rawhide or sinew thongs. When thrown, the thongs tangle in wings and limbs, immobilizing the animal until you can get to it with a club or spear.

You can make the weights in one of several ways. One is by abrading grooves into stones (see "Stone Tools," page 247) and tying them straight to the thongs. Another is by tying equally weighted stones inside little rawhide pouches. And a third is by filling wet rawhide pouches with sand. When the rawhide dries, it shrinks, leaving uniform weights that are nearly as hard as rocks.

The length and number of thongs will depend on the animal. For ducks and geese you can get by with three thongs—each two-and-a-half to four feet long, depending on the size of the bird. For larger game—especially four-legged animals—you'll be safer with five thongs and heavier weights. Tie all the thongs together at one end and attach some kind of handle for easy throwing. A loop of rawhide or sinew will do—or even a thick knot you can get a good hold on.

Throw the bolas almost exactly as you would a throwing stick, combining backward and forward arm movements into one flowing motion to give the thongs a good twirl. Again, use the overhand in thick brush and the sidearm in more open territory. With the sidearm, remember to keep the shoulders square and snap the wrist without following through. Another way is to twirl the bolas around the head, as with the slingshot. When using this weapon, keep the thongs separated and take care to avoid tangling them in brush.

Skinning and Cleaning

The procedure for skinning and cleaning most animals is very similar, regardless of size. The most important thing is to avoid contaminating the meat or other edible parts with urine, feces, or caustic substances. This means taking care not to puncture any organs—especially with skunks and other odiferous animals. Also avoid transferring such liquids to the meat with your hands or cutting instrument. A deer, for instance, has glands on the inside of its rear legs. If you touch these during the skinning process and then later handle the meat, the affected parts will spoil very rapidly. Finally, be sure you do not have any open wounds yourself that may become infected.

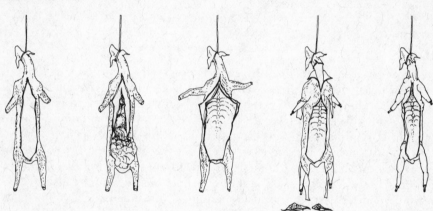

Skinning

Some animals, such as fish, don't usually have to be skinned at all. Frogs, snakes, lizards, and their relatives should always be skinned. With small amphibians and reptiles, this is sometimes just a matter of slitting the skin down the front and peeling it away from the body with your fingers. Generally, birds taste better if they're plucked rather than skinned. The exception to this rule are the diving ducks, which tend to be on the fishy side unless the skin is removed. But if you're really hungry, who cares? The fat in the skin is also good for the body after a few days of fasting. Whichever method you use, save the feathers for clothing, insulation, fletching, and bait. (A dangling wing or bunch of feathers will often entice a predator into a trap.)

Begin the skinning and cleaning process by laying the animal on an incline, head upwards. On a male animal, first tie off the penis to avoid getting urine on the exposed meat. Then, starting at the tail, make an incision just beneath the skin all the way up to the chin. Next, cut down the inside of each leg to the midline and around the joint above each foot or hoof. Once these cuts are made on small animals, you can usually just peel the skin off like a jacket. With larger animals, use your fist for this purpose, skinning first one side to the backbone, then the other. To avoid cutting through the hide, use a blade only when necessary. That way, you'll later be able to make the hide into clothing that will keep the rain out!

Cleaning

Start eviscerating the animal by making an incision just in front of the anus and sexual organs and opening the abdominal cavity all the way past the breastbone. *(Do not puncture any internal organs!)* Next, cut around the anus and free up the sex organs, tying off any tubes that might be leaking wastes. Then cut through the diaphragm and reach up into the abdominal cavity all the way to the windpipe and gullet. Once you cut or pull these out, the bulk of the internal organs can then be easily removed and stored for future use.

Everything should be pulled out and down below the animal. Put the heart, liver, kidneys, lungs, and other edible organs in a separate container so they are not contaminated. Do not be concerned if the animal has been spattered with blood, as you can wipe this with dried grasses and it will quickly form a glaze that will help preserve the meat. But look carefully for signs of spoilage. The meat will quickly turn rancid if it has been inadvertently contaminated, and it may even begin to turn green within minutes. Cut these and other discolored sections out. Also cut out any ulcerations, pustules, and badly scarred tissue. Trust your eyes and nose for this work. If it looks or smells bad, cut it out.

Once the animal is cleaned, prop open the chest cavity and hang the meat in the open air in a protected place to keep the rain from souring it. In cool weather (say, forty degrees Fahrenheit or less), you can leave the meat hanging this way for days without spoilage, as long as it is high enough above the ground to keep it away from other animals. If it gets much warmer, flies will begin to bother the meat and lay eggs on it. Maggots are not a sign of spoilage; in fact, they are even edible. But since the meat will deteriorate more quickly at such temperatures, you'll want to take pains to preserve it (see "Preserving," page 237).

Utilizing the Animal

Once you have tended to the meat, you can begin using other parts of the animal. Nothing should go to waste—not even the blood or the fat. Blood is very high in iron, salts, and other essential nutrients and can be easily added to soups or stews. Fat is rich in calories and should be part of every survival meal. It is especially important if you are forced to go for a long time on a diet of nothing but meat. Rendered fat is also extremely useful as a lubricant, wood preservative, and fuel (see "Oils," page 263).

The Head. Cut out and skin the tongue and put it in the meat pot with the heart, liver, kidneys, and lungs. Remove the cheek pads and add them to the pot. Remove the eyeballs and save them with the viscera. They contain a liquid that can be used for paints and dyes, or mixed with pitch to make a hard-setting glue. Behind the eyeball there is also a small piece of delicious fat. Remove this and store it with the other edibles. Crack the skull open and remove the brain. It is not only edible, but can be used to tan the hide (see "Brain Tanning," page 260). If you prefer, cook the entire head, brains and all.

Internal Organs. Before the viscera begin to spoil, take some time to prepare them for future use. The windpipe can be extracted for use as a blowtube for making bowls and pots (see "Coal-burning Wooden Containers," page 253). The intestines can be cleaned out, dried, and used as sausage skins for food storage. They can also be twisted and pulled into strong cordage for bowstrings and thongs. The large intestine should also be cleaned and dried for use as a container. Likewise the bladder and stomach, which not only make good storage and cooking pouches, but also excellent fishing floats. Edible viscera are especially quick to spoil. They should be cooked and eaten as soon as possible. The heart, liver, and kidneys can usually be eaten (except in areas of heavy pollution) or used as bait for carnivores.

Sinew is the tough, white connective tissue found in tendons and ligaments and in long cords along both sides of the backbone. It is the strongest natural fiber known to man. When dry, it can be pounded, separated into fibers, and used for many purposes—including thread, fishline, snare strings, powerful bowstrings, and lashing cord (see "Cordage," page 241).

Bones should all be scraped and saved. Large bones can be cracked and the rich marrow extracted and eaten. They can also be made into an endless variety of tools—including awls, hooks, thimbles, levers, needles, blow tubes, handles, whistles, scrapers, skewers, arrowheads, spikes, trap parts, digging sticks, hoes, eating utensils, knives, chisels, and many more (see "Bone Tools," page 251).

Other uses for bone are as varied as your needs. Rib cages can be made into baskets of various shapes and sizes by weaving them with dried grasses or saplings. They can also serve as frames to hold cooking pots over the fire. Jawbones with teeth intact are sometimes fashioned into saws and knife handles. The sharp incisor teeth of some rodents can be used as chisels and darning needles. Finally, bones can be crushed, boiled, and eaten in stews and soups. They can also be mashed and powdered into a calcium-rich food additive.

Antlers can be used for many of the same purposes as bone. Among other things, they make excellent awls, saws, knives, handles, arrow points, rakes, clubs, digging sticks, skewers, and buttons.

Hooves can be crushed and boiled as a source of glue and neat's-foot oil for conditioning and waterproofing leather (see "Glues and Oils," page 263).

Skin or Hide. The furred skins of small animals can be used as mittens, socks, or hats. On larger animals the hair can be removed and saved for insulation, stuffing, arrow fletching, weaving, cordage, or cushioning. The skin can also be made into rawhide for any number of clothing and utility items (see "Rawhide," page 257). Some of these include laces, straps, moccasins, leggings, ponchos, mats, pouches, and snowshoes.

The ears, tails, and hock skins of larger animals make good pouches and mittens. Hock skins also make good moccasins and overmitts with long gauntlets. Even the scrotum can be used as a pouch.

Exercises

The following exercises will help you begin to learn the skills presented in this chapter.

1. Splatter Vision. Gazing at the horizon, expand your field of vision to take in all the movements around you. Take note of these movements. This is an exercise you can do anywhere and anytime. If you practice it frequently—in forests and fields, on trails and highways, and even on city streets—you'll soon be able to alternate your focus easily from the minute to the majestic.

2. Focused Hearing. Cup your ears at strange or distant sounds and experiment with different listening angles to see what works best. One effective way of doing this is to have a friend talk softly while standing at a distance. Another is to have a friend hide and see if you can locate him or her by sound alone.

3. Stalking. Set up chairs and tables as "natural" obstacles and "stalk" a pillow in your living room. Try to move over and around obstacles with perfect form, maintaining complete control and moving each limb slowly and deliberately. It should take at least fifteen minutes to stalk the length of the room, and you should feel it in your legs when you're done. Another stalking exercise is to stand for as long as you can on one leg at a time. But most fun of all is to send somebody out to "graze" in the woods and try to stalk up and touch him without his detecting any movement or sound. Finally, practice your stalking animals—flies, birds, cats, dogs, deer, and even people.

4. Animal Habits. Study an animal a week, using library books and home references. Keep three-by-five note cards with important bits of information, including size, habits, habitat, diet, and a drawing of the animal's typical track pattern. Using observation and stalking skills, watch animals whenever you get the chance. There is no better way to get to know them.

5. Tracking. Set up a "tracking box" by fluffing, smoothing, and baiting a patch of ground. Check it periodically to see if you can identify animal visitors by their tracks. Also practice identifying and following animal tracks in the wild. The best places to begin are in muddy or sandy areas near water sources. Finally, whenever you're out in the woods, try to identify various animal highways and signs, such as trails, runs, pushdowns, and droppings. The more closely you examine these things, the more obvious they will become.

6. Trapping. Practice making and setting three basic traps before you go on to any others. These are the figure-four deadfall, the Paiute deadfall, and the rolling snare. Make these both with and without the aid of a knife. Practice baiting and setting traps for a variety of animals, using cardboard boxes for deadfalls and weak thread for snares.

7. Hunting Tools. Make several of the simplest hunting tools described in this chapter (with and without a knife) and practice using them until you are skilled with each. Use stumps or rocks as targets. When you feel comfortable with one tool, try stalking with it and see if you can still maintain your accuracy.

7. COOKING AND PRESERVING

The native Americans used plants and animals for many important things; but none was quite as important as the physical sustenance of the tribe. Through the stored energies of once-living things, tribal members continually renewed their strength and spirits. For this reason, the preparation of plant and animal foods was an important ritual. Every meal was surrounded with an aura of thanksgiving, and often with elaborate ceremony. This was only natural; for in few other circumstances did tribal members realize more fully their unique attachments to the web of life and to the flow of the "spirit-that-moves-in-all-things."

Food preparation in a survival situation is rarely elaborate. However, don't let your hunger fool you into thinking you can be careless about food preparation. If you drink contaminated water without boiling it, chances are you're going to get sick. Likewise, some uncooked edible plants can leave you debilitated with cramps, diarrhea, and other discomforts you can't afford. Contaminated meats can also take you out of commission quickly unless cooked until well done. For these reasons, as well as for added comfort and convenience, take some time to assure the safety and freshness of your food.

Cooking Methods

To start with, all animals should be skinned (or plucked), cleaned, and eviscerated before cooking (see "Skinning and Cleaning," page 228). The cooking method you use will depend on time, convenience, and available materials. Generally, stews make the best survival fare because very little of the nutrients are lost in the cooking process. However, if you don't have the containers and ingredients necessary to prepare such a meal, there are several other quick cooking methods you can try.

Spit Cooking. One of the easiest ways of cooking a small animal is by roasting it over hot coals. This can be done by running a skewer along the underside of the backbone and suspending the animal over the coals. Make sure the skewer is not a poisonous plant. For best results, first sear the animal's flesh by turning it over the flames for a few minutes. This will close off the pores and seal in most of the juices. You might sear the skewer a little, too—unless it's a pleasant-tasting wood like sassafras or spicebush. This will prevent its juices from adversely flavoring the meat.

When the animal is securely skewered, turn it evenly over hot coals until the meat is well done. One way of doing this is to prop the skewer against a rock or part of the fire reflector. Another is to suspend it on two Y-sticks on either side of the coals. Keep in mind that whenever you cook over an open fire, you're going to burn off some of the nutrients. You'll do better if you cook over hot coals instead of leaping flames, since coals will roast the meat much more evenly.

Rock Frying. Another quick cooking method is the rock frying pan. This is nothing more than a large, flat rock—the flatter and thinner the better—laid on hot coals or propped up over the flames. As the rock heats up, it transfer the heat evenly to the food. If you've found an active bird nest, you can grease the "pan" with a little animal fat and cook up some fried eggs. When cooking animals, be sure to sizzle the meat on both sides until it's well done.

Rock Oven. For still more uniform heat, fashion a rock oven by adding three sides and a roof to your frying pan. Use rock slabs as thin and flat as you can find, and keep the oven as small as possible. Ideally, it should be hardly larger than the object you want to cook. Place the oven right beside the fire with the open end just a few inches from the flames. After the flames have died down and you have a good bed of coals, you can convert this primitive appliance into a Dutch oven by placing the rock slabs onto the coals; then mounding the coals up over the sides and top. Regulate the temperature by adding or subtracting coals, or by building up or toning down the fire.

Rock Oven

Pit Cooking. All greens, roots, and meats can be cooked in a pit with very little loss of nutrients. For a small meal, dig a hole in the ground about two feet deep and two feet across. Line the bottom with red-hot rocks from the fire. After an hour or two, remove the coals and place about eight inches of green grass on top of the hot rocks. (If the rocks are too hot, first cover them with a thin layer of dirt—but then wait until the ground moisture steams away before adding the grasses, or you'll wind up with earthy-tasting food.)

Next, place your food right on top of the green grasses. Cover it first with an eight-inch layer of dried grasses, then a thin layer of bark slabs or brush, and finally with a mound of dirt. Then just leave it in the pit and forget about it for a while. There's no skewering, no tending, no worry about burning or overcooking. After about two hours, dig up the food and eat right out of the pit.

A repeated caution here: Be sure to gather your rocks from a high, dry area to prevent explosions when they are heated. Rocks should be left in a roaring fire from two to four hours before you remove them for cooking. An alternative way of heating is to place them in the bottom of the pit and build a fire on top of them. Just be sure to remove the coals before adding the grasses.

Dirt

Bark slabs

Grass

Food

Grass

Rocks

Pit Cooking

Rock Boiling. If you have a container, you can use red-hot rocks to boil water and to cook greens, meats, soups, and stews. The Indians often cooked this way by digging a hole in the ground and lining it with an animal's stomach. Boiling is an excellent way to cook wilderness meals because it doesn't burn off the food's juices. Stews are especially convenient because you can add more meats and vegetables as they are gathered and eat right out of the "pot."

Rock boiling is done by heating rocks in the fire until they are glowing red; then placing them one by one into a liquid-filled container with sticks or tongs fashioned from bent saplings (see "Wooden Tongs," page 253). One or two baseball-sized rocks should be enough to bring a gallon of water to a boil, while a rock hardly bigger than a golf ball will brew a tasty cup of pine tea. When the first rock cools off, replace it with another hot one. Regulate the boil by varying the size and heat of the rocks.

Rock boiling can be done in hollowed logs, rock depressions, animal skins, stomachs, or rawhide. If you use an animal stomach, first open it, clean it, and turn it inside-out. Then place it into a hole in the ground and stake it all the way around with pegs. Don't worry about the hot rocks burning through, as the stomach lining is surprisingly tough. Another approach, especially if you're worried about spicing your stew with wind-blown sand and dirt, is to suspend the stomach or rawhide between the legs of a tripod.

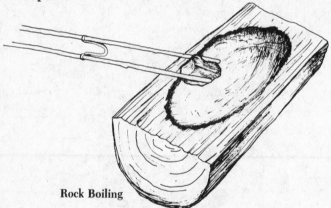

Rock Boiling

Eating Utensils. Eating tools can be as primitive or as civilized as you care to make them. Initially, you may do most of your cooking over an open fire and eat with your bare hands. But there is almost always something near at hand to make your meal more palatable. A slab of bark can often be used as a makeshift dish, and sturdy twigs make serviceable chopsticks. You can sometimes use large, nonpoisonous leaves for plates, and rocks or logs with natural depressions will hold variable quantities of liquids. Best of all are wooden pots, bowls, and spoons made through a process called coal burning (see "Coal-burning Wooden Containers," page 253).

Preserving Food

After you've taken care of your immediate food needs, you'll want to provide for the future by preserving any excess meat, fruits, and vegetables before they spoil. This becomes especially important with meats exposed to temperatures greater than fifty degrees, as they will spoil very quickly.

Drying. The simplest and most universal method of preserving meats and fruits is by drying them either by the fire or in the direct rays of the sun. Small fruits such as berries can be dried whole on flat rocks, while larger fruits should be sliced thin first. Vegetables should be eaten fresh whenever possible—or stored in a cool, dry place until needed (see "Food Storage," page 238).

Minnows and very small fish can be dried whole, although it is safest to clean them first. They can then be pounded with a hammerstone to crush the bones. The easiest drying procedure for larger fish is to crack them down the backbone and hang them up to dry, bones and all. The bones can either be pounded and pulverized or taken out later to mix with soups and stews. (Whatever you do, don't throw them away!) You can also fillet larger fish by slicing the meat off both sides of the backbone, then hanging the steaks up to dry. Use the skin, head, and tail for soups and stews.

Most birds and small mammals such as mice and ground squirrels can be dried by cracking open the rib cage and pelvic girdle and laying them flat on a rock. The rock can be propped up to receive more direct heat, but if you leave it by the fire, keep the meat far enough away so it dries without cooking. When it's dry on one side, flip the animal and dry it on the other. Finally, pound the entire animal with a rock to pulverize the bones; then dry it once more. This mashed-and-dried meat-and-bone combination can then be stored or added to soups and stews. The cooking process will soften the small bone fragments into edible tidbits.

Jerky. Larger animals should first be butchered into manageable chunks. After you have taken what roasts and steaks you can immediately use and removed all the fat (which turns rancid quickly unless rendered), cut the rest into long, thin strips along the length of the muscle. An ideal strip is an eighth-inch to a quarter-inch thick, about an inch wide, and as long as the meat suggests. The thinner the meat, the faster and more effective the drying process. Cut longer strips by slicing in spirals from the edge to the center of the meat. Then hang these strips on poles to dry. (A

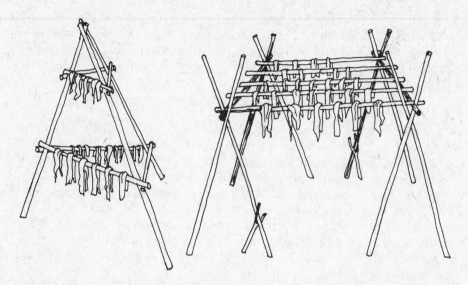

sturdy tripod lashed with horizontal poles makes a good meat dryer.)

The test for dryness is that the meat will crack or snap when you bend it. If it bends without cracking, it's still too wet. If it crumbles in your hands, it's probably a little too dry. Try to get the meat to just the right point, as dampness will bring on spoilage and overdrying will burn off some of the nutrients. After they are thoroughly dry, these strips of "jerky," as they are called, can be moistened and eaten as snacks or rolled up and stored indefinitely for later use in soups and stews.

Pemmican. The Indians, mountain men, and pioneers of old used to mix equal portions of jerky, partially dried and pounded berries, and rendered animal fat to make a long-lasting and highly nutritious food called pemmican. Pemmican could be kept for such long periods that it became a standby meal on trips lasting up to several months. In fact, I recently met a man who unearthed a cache of still-edible pemmican that was dated at more than four hundred years old. You probably won't be interested in preserving yours that long, but it's reassuring to know that you could.

The key ingredient in pemmican is the animal fat. It is heated until it becomes liquid and then filtered twice through dried grasses to yield a pure tallow. When the tallow cools, it hardens just like bacon grease. Mix this in with equal amounts of jerky and dried, crushed berries; then store the mix inside a cleaned, airtight intestine as explained below.

Food Storage

For short wilderness stays, you'll probably use most of your food resources as you get them. For more extended survival tests, though, you'll want to store your excess food in a place where it will stay dry and beyond the reach of hungry animals.

Stomach Pouch. One way to store food is to stuff it inside the stomach or intestine of a large animal and hang it up high. First clean the organ well, then turn it inside-out and dry it. Most animals will not be attracted to such containers, since they have very little food value; but as added insurance you can smoke the organ or wash it in tannic acid water.

Once the pouch is prepared, stuff it with dried food and tie the ends tightly with cordage. Grease the ends with tallow to completely seal them off. Then suspend the pouch with cordage from the branch of a tree. Make sure it's hanging free and cannot be reached by squirrels or bears. These storage containers can also be hung from the apex of a large, sturdy tripod. In this case, it is also advisable to set several traps in the area to take advantage of any animal visitations brought on by the smell of the food.

Storage Pit. A longer term method of storage is to make a pit. Dig under a rock outcropping or in the floor of a cool, dry shelter. Rid the pit of ground moisture by lining the bottom with hot rocks and allowing it to steam for a while. Leaving the rocks in place, line the pit floor and walls with a thick layer of dried grasses. Place the food inside the pit and cover it with any kind of non-poisonous, dried bark. (Ideal is cedar bark, which

contains enough tannic acid to repel most insects and worms.) Cover this with dried, aromatic, non-poisonous leaves such as mint, sagebrush, or evergreen needles. These will disguise any remaining food scent. Lastly, cover the pit with a six-inch layer of dirt and weight it with heavy rocks as a final precaution against animal intruders.

Exercises

Following are a few ideas that will help you to learn the skills presented in this chapter.

1. Backyard Survival. Try living on your patio or in your back yard for a weekend. Build a fire without matches, make your own coal-burned containers, and roast a skewered chicken on your homemade spit.

2. Cooking Methods. On an extended campout, try different cooking techniques each evening. Experiment with various methods until you're familiar with the relative advantages of spit cooking, rock frying, rock oven, pit cooking, and rock boiling.

3. Rock Boiling. Practice rock boiling with various sizes of rocks and containers until you have a good sense for the best combination.

4. Preserving. Make a supply of jerky or pemmican at home. For realism, store the pemmican in commercial sausage skins—or better yet, stuff some into a cleaned rabbit intestine or stomach.

8. TOOLS AND CRAFTS

A wilderness environment can take you back thousands of years. Like the stone age people of old, you may suddenly find yourself without any modern conveniences. In such a situation, your survival depends partly on your ability to fashion natural resources into useful tools and materials.

However, it is a joy to discover how little we really need and how abundantly it is provided. Learning to shape natural materials into usable items is not just survival insurance; it is like reclaiming a lost heritage. Such skills connect us with the countless generations of humans who have lived before and help to remind us that, beneath the trappings of civilization, we, too, are creatures of the earth.

Cordage

Cordage is one of the most indispensable items in a survival situation. Among other things, you'll need it for bows, fishing line, trap triggers, snares, and lashings. Most people despair when they think of trying to make their own cordage. Yet the materials are plentiful in most places and the means of making it actually quite simple.

Materials. Generally, any strong, flexible plant fiber makes good cordage. The dried inner bark of just about any tree will supply you with workable material. Some of the best are basswood (linden), elm, walnut, cherry, aspen, cottonwood, maple, and cedar. Look for trees with dead bark, and strip off long sections of the fibrous cambium layer. If you can't find dead trees, strip sections of the inner bark from live trees (easier in spring, when the sap is running) and dry them before using. However, take only a few thin strips from any one tree—and do not cut clear around the trunk, as this may kill the tree. If you have trouble separating the inner from the outer bark, soak the strips in warm or boiling water until the fibers come apart.

The dried inner bark of fibrous plants also makes useful cordage materials. Excellent ones are dogbane, milkweed, velvet leaf, wild hemp, evening primrose, stinging nettles, fireweed, and sagebrush. Dried rushes, grasses, and fibrous leaves from plants such as yucca and cattail are good, too. With pithy plants such as dogbane and milkweed, you may be able to strip the fibrous material from the stalk in long ribbons. If it's dry, a better method is to crush and open up the stalk; then break off short sections of the woody core, leaving a long ribbon of fibers in your hand. For non-pithy plants such as nettles and rushes, the best method is to place the dried stalk on a piece of wood and pound it with a rounded rock. (Do not use a sharp instrument, as this may cut the fibers.) The fibers of annual plants will usually be shorter than those from trees, but by splicing them together you can make cordage of any length or thickness.

241

Sinew. Animal sinew makes the strongest cordage of all. A strand as thick as a carpet thread will hold the weight of an average man. This makes it especially useful for bowstrings, fishing line, snare strings, wrappings, and threads. Another useful property of sinew is that, when wetted with saliva before wrapping, it shrinks and dries as hard as glue. This often makes it unnecessary to knot the ends. (Rawhide is also very strong and shrinks as it dries. See page 257).

The longest sinew is found in the two white cords on either side of the backbone, but you can get shorter lengths that are just as strong from the tendons and ligaments attached to muscles and bones. Simply cut out the sinew, remove its protective sheath, and clean and dry it. When it's dry, the sinew will be very hard and brittle. To separate the individual fibers, pound it with a rock as explained above, and put it in hot water.

Wrapping. First decide how thick and long you want your cordage to be. If all you need is a piece of dental floss or a trap trigger, you might get by with only a few fibers. In most cases, though, you will want stronger cordage—and strength is given by wrapping fibers together. In order to do this, you must first break down the original material a little more. If you have a ribbon of inner bark or leaves, separate the fibers by rolling them between your palms or against your pant leg. This will also get rid of any remaining non-fibrous material. For better friction, dampen your skin. Work along the entire length of the material until you have a long, thin bundle of fibers.

Single Wrap. For a fast wrapping job, hold on to the end of the fiber bundle and roll it against your pant leg in one direction. With repeated

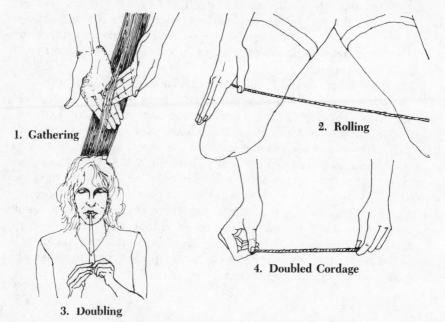

1. Gathering

2. Rolling

3. Doubling

4. Doubled Cordage

strokes along the entire length, you should be able to twist the fibers into a strand of makeshift cordage that is many times the strength of the original material. To secure the twist, take the middle of the strand in your teeth (make sure it's non-poisonous) and bring the two ends together. When you let go with your teeth, the doubled cordage will twist around itself naturally.

Reverse Wrap. For a much tighter, stronger wrap, start by twisting the fiber bundle in the middle until it kinks. Hold the kink between the thumb and index finger of one hand. With the fingers of the second hand, twist the bottom strand toward you and wrap both strands once around each other in the other direction. Then hold this wrap with the first hand, twist the new bottom strand, and continue along the entire length. If you need only a short, thin string, tie a knot at the end of this double-wrapped cordage and use it as is.

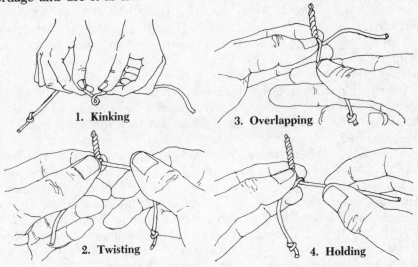

1. Kinking   3. Overlapping

2. Twisting   4. Holding

Splicing. For longer cordage, splice together as many pieces as necessary in the following way: First, twist and kink the bundle so that one end is twice as long as the other. This will prevent parallel splices that weaken the cordage. Using the reverse wrap, wrap to within about an inch or two of the short end. Separate the fibers of the short end with your fingers so they spread out like a broom. Then attach another bundle of equal thickness by spreading and fitting its fiber ends into those of the first. (To keep a uniform thickness in the cord, pull or cut out half of the fibers in each strand before pushing them together.) Then, taking care not to pull the strands apart, continue twisting and wrapping as before. When you come

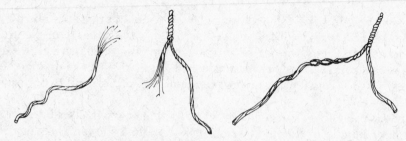

to another end, add a second piece, and so on. Make sure, however, that you never have two splices in the same place. A splice must always be wrapped with a solid strand.

Doubling. To get stronger cordage, you might logically think all you need to do is use bigger fiber bundles. However, this is not the case. Strength is produced just as much by twisting and wrapping as by greater thickness. As explained above, one thing you can do is twist and double the strand you've already wrapped. (The Plains Indians often made bowstrings by splicing sinew strands to three or four times the necessary length, then twisting and doubling them twice.) For cordage of greater strength and thickness, take two reverse-wrapped strands and join them together with another series of reverse wraps. By repeated splicing and doubling, you can make cordage of any length and thickness you like. In fact, eventually it may be hard to imagine that such cordage is made from the same frail material that once broke so easily in your hands.

Finishing. When you're done with all the wrapping and splicing, you'll probably have a lot of unsightly fibers sticking out along the length of the cordage. To get rid of these, run the cordage quickly through a flame and they will burn off without damaging the main fibers. To keep the ends from fraying, either weave them back into the twisted cord, secure them with simple overhand knots, lash them onto the tool or material you're working with, or "whip" the ends by wrapping and tying them off with smaller pieces of cordage (see "Knots," below).

Knots and Lashings

For most survival purposes, you'll need three kinds of knots. These include knots to join two pieces of cordage, knots to attach cordage to another object, and knots to secure lashings. Following are illustrations showing some of the easiest and most useful knots in each of these categories.

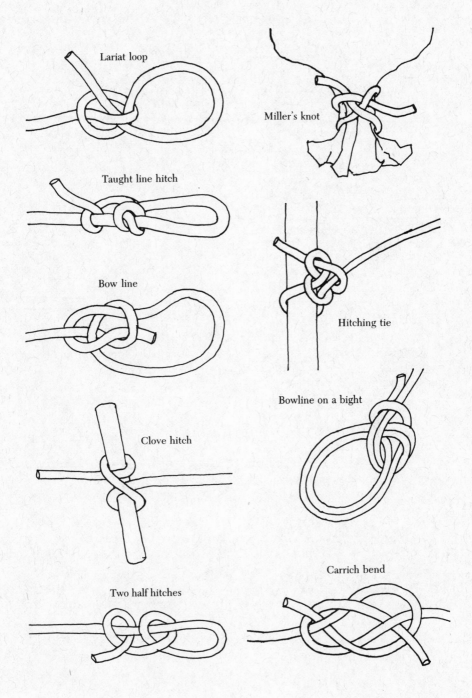

Lariat loop

Miller's knot

Taught line hitch

Bow line

Hitching tie

Clove hitch

Bowline on a bight

Two half hitches

Carrich bend

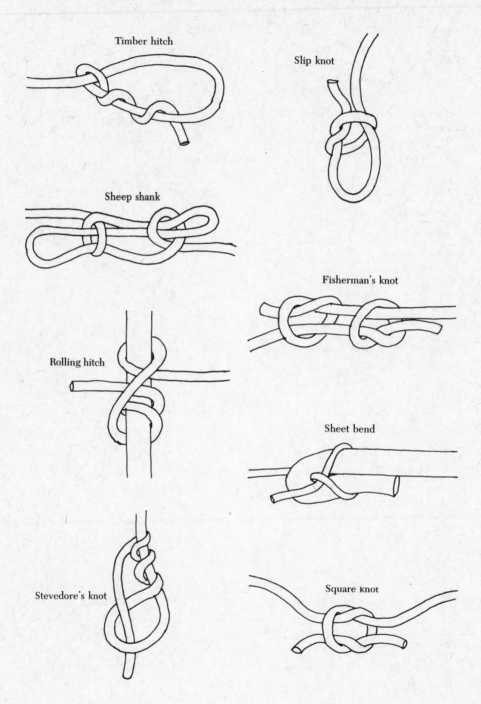

Timber hitch

Slip knot

Sheep shank

Fisherman's knot

Rolling hitch

Sheet bend

Stevedore's knot

Square knot

Stone Tools

I sometimes like to kid my survival students when we're walking along a riverbed by pointing to the rocks and saying, "Look at all those Craftsman rocks!" But in a way it's true—you can pick up almost as many different kinds of pounding, cutting, and sanding tools from a pile of rocks as you can from the shelves of your local hardware store. Certainly the rocks are still in crude form, but with a little imagination, skill, and patience, you can fashion them into all kinds of useful items.

Sharp Blades. The most important tool of all is the sharp blade. For the myriad cutting and carving jobs you will face in a survival situation, some kind of knife is indispensable. You may also find great use for related tools such as axes, arrowheads, and scrapers.

The simplest and crudest blades are made by smashing one rock against another until you break off one that has a usable edge. Don't worry at first about finding the ideal rock, since they are often hard to come by. Just experiment with whatever rocks are available until you find one that breaks with a cutting edge.

If you want a more distinct blade, choose an egg-shaped rock and strike it across the end with a harder rock. If you hit it hard enough with a circular, glancing motion, you will knock off what's called a discoidal blank—a circular chunk with sharp edges that is flat on one side and round on the other. This will be easier to use for carving and cutting.

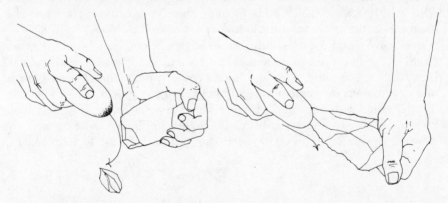

Best of all for cutting are the sharp-cleaving stones such as obsidian, jasper, chert, agate, and quartz. If you find one of these, you can fashion a razor-sharp blade by carefully flaking the edge on both sides. A crude way of doing this is with repeated blows from another rock at slightly less than right angles to the edge. But if you use this method, you must have a feel for where the rock will cleave or you may ruin the blade. More accurately, you can flake the edge under pressure with a piece of bone or antler.

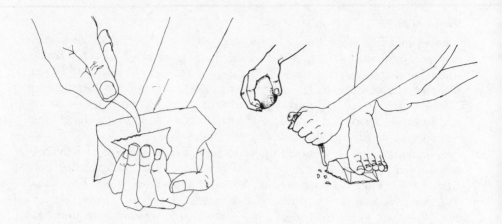

Gently push in and down with a slight twisting motion, knocking off little flakes that leave a tapered edge. Whenever working with sharp-cleaving stone, be sure to protect your hands from cuts by holding it with a piece of rawhide, clothing, or a slab of bark or wood.

The blades of rocks such as obsidian and jasper will probably be so sharp they won't need further work. Large-grained rocks, though, can be sharpened further by sanding them against softer stones. The various grades of sandstone are excellent for this purpose—especially when used with a little water, which adds to their abrasive qualities. They are also ideal for abrading wood and sanding hides (see "Rawhide," page 257).

Grooves and Depressions. At some point you may want to attach handles to your stone implements, or fashion shallow rock bowls (called metates) for pounding grain and meat. You can make the needed grooves and depressions in coarse-grained stones through a process called pecking. This is done with repeated glancing blows from a harder rock, or hammerstone, slowly knocking away the grains until you have formed the desired groove or depression. Save the grains and dust to help make a

hard-setting cement (see "Glues and Oils," page 263). Admittedly, this can be a long task; but it is a worthwhile occupation when you are not involved with more pressing needs. Many Indian tribes called December the "Moon of the Clacking Rocks," because that was the time they chose to fashion most of their stone tools.

Handles. Knifeblades can be attached to their handles in many ways. One of the easiest is to groove or split a short length of sapling and fit the flattened, blunt end of the knife down into it. This can then be further secured with glue and cordage in much the same way as with arrowheads (see page 222).

One of the simplest (though not the strongest) handles for heavy stone tools can be made by grooving the tool and bending a green sapling around it. To do this, pick a sapling that is strong and resilient. Bend it gradually, softening it over a fire as you shape it to the groove in the tool. This can be made easier by thinning the inside of the sapling first. With repeated heating, you should be able to bend the sapling in half without cracking it. Bend it all the way around the groove in the head, then lash the two halves of the handle together with cordage all the way up to the head. For added security, wrap the handle twice around the head before lashing the halves together. This handle is especially useful for small stone tools such as hammers.

You can make a serviceable scraper by lashing a rounded blade to the flattened top of a T-stick that fits comfortably in the hands (see "Rawhide," page 257). For larger tools that must withstand heavy blows, you will want to fashion more durable handles. These should be made from thick, sturdy saplings that are grooved or split at the end to fit the implement. Groove the stone and lash it on tight with strong cordage—preferably a rawhide thong or thick strands of wet sinew. As these materials dry, they shrink and bind even tighter. For best holding power, wrap tightly around the handle on both sides of the stone, crisscrossing several times in the middle. Finish with several half hitches.

Another way of making handles is by splitting a sapling near the end, then fitting and lashing the grooved stone right into the split. If the stone is exceptionally thick, you can also notch and lash together two sturdy saplings to hold it.

This should give you some ideas for handles, but you will have to use your ingenuity to discover what works best for specific tools. Remember also that the more patient you are while grooving the stone, the better the handle will hold and the less likely it will be to flip out when you least expect.

Handles

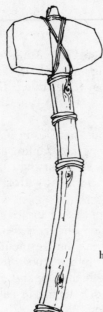

heavy head attachment

securing knife handles

bent sapling method

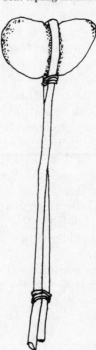

Bone Tools

Bones and antlers have qualities that make them especially useful tool-making materials. They are hard enough to hold sharp edges and points, but soft enough to be abraded rather easily with stone. They can also be broken and splintered into pieces of many different sizes and shapes. Small bones can be shaped into tiny tools such as needles and hooks simply by snapping them with the fingers and scraping them against a rock to produce the desired sharp points and barbs (for specifics on fishhooks, see "Fishing," page 203).

Large bones, on the other hand, often have to be sectioned before they can be fashioned into tools. You can usually do this by scoring both sides of the bone with a stone knifepoint and then tapping along the groove with a hammerstone until the bone falls in two. It's a lot like scoring and breaking a pane of glass. After the bone is sectioned in half, you can then break it down further, into whatever instruments you need.

Bone is especially useful for making long, sharp-pointed instruments such as awls and leather punches. To fit these with wooden handles, flatten the non-working half of the bone and insert it into the deeply notched or split end of a dowel-shaped sapling. For added security, use plenty of glue (see "Glues and Oils," page 263). Then lash the sapling tightly together with cordage. This should stay firmly in place even with considerable twisting and turning. In fact, you can make bone drills using this same procedure. Just split the end of a wooden spindle and lash the flattened end of a long, sharp bone into it. You can use this drill to make

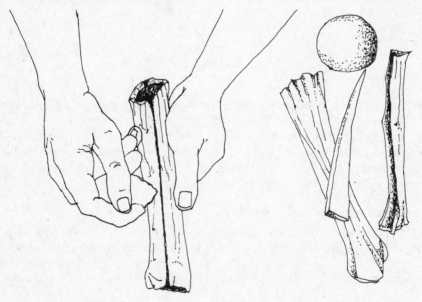

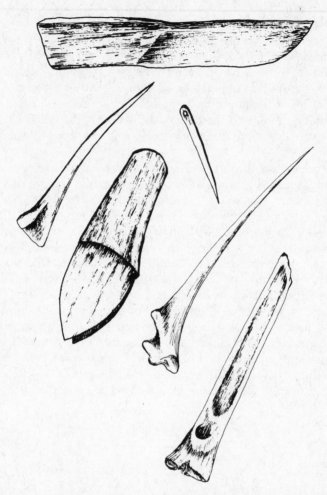

holes in bone or wood, employing the same form and technique as you would to make a fire (see "Bow Drill," page 66).

Bone also makes excellent arrowheads. These can be shaped and sharpened by abrading on stone, then secured to the shafts as explained in "Arrowheads," page 222. With careful sanding, you can make surprisingly sharp knife blades and scrapers out of bone, too.

Firehardening Wooden Tools

The points and working ends of tools made from green wood should be hardened with fire before use. Do this by holding the point of the instrument a few inches above a bed of hot coals—or by pushing it into hot dirt or sand under the coals—and slowly turning it as you might a skewer.

Gradually the wood will begin to hiss and steam, and you will be able to see the moisture escaping.

Firehardening makes the cells swell and the sap thicken, which in turn makes the wood much more resistant to abrasion and concussion. This is especially important with such tools as digging sticks and wooden spearheads and arrowheads. Take care during this process not to char the wood, however. You only want to turn it a light brown. Check for hardness periodically by pushing your thumbnail into the wood. Also remember that you need to harden only the very tip of the instrument—little more than an inch in most cases.

Wooden Tongs

Wooden tongs are especially useful for handling red-hot rocks and coals. They are easily made by bending a length of green sapling into a "U" shape and beveling the ends slightly. To bend the sapling without splitting it, first thin the bending area, then alternately heat it by the fire and work it slowly into the desired shape. To maintain this shape, tie the tongs in place with a piece of cordage a few inches up from the bend.

Coal-burning Wooden Containers

It is very difficult to carve depressions in wood with a stone tool or a knife. However, wooden pots, bowls, cups, spoons, and other containers can easily be made through a process called coal-burning. Using a slab of bark, two sticks, or a pair of tongs, place hot coals over the area you want to hollow out. Then blow on the embers with a thin, steady stream of air to keep them glowing. If available, use a thin reed or length of hollow bone to direct the stream of air. After the coals have burned down, scrape out the charred wood with a knife or sharp rock. Repeat this process with

fresh sets of coals until the depression is fully formed. Using this method, you can make a sixteen-ounce cup from a softwood such as pine in less than an hour; and you can burn out a one-gallon container almost as quickly if you use a lot of coals.

Be careful, of course, not to make your container from part of a poisonous tree such as yew, cascara, or some varieties of locust, because the wood's toxins may spoil the water. The coal-burning process works best with logs, stumps, and chunks of wood that are thoroughly dry. Green wood is usable, but it tends to crack much more—especially if the coals are too hot. Keep the coals glowing evenly, but don't blow too hard. As you near the bottom of the depression, you can minimize cracking and splitting by using red-hot rocks instead of coals.

If you plan to eat from the container, you can keep it from absorbing food material by applying a layer of pitch glue mixed with wood ashes (see "Glues and Oils," page 263). Just pour in the molten mixture, spread it in the depression with a stick, and rub it in with your fingers as it dries. You can rework the glue simply by reheating it. However, don't seal your container this way if you plan to use it for rock boiling—that is, unless you want to thicken your stew with a little pitch glue. A better procedure is to seal it with double-rendered fats. Add a little fat after each cleaning to help seal it and keep it from cracking. (For further discussion of containers, see "Rock Boiling," page 236, and "Eating Utensils," page 236).

Weaving Clothes and Baskets

It is common in a survival situation to find youself in need of extra clothing. There may also come a time when you will want such things as blankets, mats, backrests, baskets, and a host of other useful items. Many of these things are as near as the closest patch of vegetation if you know

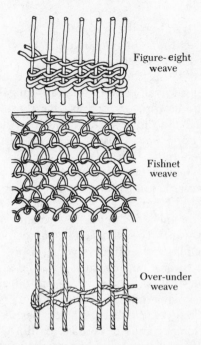

Figure-eight
weave

Fishnet
weave

Over-under
weave

how to weave natural materials. Fortunately, there are two simple weaves that will provide for most of your needs.

Over-Under. The over-under weaving process is aptly described by its name alone. It is especially useful for thick or brittle materials such as saplings or cattails. Start by laying a series of strands parallel to each other on the ground. Then interweave another series of strands at right angles by simply lacing them alternately over and under the parallel strands. After you have woven several of these, the network will begin to hold together and you can tighten the weave by pushing the strands closer together. The more flexible the material, the tighter you'll be able to get the weave. However, the tightness should depend on your needs. If you're making a doorframe, you'll probably weave a fairly loose network of stout saplings. If you're making a mat or blanket, you'll most likely choose more flexible materials and a tighter weave.

Figure-Eight. The figure-eight weave is tighter than the over-under, which makes it more useful for baskets and clothing items such as sandals, leggings, and shawls. It works best with more flexible materials like grasses, vines, and cordage. Like the over-under weave, the figure-eight begins with a series of parallel strands. However, instead of single strands at right angles to these, weave in double strands. These go over and under in opposite directions and cross over each other between each parallel strand. With long, fibrous strands, an easy way to do this is to weave over and under with one strand on the way out, wrap around the last parallel strand, then cross over the "outward bound" strand with each over and under movement on the way back.

Survival Baskets. Using the weaves described above, you can very quickly manufacture survival baskets for gathering greens, seeds, and other edibles. The framework or "splints" for these can be made from thin, resilient saplings, and the rest from almost any flexible material such as grasses or vines. For a small basket, start by weaving together eight long splints in the over-under style—four parallel and four at right angles, as described above. Then, using your lap or a hollow log, press down on the middle of this network so the sides start to bow upward. Maintaining pressure on the middle, begin interweaving rows of cordage.

As you weave, bow the sides upward more and more until the basket holds the shape you want. Then finish the basket by weaving over and under with whatever material best suits your purposes. If the material is too short to weave clear around, just tuck it in and grab another handful.

Initially, your survival baskets (made in haste from the materials immediately at hand) may look quite shabby. But don't worry if the weave is loose and bulky as long as the basket holds berries. For more tightly woven baskets, use long strands of cordage or fibrous material with the figure-eight weave. If you weave closely enough, you can even make watertight containers this way. Some materials naturally swell up when they get wet, reducing the size of the pores even further. For absolute watertightness, brush or dip the basket in molten pitch (see "Glues and Oils," page 263).

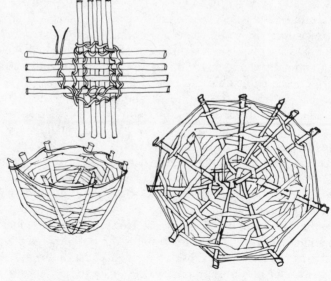

Improvise! Experiment with these two basic weaves to make your clothing items and baskets more functional. For example, you can make a serviceable blanket from cattails using the over-under weave; however, you will find it warmer and more flexible if you use the cattails for the parallel strands and wrap them together with cordage (see "Thatched Blanket," page 38)—perhaps using the figure-eight weave for extra security.

By the same token, a basket's size, shape, and tightness depends on its purpose. Baskets for food gathering are generally deep and moderately tight. Those for winnowing seeds or catching fish should be wide, shallow, and more loosely woven. In making a basket trap for fish, you will probably use a weave that allows an inch or more between strands (see "Fishing," page 203). Whatever the article, let the function dictate the form.

Rawhide

Like thick, form-fitting coats, animal hides protect their bearers from the elements, maintain body warmth, and allow for the free and supple movement of limbs and bodies. To perform these functions, hides must be very strong and elastic. These same qualities make rawhide one of the most useful and versatile materials in a survival situation. Fortunately, the process of making it is fairly simple.

Soaking. You can make rawhide either with or without the hair. Whether or not you remove it depends on how you plan to use the hide. If you want to make a warm blanket or covering for your entryway, you'll probably want to leave the hair on. You may also want to leave it on just to save time; for then you will only have to work on one side. If you plan to remove the hair, soak the hide in water for a day or two until it pulls out easily. Otherwise, soak it only long enough to make it soft and pliable—usually only a few hours.

Stretching. Next, stretch the hide out on hard, cleared ground and stake it down every few inches so that it is well secured. Better yet, "rack" it out with cordage—preferably rawhide strings—on a sturdy rectangular framework. Do this by notching and lashing four poles together, or by lashing horizontal poles between trees. Stretch the hide inside the framework by punching small holes around the edge and tying it on with separate loops of cordage. This is easier if you first stretch out the four ends of the hide, then fill in the gaps. Whether on the ground or on a framework, though, stretch the hide tight all the way around. You may have to reset the stakes or tighten the cords periodically.

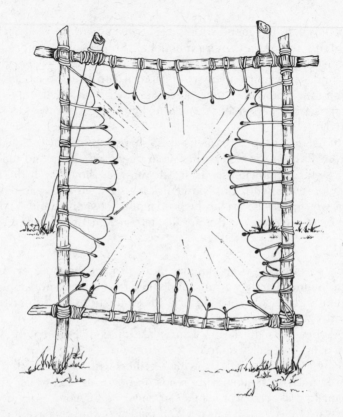

Scraping. While the hide is still wet, remove as much of the hair as you can with your fingers. This may be very easy or a real chore, depending on the hide. If it is too difficult, soak the hide some more or remove the hair with a scraper, described below. On the other side, peel off all the fat and excess material so that it doesn't burn into the hide. Then let the stretched hide dry out completely.

Next, using a scraper of some kind—ideally, a wide, rounded blade of stone or bone fitted with a sturdy handle—scrape off the outer membrane until the surface is smooth and fluffy, like suede. This final process takes a lot of elbow grease, so be patient and keep scraping. Also be careful not to cut or puncture the hide. Use the tool as you would a plane or drawknife, holding the blade at right angles to the hide and pulling down without applying too much pressure. When fully dried, the resulting rawhide becomes hard and stiff and can be used for a multitude of purposes. Save the scrapings to make glue (see "Glues and Oils," page 263).

Uses. Because of its tendency to shrink and dry hard, rawhide is one of the best natural binding materials. It makes strong cordage for the most demanding jobs, including bowstrings and lashings for axeheads and ham-

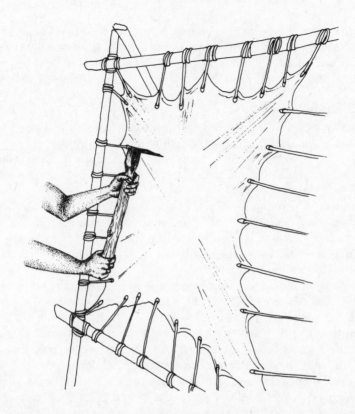

merheads. It has even been used to secure wooden beams in major construction projects such as the Mormon Tabernacle Church in Utah.

To cut a length of thong, lay the rawhide out flat on a hard surface such as a log. Then, beginning on the outer perimeter, cut gradually in a spiral toward the center. This way, you'll be able to get a much longer piece of cordage than by cutting straight parallel strips. The width of the thong depends on how you plan to use it. A half-inch strip twenty feet long can be soaked, then twisted and stretched into a much longer and thinner cord. If you lash it on wet and tie it well, it will shrink and dry as hard as cement.

Rawhide can also be cut to pattern and sewn into an endless variety of tough articles. It makes durable soles for footwear, excellent cooking and storage containers, useful shelter material (tarps, doors, rugs, roofing, etc.), and stiff but serviceable clothing items.

To make small rawhide containers, soak the material in water, shape it into a pouch, and fill it with wet sand. Wrap cordage around the mouth and allow it to dry. Gradually, the rawhide will shrink to about half size. When it's dry, pour out the sand and use the container for whatever you like. You can make larger containers by pushing well-soaked patches of rawhide into the ground and filling them with sand or stones. When dry, such pots and pans can be used to hold either solids or liquids—or even for boiling and cooking (see "Rock Boiling," page 236).

Brain Tanning

For short-term survival purposes, it is unlikely that you will need to know how to tan hides. However, even a rudimentary knowledge of tanning will allow you to make soft clothing items—which, for an extended wilderness stay, is a very useful occupation. For this reason, I include the following short description.

Braining. Fortunately, much of the tanning process is already complete when your rawhide is finished. In fact, the main purpose of tanning is to soften rawhide so it can be used for clothing. But from rawhide to buckskin is a remarkable transformation—all the more so because it is done with the animal's own brains.

There is an old saying that every animal has enough brains to tan its own hide, and this is generally true. First, soak the rawhide in water until it is soft and pliable. Then, over low heat, mash the animal's brains into a slimy paste and rub them thoroughly into the wet rawhide. During this process the hide will become softer, thinner, and more translucent.

If you have taken the hair off, treat both sides. Then add a little water to the remaining brains and soak the hide in this mixture for two to three hours—or even overnight if it's especially cool. Finally, wring the hide out well (perhaps twisting and stretching it between two poles), and rack it out tight again. If you've left the hair on, just treat the bare side with brains and omit the soaking process. But make sure the hide is well permeated by the brain mixture.

Staking. Now stroke, push, and stretch the hide continually until it is dry. This may take a long time, so be prepared to use a lot of elbow grease. Work the hide with the smooth, rounded end of a stick until all the fibers are soft and pliable. You can even use your own fists to some extent, although you may tan your own hide if you're not careful. Push in and down with long, even strokes, working both sides of the hide and giving special attention to rough, scaly spots. Apply plenty of pressure, but be careful not to puncture the hide. Keep pushing, stroking, and punching until the hide is completely dry. A good test for dryness is to touch the hide with the back of the hand. If it still feels cool, apply more elbow grease. If it feels warm and soft, it's probably dry enough.

Smoking. Once the hide is dry, take it off the rack and smoke it over a small fire of green boughs and leaves. This can be done by building a tripod over the fire and draping the hide around it. Keep the fire as low as

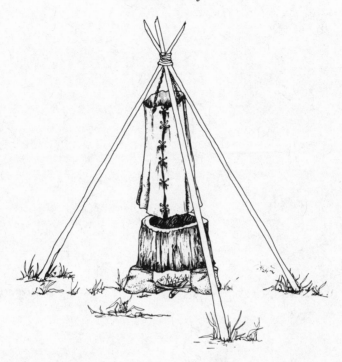

possible—you want smoke, not heat. Turn the hide from time to time, but don't worry about over-smoking it. This process will cure and set the brains.

Buffing. Finally, buff the hide thoroughly by running it rapidly back and forth like a shoe-shine cloth around a smooth pole or thick loop of cordage. When you're done, the hide should be soft and pliable enough to use for a variety of clothing items, from shirts and leggings to mittens and moccasins.

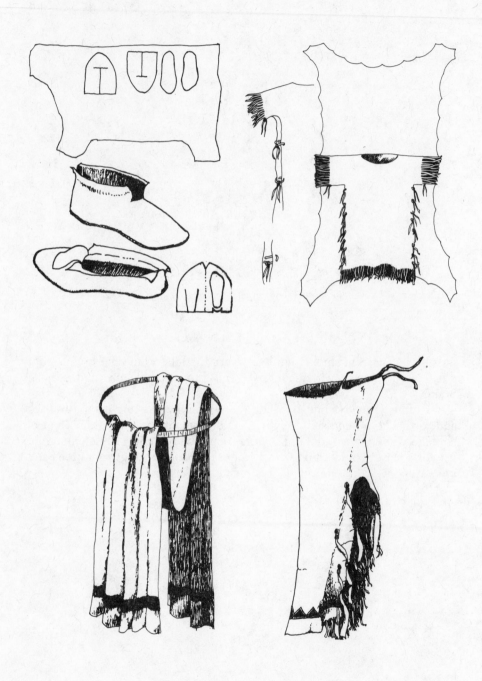

Glues and Oils

The uses of glues and oils are just as varied in the wilderness as they are in your own home. But where to find them? Fortunately, nature provides these just as readily as she does all other needed items.

Pitch Glue. The sap from conifers such as fir and pine makes excellent glue when boiled and thickened. Gather it with sticks where it seeps from wounds or swells into blisters beneath the bark's outer skin. Heat the sap in a container so it melts into a liquid. As it heats up, you'll smell the turpentine evaporating, leaving only the thick, viscous rosin behind. When the pitch has turned to liquid, filter out any bark or debris by pouring it through a strainer of dried grasses.

Now you'll have a thick, gluey substance, but it won't really harden unless you add a catalyst. A handful of finely powdered wood ashes will give it what it needs. Mix these in while the liquid is hot; then pour or brush it on and let it set. Most pitch glues set within a minute or less, so it's best to work quickly.

With experience, you'll discover that different pitches have different qualities. Pine is one of the strongest. Spruce tends to be brittle unless you add animal fat to keep it from crumbling. Some pitches make light glues, others very heavy ones. By adding different materials to molten pitch, though, you can either change the quality of the glue or the final product. For example, pitch mixed with wood ashes makes a very stiff, brittle glue that will crack if you try to bend it. Pitch mixed with charred, powdered eggshells produces a very strong, flexible bond. If you add sand, you can make sandpaper. With powdered rock you can make a weighted fish lure. Experiment with different materials to see what you can come up with.

Hide Glue. If you're blessed with a large animal, you can make glue by boiling hide scrapings or rawhide. Put the materials in a container, cover them with water, and boil them furiously. Add water as necessary during the boiling process. Gradually, the boiling breaks down the skin and leaves a thin, water-soluble glue that is excellent for moccasin bottoms and other flexible items.

Hoof Oil and Glue. The hooves of large animals such as deer and elk can be crushed, mashed, and boiled to yield small amounts of neat's-foot oil. This oil forms as a dirty film on the surface during the boiling process. It is then scraped off and used as a preservative and waterproofing for such things as bows and rawhide goods. It can also be mixed with the wash water to replace natural oils lost from various garments. After removing the oily film, the liquid beneath can be boiled into a glue that is very much like hide glue.

Exercises

Following are a few suggestions to help you review and practice the skills presented in this chapter.

Cordage. Keep your eye out for potential cordage material in tree bark and fibrous plants. Test these materials whenever you find them and wrap a short length of cordage to see how they hold up. When you have time, gather large amounts of material and practice splicing and doubling. With a little practice in this art, your skill and speed will increase dramatically. You'll also begin to get a sixth sense for how strong your cordage is. For an accurate reading, attach it to a poundage scale and pull.

Stonework. Next time you find a good supply of rocks, test a few of them for hardness and cleavage by hitting them with other rocks. Try a variety of rocks with a variety of blows—straight on, glancing, etc.—until you get a feel for their properties and uses. Then, using the skills described above, make a knife and a hammer and fit them with handles.

Bonework. Next time you have chicken or leg of lamb for dinner, save the bones and practice scoring and splitting them into useful tools. Make and try out a variety of things—needles, awls, tubes, scrapers, knives, etc.

Coal-burning. In your backyard or basement, practice making coal-burning containers and utensils of various sizes. You can use almost any wood for this, the most convenient being the fuel for the fire itself.

Firehardening. Get a feel for firehardening by turning the point of a stick over hot coals. Notice how the sap is forced out and the point becomes more solid. Test its hardness with the edge of a thumbnail. Compare this with a point that has been "hardened" in flames.

Weaving. Make some small mats and baskets using the over-under weave and the figure-eight weave. Try a variety of materials, including grasses, reeds, leaves, and bark.

Rawhide. Order an animal hide from a supplier (most of these would otherwise go to waste) and make it into rawhide. Use the material to make cordage, containers, or other items that will come in handy as you practice your survival skills.

Glue. Practice spotting sources of pitch in the woods. Then gather and boil various kinds into glue. Try these out on different surfaces—wood, paper, bone, etc.—to see how they hold. Then experiment with various additives, such as ashes and ground- eggshells, to see how they change the properties of the pitch.

9. CAUTIONS AND SUGGESTIONS

Whether you're in a survival situation or not, there are several major precautions you should take when traveling the backcountry. All of these things will help you get out of trouble if an emergency arises. But more important, they will help you *avoid* trouble in the first place.

Hypothermia

The simplest but most important concept in wilderness survival is to stay warm and dry. In some ways, a life can be likened to a fire that needs a constant supply of combustible fuel to keep burning. When the fuel reserve gets depleted or adversely affected by the elements, the fire dies down and produces less heat. Eventually, the fire may go out altogether.

Hypothermia (also called exposure) is a dangerously cooled body core, very similar to threatened coals at the heart of a fire. It can be caused by a number of conditions, including exposure to wind and rain, body contact with cold objects, unusual exertion, and lack of food.

Keeping these things in mind, you can avoid hypothermia by following a few simple rules: (1) Stay out of wind and rain. Cold water can douse your internal fire just as surely as a campfire if you don't have a good shelter; and cold wind can numb your body as fast as a winter chill. (2) In cool weather, don't sit on exposed rocks and bare ground without some kind of insulation under you. (3) Conserve your energy. Don't exert yourself any more than necessary. Plan your activities so that you make every move count (see "Economy," page 271). (4) Avoid overheating. If you start to sweat, slow down and open your clothing to allow air to circulate. Accumulated moisture under your clothing will only cool and sap your energy later on. (5) Eat plenty of nutritious food to keep up your energy reserves.

If food is scarce or unavailable, this does not mean you will get hypothermia. The body can function for several weeks without food under normal conditions. However, be especially certain in cold weather that your clothing and shelter are well insulated, and that you do not exert yourself to the point where the natural cooling effect of your body leads to chilling. Also be aware that hypothermia can creep up on you even at temperatures above fifty degrees if you are exposed to severe wind or rain.

Finally, just as it is easier to keep a fire going than to build a new one, it is much easier to prevent hypothermia than to cure it. In fact, a person who is severely affected by hypothermia does not usually have the coordination or presence of mind to do anything about it. That's why it is so important to recognize the symptoms—fatigue, shivering, stumbling, slurred speech, disorientation, hallucinations, blue skin, and drowsiness—before it's too late.

If you are with someone who shows signs of hypothermia, get that person to a shelter immediately and warm him up with hot liquids (nutritious soups are excellent) and plenty of insulation around the body. If you can, build a small fire to warm both the air and the patient. If the patient is unconscious, warm the body with your own—skin to skin—and administer hot liquids very gradually only after consciousness is regained.

Clothing

If necessary, you should be able to survive in the wilderness without any man-made articles. But most survival situations arise from recreational use of the wilderness, and it would be foolish to go into the woods unprepared. Therefore, I would like to mention a few articles of clothing— some of them commercial—that will make a forced survival stay more comfortable and that could even mean the difference between life and death.

One of these items is wool. Unlike cotton or most synthetic fibers, wool maintains its insulating properties even when wet. Since you never know when you'll be faced with a survival situation, wearing wool serves as an ounce of prevention. Wool is also a very economical, energy-saving fiber. Though initially expensive, it's warmer and lasts longer than many other materials.

In like manner, fiberfill garments and sleeping bags are much safer than down items. Fiberfill is heavier, but it maintains a layer of thick insulation even when sopping wet. What's more, you can wring it out and increase its loft even more. Pile is another material that holds its insulating loft very well.

However, if you should be caught in a survival situation wearing wet jeans, denims, cotton T-shirt, down parka, or any other clothing with inadequate insulating properties, don't despair. You can still warm yourself by stuffing your shirt and pants with any insulating material at hand— leaves, grass, moss, fir branches—anything that will keep the wet clothing from your skin and trap the warmth from your body (see "Insulation," page 28). You can also fashion emergency clothing items from materials such as bark, rushes, and cattail stalks (see "Weaving Clothes and Blankets," page 254).

Another item I might mention, though you may not have the time or resources to make it in a survival situation, is buckskin. Like wool, it keeps you warm even when wet; and it makes especially wonderful wilderness garments because it is so soft, light, and pliable. Unlike most synthetic garments, buckskin is virtually noiseless while you're moving, which makes it excellent for hunting, trapping, and undetected nature observation. In fact, the ideal wilderness clothing would be wool undergarments and buckskin outer wear. (For details on how to make buckskin, see "Brain Tanning," page 260).

Footwear should be one of the first concerns of any outdoor enthusiast. Possible brands and types are even more varied than uses. But for all around backwoods use, you'll do fine with a pair of light, high-top boots with Vibram soles. If you're going to carry lots of weight, make sure the boots are sturdy enough to give you plenty of support. Most people, I notice, use a lug pattern on the sole for greater traction. I prefer flat soles because lugs tend to chew up the landscape quite badly.

To tell the truth, the footwear I enjoy most of all are handmade moccasins. In cold weather, I also use high-topped, fur-lined mukluks that keep my feet warm even when soaking wet. Both of these are thin-soled and feather-light, allowing the feet to feel the ground (which is critical for stalking). Both also allow a wonderful, free movement that makes for a natural and healthy walk. I wouldn't use them on a hard-packed trail, of course, or they would be beat up in no time. But they will last for quite a while in untrodden wilderness areas.

Finding Your Way

Every year, thousands of people of all ages get lost in the woods. Most people could avoid such mishaps if they would pay more attention to the landscape.

Read the Landscape. There is no such thing in people as a sense of direction. A good way to prove this is to put in earplugs, cover your head with a paper bag, and try to walk a straight line across a football field. Theoretically, a person with a good sense of direction would be able to walk from one goal post to another. There is no such person. Sight, hearing, touch, and smell are the real senses of direction. What actually happens in a person with a "good sense of direction" is that, consciously or unconsciously, he or she notices and remembers significant landmarks in the terrain. Anyone can learn to do this.

I repeat: *anyone*. Many people hypnotize themselves into believing they have a "poor sense of direction" when in fact the only thing lacking is an attention to detail. The first thing to do, then, is to be aware. Keep a running account in your mind of just where you're going and where you've been. You should always be able to follow your own trail back to its origin. Never get so closed-minded or preoccupied with one thing that you fail to take note of the landmarks around you: a dead snag, a creek you've crossed over (each has its own distinct sound), a patch of colorful wildflowers (and their fragrant smell)—whatever seems like something you'll notice and recognize on the way back.

Do this not only with objects along the trail, but with the overall landscape. Look up from the trail often and let the terrain soak into your subconscious. Take note of prominent features—the shape of mountains, the slopes of hillsides, bold rock outcroppings, colorful patches of vegetation—any permanent or semi-permanent thing that will be a signal to you. Do this not only looking ahead as you go, but frequently looking back. The trail looks entirely different in the other direction.

Finally, stop every so often and take a look around. Look at the way the trail bends and winds. Turn around and take in the whole landscape. Imagine you're an eagle looking down on the entire area. Try to picture what it would look like from the air and where you would be in relation to specific features—especially man-made things such as highways, roads, and dwellings. This exercise is tremendously valuable, and it becomes quite a bit easier if you have familiarized yourself with a map before your outing.

If all this seems tedious, it needn't be. You don't have to make a written inventory of the landscape. Just pay attention to it. On the way back, you may not even remember most of the things you've catalogued, but they will look at least vaguely familiar. And if you are able to positively identify even a few of them, you will be able to find your way.

Sun. Keep track of the sun's movement across the sky and its relation to the landscape at various points. Generally, the sun rises in the east or southeast (more toward the south in the winter months), and moves in a smooth arc across the sky toward the west or southwest. Oftentimes you can take note of the sun's position on the way out and imagine what it will look like in relation to the landscape later on. The sun is also a good time indicator, letting you know generally when you should prepare to make camp, search for signs of animals, bed down for the night, and so on.

Stars. Likewise, stars are good general direction indicators—especially the bright North Star. Find it by locating the Big Dipper and sighting up along its front edge about twice the length of the barrel. When you're looking at the North Star, you're facing in a northerly direction. If you know what direction you want to travel, you'll be able to orient yourself and walk out by lining up landmarks, as explained below.

Wind. Wind and other meteorological features such as clouds are so changeable that they are usually unreliable direction indicators. However, most areas have a prevailing wind direction, and this can help to indicate your position. For safety's sake, keep track of the weather with frequent glances into the sky. Do this as a matter of course so you know when to find shelter and how to organize the day.

Lining Up Landmarks. When traveling on unfamiliar terrain without a map and compass, most people do not walk in a straight line. Instead, they are either drawn to the right or the left, depending on whether they are right- or left-handed. Strange as this may sound, it's true. I have found many people who were hopelessly lost wandering in circles no greater than a quarter of a mile in diameter. You can avoid this circling syndrome in a survival situation by lining up trees or other prominent landmarks. Simply choose a landmark in the direction you want to go and walk to it. Then pick another distant feature in the same direction and repeat the process. Verify your direction by sighting back and lining up landmarks. This will keep you from circling.

If you come to an impassable obstacle such as a lake and you're afraid you'll lose sight of your landmark as you walk around it, count the number of steps you have to go out of your way, then retrace the same number of steps after you've cleared the obstacle. Don't be afraid to climb a tree to help in sighting landmarks.

Probing. Generally, I recommend staying put when you first discover you're lost. But if you are certain you're not far from civilization, you can systematically probe for a known trail or highway by lining up landmarks, as explained above. Do this in a systematic way. Imagine your shelter as the center of a circle or the hub of a wheel. Walk out from it in the most likely direction a specific number of steps. Be sure to leave an easily identifiable trail—perhaps with prominent scuffs, arrows, or cairns. If you find nothing, return to your starting point. Then make a beeline at a ninety degree angle to the first two lines—and so on, gradually adding more spokes to your "wheel." Chances are, using this method, you will come upon a thoroughfare somewhere along the first few lines you walk. If not, return to your shelter and make the best of the situation.

Signaling

If you're lost, you will have to pay some attention to letting searchers know where you are. This is especially important if you're in thick woods or in an area where you aren't likely to be noticed easily. Natural shelters are very little help to most searchers. They blend in so well with the landscape that they are virtually undetectable. For your own safety it's a good idea to flag your shelter with a light-colored piece of clothing, if you can afford it, or a patch of light, woven bark. Suspend this marker high enough so it can be seen from all directions—both by searchers and by you when you're returning from hunting or trapping forays.

The most effective signal from a distance is a fire with lots of billowing smoke. For this reason, it's a good idea to keep your fire going constantly. When you're not using it for cooking or other survival purposes, feed it with wet and green wood. This will produce plenty of smoke and keep it burning longer (see "Maintaining the Fire," page 78).

Walking Out

Very rarely do I recommend trying to walk out of a survival situation, primarily because it consumes so much energy with no guarantee of success. Many people who try to walk out only become more hopelessly lost. For these reasons, try walking out only if (1) rescue is unlikely; (2) you are already familiar with the land and are fairly certain of the direction and distance you will have to travel; and (3) you have adequate provisions or enough survival skills to live off the land indefinitely.

On the positive side, this country is so crisscrossed with roads and highways that there is hardly a wilderness area in existence (other than Alaska) where you would have to walk more than seventy-five miles in a straight line before hitting a trail or a roadway. Remember that most thoroughfares tend to follow the easiest terrain—alongside waterways, through mountain valleys, etc. If you come to a place that looks like a road could be built, chances are there'll be one.

Illness and Injury

Treatment for illness and injury is always minimal in a survival situation, and a relatively minor problem in the backwoods can seriously threaten your life. That is why it's so important to think before you act—to walk as if you might trip or fall with the next step. Almost all sprained ankles and broken bones, for example, could be avoided if people first looked where they were going and stepped more carefully (see "The Fox Walk," page 168). You cannot move in the woods as you would on a paved sidewalk or street and expect to go long without injury.

Likewise, cuts can be avoided by taking care with sharp-bladed instruments. Fit all blades with handles, or hold them in a protective piece of clothing or rawhide. When carving, always make the stroke away from the body and keep all limbs and fingers away from the moving blade.

Internal problems are usually caused by ingesting bad food or water. These can be especially debilitating. If you have a broken arm, you can splint it and still provide for yourself; but if you poison yourself, you may be laid up for days without adequate food or shelter. Fortunately, you can easily avoid such misfortune by following the cautions outlined in previous chapters (see "Water," page 47; "Plants," page 81; and "Animals," page 145). For additional preparedness, I highly recommend a standard first-aid course.

I might add that you will probably be surprised to see how much more careful you are when you realize there is no recourse to modern medical care. I believe many people bring on illness or injury in society to avoid unpleasant circumstances. This rarely happens in a wilderness setting because you simply can't afford it. At times, in fact, the body seems to look out for itself without any conscious prompting from the mind. When this begins to happen, you will find yourself following terrain and weather with a depth of awareness you've never felt before, and getting hunches about hazardous conditions that indicate a new—or perhaps much older—level of attunement to nature.

Economy

Always be alert to things you can do to conserve energy. One evening, a friend of mine who owned a bar was trying out a couple of bartending prospects. He pointed them out, saying they both had the same amount of experience, and assured me that within five minutes he would know which one to hire. I asked him how, and he said, "Just watch."

Almost immediately, I began to see what my friend was getting at. Both of the bartenders were equally skilled at mixing, pouring, and serving drinks. But there was a big difference in the economy of their movements. One man served a drink, came back to the bar, went out to get another order, came back to the bar to pour the drink, served the second drink, and so on—doing one thing at a time. The second man, though, was always on the lookout for things he could do to save time and energy. After serving a drink, he picked up several dirty glasses, took another order or two, and then came back to the bar. There, he washed the dirty glasses, mixed several drinks, and took them around to various customers all in one trip. It was easy to see why this man got the job. He was much more valuable to his employer—and he wasn't nearly as tired as the first man when the evening was done.

This kind of economy is critical for survivalists. In the wilderness, it's not just a matter of your job, but your life. When you're building a shelter, then, also look for a good throwing stick and firebuilding materials. When you're out setting traps, stuff your pockets with edible plants. When you're hunting, keep your eyes open for toolmaking materials—and so on. This kind of "multiple" awareness may seem cumbersome at first, but with practice it becomes a habit-knit part of survival living that saves tremendous amounts of time and energy.

Survival Belt Pack

Once you master the skills described in this book, you should be able to survive in any wilderness area in North America with nothing but your knowledge and the natural materials provided by the good earth. However, don't get so overconfident that you neglect to take normal emergency precautions. Survival skills are not meant to replace standard safety measures, but to give you something to fall back on if all else fails. Unless you are an expert survivalist (able to live in the wilderness indefinitely, starting with nothing), you would be very foolish to go on a wilderness trek without minimal emergency equipment.

Fortunately, such essentials are few. In fact, they can all be easily placed in a small belt pack that you can carry with you almost anywhere. At the least, such a pack should contain the following:

Pocketknife
Waterproof matches
Candle
Strong cordage (fifty feet)
Compass
Monofilament fish line (fifty feet)
Solar-still items (see page 52)
    Clear plastic sheet (five-by-five feet)
    Plastic or surgical tubing (six feet)
    Collapsible plastic cup

These items alone will assure you the tools you need to obtain fire and water, and to fashion critical survival tools such as traps, snares, and hunting implements. Depending on your skill level and the size of your belt pack, you may want to add other items you consider important—for example, flint and steel, a first aid kit, sunglasses, high-energy food items, or even an emergency shelter. Wherever you go, take this little kit with you and you'll always be prepared for the unexpected outdoor emergency. Just remember, though: A survival kit does you no good at all in an emergency situation if it's been left behind in a closet or backpack!

CONCLUSION

Before I send you out into the woods on your own, I would like to pass on a few final thoughts about the art of wilderness survival. First I want to reemphasize that this book cannot do your surviving for you. A real survival test is much more than an examination in school. To pass the test, you must have a working knowledge of the necessary skills. That means you must practice them until they become as habitual as playing baseball, driving a car, or performing any other familiar but complex skill.

However, once you have mastered the skills presented in this book, I am confident that you will be able to survive indefinitely almost anywhere on this continent at any time of the year and in any weather—even if you are caught without proper clothing, food, or tools of any kind. With a reservoir of knowledge and experience, you will be able to ward off panic, establish priorities, and plan to meet your most critical needs with a calm mind. You will be able to build a warm shelter from a variety of natural materials, find water in the most arid environments, and make a fire without matches even in wet weather. You will be able to recognize a variety of edible and medicinal plants and call on a wealth of fishing, trapping, and hunting skills to provide you with healthful and sustaining meals. You will be able to make tools such as knives, baskets, and bows and arrows with nothing but your bare hands and the natural resources available to you. In short, you will be able to care for your body, mind, and spirit as long as you are living in a survival situation. What is more, you will have the security of knowing you can take care of yourself and those around you even if the need should never arise.

If this book helps to save a life, it will have fulfilled its basic purpose. However, as you may have gathered, I have a deeper purpose; and if you have practiced the skills in this book, you have already begun to fulfill it. You have learned that survival need not be a struggle and that nature will provide everything you need for fruitful and harmonious living. You have learned to flow with nature rather than resisting or fighting it. Your senses have become more alert and alive. You now see, hear, and feel more in the environment than ever before. Most important, you have felt the flow of the spirit-that-moves-in-all-things and begun to realize that survival is only the beginning of a much deeper relationship with nature that can permeate your entire philosophy of life.

Likewise, this book is only a beginning. In these pages I have had room to pass on only the most basic survival skills. There remains much to say, both about wilderness survival and about other subjects having to do with our intricate connection to the earth. It will take many more pages before I am satisfied with what I have tried to teach. But ultimately I will

273

feel satisfied only when I see a redirection of attitude toward nature—a reversal of our present tendency to exploit the land and our fellow creatures and the beginnings of a life ethic based on wisdom, respect, and reverence for all things.

These are lessons of the spirit, and they cannot be taught directly by any book or individual. They can only be learned through the love and humility implanted in human hearts by wild nature itself. But no one who looks at the world situation today can seriously doubt that we are in need of such a transformation. And when it comes—as I believe it will—then I will be truly content. For that will assure the survival of us all.

PLANT GLOSSARY

Following are some definitions you may find helpful in familiarizing yourself with the plants described in this book:

Alternate—Only one leaf growing from each joint in a stem.
Annual—A plant that flowers, produces fruit, and dies in one year.
Axil—The angle between the upper side of a leaf and the stem from which it grows.
Basal—Arising from the base of a plant.
Biennial—A plant that takes two years to flower, produce fruit, and die.
Bract—A leaf (usually small) located at the base of a flower or its stem.
Calyx—Outer circle of sepals, or floral leaves.
Compound—Divided into two or more leaflets.
Corolla—Circle of flower petals inside the calyx.
Deciduous—Foliage shed each year; not persistent or evergreen.
Disk Flowers—Tight central cluster of tubular flowers surrounded by ray flowers (as in the sunflower family).
Evergreen—With green leaves or needles all year; not deciduous.
Fruit—The ripened ovary containing one or more seeds.
Head—Dense, round cluster of flowers without stems.
Herbaceous—Fleshy, succulent, non-woody.
Lanceolate—Three to four times longer than wide, tapering to a point.
Leaflet—One of the divisions of a compound leaf.
Linear—Very narrow, five or more times longer than wide, usually with parallel sides (as with grasses).
Oblong—Two to four times longer than wide, usually with parallel sides.
Obovate—Egg-shaped, with the narrow end at the base.
Opposite—Growing on opposite sides of one stem joint.
Ovate—Egg-shaped, with the wider end toward the base.
Palmate—With three or more divisions or leaflets growing from a common point.
Perennial—A plant that lives longer than two years.
Petal—One of the parts of the corolla, or inner flower, usually colored.
Pinnate—With leaflets growing on both sides of a common stem.
Ray Flowers—Strap-shaped flowers encircling central disk flowers (as in the sunflower family).
Rootstock—Long, trailing underground stem that produces roots below and shoots above.
Rosette—Cluster of basal leaves arranged in a circle.
Sepal—A single part (or leaf) of the calyx, sometimes resembling a petal.
Shrub—A woody, bushy, plant (up to about fifteen feet tall) with several main stems.

Taproot—A single large, thick root (such as a carrot) growing vertically downward.
Toothed—Notched around the edges.
Tuber—Short, thick root with many buds (like a potato).

RECOMMENDED
PLANT BOOKS

Following are some books you may find useful
in identifying wild, edible plants.

Fernold, Merritt Lyndon, *Gray's Manual of Botany* (largely rewritten and expanded). New York, Cincinnati, London, Toronto, Melbourne: D. Van Nostrand, 1970.

Gibbons, Euell and Gordon Tucker. *Euell Gibbons' Handbook of Edible Wild Plants*. Norfolk: Donning and Company, 1979.

Hitchcock, C. Leo and Arthur Cronquist. *Flora of the Pacific Northwest*. Seattle: University of Washington Press, 1976.

Medsger, Oliver Perry, *Edible Wild Plants*. New York: Macmillan Publishing Company, Inc., 1966.

Newcomb, Lawrence, *Newcomb's Wildflower Guide*. Boston: Little, Brown, and Company, 1977.

Niehaus, Theodore F. and Charles L. Ripper, *A Field Guide to Pacific States Wildflowers*. Boston: Houghton Mifflin Co., 1976.

Niering, William A. and Nancy C. Olmstead, *Audubon Society Field Guide to Wildflowers of the Eastern Region*. New York: Alfred A. Knopf, 1979.

Peterson, Lee A., *A Field Guide to Edible Wild Plants of Eastern and Central North America*. Boston: Houghton Mifflin Co., 1977.

Peterson, Roger Tory and Margaret McKenny, *A Field Guide to Wildflowers of Northeastern and North Central North America*. Boston: Houghton Mifflin Co., 1968.

Spellenberg, Richard, *Audubon Society Field Guide to Wildflowers of the Western Region*. New York: Alfred A. Knopf, 1979.

INDEX

279